Acknowledgements

This book is dedicated to my wife Karen (1953 to 1990), who was always supportive and would have been very happy and proud for us. It is also dedicated to my son Aaron J. H. Martin.

"I am a part of all that I have met." -- *Tennyson, Ulysses.* Thanks to all my students for the past 30 years. We exchanged experiences and ideas in a hopefully mutually beneficial learning process. Thanks to everyone who helped me with the initial proof reading of this book. Second printing proof reading and editing may be fully blamed on the author. Finally, thanks to all my friends and colleagues at Full Sail University in Winter Park, Florida.

About The Author

James R (Jim) Martin is an Emmy, award winning Producer, Writer, Director of Film, Television, Video, Multimedia and Digital Media Productions. He is currently Director of the Documentary Filmmaking Course at Full Sail University in Winter Park, Florida. Prior to coming to Full Sail University, Professor Martin taught film production at Columbia College in Chicago for 13 years. He also taught Directing at University of Central Florida as adjunct faculty.

Credits include two Emmy nominations and an Emmy Award for Nationally aired PBS documentary - *Fired-up Public Housing is My Home* and Chicago Film Festival, Golden Plaque for Best Network Documentary for Emmy nominee, *Wrapped In Steel* also seen nationally on PBS stations. 2008 Telly Award of Best Short Documentary on Make-A-Wish Foundation.

Jim Martin has worked as an editor and cameraman in both film and video production and he has taught film and video production for thirty years. He has written, produced and directed a feature film, Public Television documentaries, commercials, feature short films, corporate and industrial films and videos.

HOW TO USE THIS BOOK

This book is published as an interactive, multimedia publication. It has two main components, a print version and a digital version. The print (hard copy) and the digital version may be used together or separately. It is recommended that they be used together. Many of the photographs, illustrations and film clips included or referred to in the print version become interactive in the digital version. For example: if the cursor turns into a hand when over a photograph, clicking on the photograph may bring up an audio recording, video or other presentation.

Each chapter in Create Documentary Films, Videos and Multimedia covers a specific area of documentary production.

Case studies cover a range of documentary projects and actual documentaries. The case studies are first hand accounts that detail the preproduction, production and postproduction of each production.

Documentary storytelling methods may also be used for all types of presentations, exhibits and events. Chapters in this book detail how to apply theses techniques in a diverse number of situations.

The Filmography of recommended documentary films is comprised of about one hundred documentary films of al l types and are meant to give examples of the wide range of storytelling applications that fall under the documentary and nonfiction genres. For detailed reviews go to JRMartinmedia.com (Reviews).

CreateDocumentaryFilms.com   **JRMartinMedia.com**
Info@jrmartinmedia.com   **RealDealPress@gmail.com**

TABLE OF CONTENTS

TABLE OF CONTENTS

TABLE OF CONTENTS

This chapter is a brief introduction, discussion and summary of the history and evolution of the concept of documentary and nonfiction filmmaking.

To this end it is necessary to look at the many issues that deal with the telling or reporting of nonfiction realities via the many methods of conveying such realities in films, videos, books, magazines, newspapers, television and the internet. These issues deal with personal and public expectations as to how information is reported and disseminated in our culture.

(Above) Nyla and Child – Nanook of the North
New York Museum of Modern Art

CHAPTER 1

DOCUMENTARY/NONFICTION
STORYTELLING

CHAPTER ONE

CHAPTER 1

Documentary Storytelling

Documentary storytelling is as old as human life, older than cave paintings, older than Neolithic nomads passing on hunting skills and survival stories. It is perhaps one of our most important ways of handing down information and exploring reality.

Think about it for a moment and it becomes obvious that even early folklore and fiction were metaphors for human experience and intellect that reflected or tried to understand nonfiction realities.

Thirty-two thousand year old cave paintings of animals have been documented in Chauvet-Pont-d'Arc Cave in southern France. "Cave of Forgotten Dreams" 2011 Documentary - by Werner Hetzog

Documentary stories were told orally when there was no written language. Someone actually experienced being chased by a bear, was able to survive and pass on the account from his or her own point-of-view (POV). They traced the route or location of the chase in the earth or drew the bear on a cave wall as they told the story so everyone knew where the bear looked like and might be lurking. This story would be passed down to the next generation, to the neighbors or other families in the vicinity until it became legend, embellished by each generation no doubt. With the resources available today, there would be an interview with the person who encountered the bear at the location, graphics to show the route and maybe a look at the bear if it was still around.

This book explores many ideas, techniques and styles that make up the complex world of documentary and nonfiction storytelling.

Louis Lumier Created First Documentary

DOCUMENTARIES AND NONFICTION

Documentaries explore reality in the hope of revealing some truth. To do this they record or "document," actuality, that which is actually happening at the moment. Documentaries do not employ actors or stage events. Interviews are not rehearsed or coached. The information collected on film, video, still photography or some form of audio recording is edited into a story which the author feels represents the actuality he or she experienced and observed.

In general terms when documentary formats are employed there is some latitude in presenting the subject matter and how the subject matter is defined. Nonfiction films or videos are found in the humanities and social sciences and also in the form of corporate training, public relations and sales projects. The big difference is in the level of subjectivity or point-of-view.

This book will look at some classic documentaries, however, this is not an exploration of the history of nonfiction filmmaking.1 This story is about making documentaries in a number of ways and techniques, for a number of purposes and reasons that the author learned and experienced over a lifetime, as a student filmmaker, fiction and nonfiction writer, reporter, interviewer, teacher and documentary filmmaker.

ACTUALITY

In a pure sense a documentary film is a story that uses actuality sources to create a nonfiction documentation of some reality. Actuality meaning something that "actually" happened and was in some way recorded on film, video, still photographs, audio, or other medium. It is a nonfiction reality, somehow witnessed and recorded.

A documentary does not employ actors to recreate reality. As soon as actors are employed, or a script is written detailing what's going to happen, even if it is based on a true story or event, it becomes a fictional recreation. A documentary or nonfiction story explores actual events witnessed and/or recorded in some fashion. The documentary takes these actual events and presents them in a nonfiction context.

A script may be written to indicate how the subject will be documented.

USING DIFFERENT MEDIA

Nonfiction or documentary style stories may use a number of different media in combination or alone to create a documentary story. For example film, video, audio, slides, photographs and other media alone or combined might be used for a multimedia presentation.

POINT-OF-VIEW (POV)

In many ways film or video documentaries are like visual nonfiction books. The stories they tell can be about a number of different subjects. They can be informative, educational, entertaining, political, and on any topic found in the nonfiction area of a library or bookstore. Like a nonfiction book documentary films make their POV known to the viewer.

Documentaries are subject to having their POV or premises accepted or disputed by the viewer. Just because they use actuality materials to present a view of reality on a given subject doesn't mean that the reality they show is objective in anyway. It cannot help but be subjective.

In 1874 French Astronomer Pierre Jules Cesar Janssen documented the movement of Venus on a plate revolving cylinder shaped camera. This was the first known attempt to document motion.

---

1   A fantastic book on this subject is The History of Nonfiction Film, 2nd edition by Eric Barnouw.

Nonfiction work, including documentaries, newspaper articles, TV news, history textbooks and many other works are not objective, they all have a POV. All are subjective interpretations of what an individual or group of people believe to be reality. Humans have subjective minds; they perceive reality though their own experience, cultures, heredity, and other factors.

No two people perceive reality in exactly the same way. Start with the fact that no two individuals have the same amount of rods and cones in the macula of their eyes. Rods perceive motion in black and white and are located toward the outside edges of the macula. Cones perceive color, give us focus and are located toward he center. The number of these sensors differs greatly in each individual. Many individuals don't have all the cones that perceive every color. Humans have the most versatile eyes of any creature on the planet but they don't see things exactly the same. Add all the varying life experiences each person has and it's not difficult to understand that in a roomful of people each person is experiencing that reality from their own point-of-view. Each persons's mind is in a different reality and will come away from the experience with their own interpretation of what happened or was said in that room.

Rashomon Effect

Rashomon is a 1950 Japanese film directed by Akira Kurosawa, working in close collaboration with cinematographer Kazuo Miyagawa. It stars Toshiro Mifune, Machiko Kyo and Masayuki Mori.

The film has a narrative structure that reflects the impossibility of obtaining the truth about an event when there are conflicting witness accounts. Psychologists use the term *"Rashomon Effect"* to describe any situation in which the truth of an event is difficult to verify due to the conflicting accounts of different witnesses. Police are reminded of this phenomenon when trying to get eye witness statements.

The film is based on two stories by Rynosuke Akutagawa. Rashomon provides the setting, while *"In a Grove"* provides the characters and plot. Rashomon can be said to have introduced Kurosawa and Japanese cinema to Western audiences, and is considered one of his masterpieces.

Subjective and Objective Reality

Philosophically there are numerous arguments about human subjectivity and objective reality[2] but what does it all mean to

2 *On Truth* by Harry G Frankfurt - interesting book on subject.

documentary and nonfiction storytellers? Why is it important to understand these concepts?

It is important to discuss these issues because of the need to explore reality and develop a point-of-view that attempts to find truth in those realities when truth is an issue. To not be aware of the subjective nature of people or ignore it on purpose facilitates creating fiction or propaganda. Propaganda distorts or skews reality, actuality and fact to present an alternative reality that is false. Intentionally or unintentionally it is possible to create stories which seek to manipulate the viewer by altering facts to the point where the story becomes fictional.

Proponents of certain philosophical concepts contend that despite our subjective natures and realities there is "objective reality." There is the notion that despite everything there are facts which when examined are true or false. So that no matter how subjective our realities might be these "objective realities" cannot be ignored. An example might be that if someone stands in front of a speeding train it is true that if it hits them, they will be killed despite any reality they may perceive. If someone lives at a certain address and states they live someplace else, what they have claimed is factually not true, therefore false. They have failed the test of objective reality.

Some philosophers contend that all reality is subjective, that whatever is believed to be reality, is reality and therefore there is no true or false, only what is perceived to be true or false.

Count Yourself In

"We cannot withdraw our cards from the game. Were we as silent and as mute as stories, our very passivity would be and act." -- John-Paul Sarte

"Philosophy is the science which considers truth." --Aristotle

Ethics and Standards

Documentary filmmakers or nonfiction story tellers, dealing with issues that pertain to the human condition, social, political and other critical areas need some standards, considerations and ethics to guide them in their storytelling pursuits. They need to come to terms with their own realities, biases, and cultural prerogatives. Perhaps individual point-of-view can be examined in a way that allows recognition of an other point-of-view. That new point-of-view can then be explored.

Propaganda

Most documentary filmmakers do not get involved in making propaganda because its purpose is to manipulate others in to believing one point-of-view which is distorted to the point that it is fictional and directly related to what is called "spin" today. Propaganda often skews reality to promote one ideological, political or religious view.

Propaganda -- Distorting or skewing reality, actuality and facts to present an alternative reality that is false.

Propaganda -- Skewed toward a bias that a government, cause or ideology espouses. Showing only one biased and usually undisclosed point of view.

Propaganda films seek to manipulate the viewer by altering reality with untruths and distortion to create a reality favorable to whatever ideology it favors.

A group or organization may make an indoctrination or informational nonfiction film to be used to *"educate"* individuals who are members of that group. However, if it is used to promote that ideology to individuals outside the members of that group it becomes propaganda by definition. Any "documentary" made by a government, political group or religion for dissemination to the general public is propaganda.

Many ideological and political groups promote intolerance, racial or religious hatred and distorted realities to convince others that their reality is the only reality. They create fictional realities they claim are objective and righteous to convince others that their way is the "true" one and that everyone else is some how evil. German propaganda films before and during WW II are a classic example, in that they depicted Jews and other ethnic groups as evil and inferior to Germans.

Objectivity

If it is not possible to be objective, how may a conscientious documentarian can approach working with any hope of preserving truth? Maybe by giving up the notion of being arbitrators of what is true and false. Adopt a point-of-view from the inside looking out and explore the realities of others using humanistic priorities, while at the same time exploring with few pre-conceived notions. Allow the reality to tell its own story.

How does this idea compare with journalistic ethics and concerns? Ideally they are similar. There was a time when journalists working for newspapers had a code of ethics, where they tried to be "objective" in some way, to report the facts about events they were covering. Opinions were supposed to be confined to the editorial page. In this day and age of cable news and the fact that only a small percentage (27%)[3] of the US population still reads newspapers it is hard to find non-opinionated news.

Newspapers and news magazines have never been without opinion in their reporting of the news. Newspaper owners hire editors who represent their way of thinking and political beliefs who in turn hire reporters who see the world the way they do. So facts are reported but not all the facts. The news that is reported tends to be without the other side of the story, so what is not written is often more interesting than what is written. When the other side is reported it is usually "framed" negatively.

3   Check out source for actual percentage of people who still read newspapers. It's around 27% heard on Bill Maher show March 16th, 2007.

"Framing" is a technique of placing facts in a framework which frames the discussion. Calling the Inheritance Tax the "Death Tax" changes the idea to make it appear that there is a tax you must pay when someone dies. In fact the inheritance tax is a tax on large estates and does not apply to immediate family members. Framing goes hand-and-hand with "spin." George Carlin is quoted as saying "Whenever the other side has you talking their language, they've got you. That, to me, is what it's about in a nutshell and it's almost that simple."[4] Other classic frames are "tax relief," "personal accounts, "Pro-Life" and "Pro-Choice."

Yellow Journalism, Newspapers, Radio and Television

According to Frank Luther Mott (1886–1964), American Historian and Photojournalist, "yellow journalism" may be recognized by scare headlines, about minor news items, in huge bold type; fake pictures or drawings; faked interviews; misleading headlines, fake science from fake experts among other things. – Source Wikipedia

"The greatest deception men suffer is from their own opinions."

Leonardo da Vinci

Certain tabloid newspapers practicing what is known as "yellow journalism" have always sensationalized the news and distorted political issues. Other newspapers do it in a slightly more subtle fashion. A look on the editorial page reveals who owns the newspaper and reading the editorials helps to understand the point-of-view of that newspaper. In a way they are saying what their point of view is, so when you read that paper you have an idea how to evaluate what they report.

When you read *The Wall Street Journal*, once owned by the Dow Jones Corporation, it's understood that it's coming from a conservative, business oriented perspective. What it chooses to report, not so much how it reports it, is going to be conservative or cater to those with conservative business interests.

Editorial Page

On the other hand a newspaper like *The New York Times*, is known for a more progressive editorial policy. Compare what is reported in the *NY Times* and the *Wall Street Journal* newspapers and it appears that they each often neglect to report certain stories or they report them in different ways paying more attention to certain facts more than others. Knowing what's on each of their editorial pages may actually give some perspective on a particular subject in the news.

---

4   George Carlin in an interview with Tim Russert, when asked why he thought the Democratic Party and John Kerry failed to connect with the voters. (November 23, 2004) The Nation BLOG I Posted 07/18/2005 @ 11:52am Debunking the Spin About Framing

Differences between Documentary Storytelling and Television Nonfiction Programming

Nonfiction storytelling – Documentary – is about exploring reality, current issues and other subjects with the purpose of informing and possibly bringing candid insights to the viewer. Hopefully giving the viewer choices regarding how they may end up feeling about the subject. Documentaries are very different than the news or so called "Reality" programming in that documentaries are about conveying actuality information in a narrative form. Some documentaries can be both informative and entertaining.

Television in the United States is an entertainment medium. People watch television to be entertained. It seems that American Television has turned the news into entertainment because that's how they get ratings and advertisers. Not only is the news turned into entertainment it is exploited by individuals, corporate and political groups; so the end result is entertaining propaganda.

You can often tell where a newspaper is coming from by looking at its editorial page

Unlike a newspaper the editorial policy of Cable News Channels and Network News Channels is not made clear by the broadcasters. Certain Cable News channels are the television version of a "yellow journalism" tabloid newspaper. In some cases they are no more than propaganda organs for one political point-of-view. Viewers who watch tabloid television news want to be entertained more than informed. There are number of so-called television anchors, personalities, and self-proclaimed experts or "pundits" who also use this tactic to promote themselves and make money. They have little integrity, or real political insight. They often fabricate news stories or "spin" events to fit a sensational faux-partisan mold. This is "news" as much as "professional wrestling" is Olympic wrestling. The first is a show, the second athletic competition. Documentaries do not fabricate events or purposely "spin" information to the point that it means the opposite of what the facts indicate.

Always remember Television is about enterainment not reporting the news.

Broadcast radio is no exception. "Talk Radio" hosts and faux-pundits, whose bombast and vitriol has no substance or relevance, are the equivalent to tabloids and "yellow journalism." Most of these "hosts" have no more insight into the issues they discuss than the average man or woman on the street.

Television news reporters are not hired for their knowledge of current events, politics, history, government or background in journalism. They are hired for their looks or "personalities or political views." Many have no idea what they are talking about as they read the teleprompter. One need only watch the faces and verbal intonation of reporters on CNN, FOX or MSNBC to know their POV on the news they are reporting. Questions asked of some interviewees reflect either an accusatory cynical tone of voice or patronizing whine. Hours are spent on news stories that barely deserve mention.

"Everyone is entitled to his own opinions -- but not his own facts"

Attributed to "Murrow Boys" by Peggy Noonan -- Wall Street Journal 10/28/07

Nighly News on Cable Channels CNN, MSNBC, and FOX report varying versions of the news. MSNBC at this prime time hour features Chris Mathews who is a commentator and opinionated. CNN and Fox purport to be reporting the News at this hour but tend to sensationalize the facts.

It's interesting to note that Steven Colbert and the *Daily Show, with Jon Stewart*, which bill themselves as comedy and present a self-proclaimed "fake news" program, may give you, with their subjective satirical approach, more insight into current events than the actual news programs. But the news is still being "spun" for entertainment value and reflects opinions and biases of the shows writers.

"Reality Show" programs are scripted and produced. Stereotyped individuals or actors are hired to participate. Events and outcomes are manipulated. This is fiction programming.

"Reality TV"

The news as reported on most cable news networks, broadcast networks and local television news stations to a large extent reflects the editorial point-of-view of the owners of those entities. In some cases these are the same corporations or individuals who own chains of newspapers and magazines. General Electric who once owned

NBC, and MSNBC (sold to Comcast in 2009) donated heavily to the campaigns of G W Bush. But NBC or MSNBC do not make that known when they report the news. There isn't an editorial page to view.

Fox "News" is owned by Rupert Murdock's News Corp, which also owns 22 television stations, tabloid newspaper New York Post and holdings in other areas as well.[5] Murdock owns a vast international media empire and has purchased the *Wall Street Journal*.[6] The point is that some people tend to take the news they see and hear on television as being unbiased; perhaps because it seems they are seeing it for themselves. The truth is that only what the owners of these television stations want to air is seen or heard. They tend to promote their point-of-view. So how does this differ from propaganda since you are seeing sensationalized reporting of one point-of-view with a political agenda?

In one well documented instance in late 2009 a Fox cable news program took footage from several political rallies and used it as if it all happened at one political rally to make it appear that it was attended by thousands of protesters rather than hundreds. They regularly over estimate crowds at their favorite political rallies. The management of Fox News has publicly stated its political position and that this is the view Fox will promote. This is not a "news" channel, it's a propaganda outlet with advertisers!

Granted some cable news networks have newscasters with varying political views, who have a point-of-view on various subjects, but most of the news time is given over to a subjective reporting of the news. The notion that the television, newspapers and other media are "liberal" is a myth and used in many cases to intimidate journalist who report actual facts contrary to conservative ideology.

Documentary and nonfiction programming are mostly missing from commercial cable and television. There are some exceptions to this rule on public television and a few cable channels like the *History Channel, National Geographic Channel* or certain *HBO* documentaries. But even on these venues there seems to be programming that is "based on a true story" reenactments, other scripted programs and "Hybrid Documentary" situations. A hybrid documentary sets up a situation and then documents the actuality that results from that event. Also hybrids are highly edited and the subjects involved in the

5   Source: http://www.cjr.org/_deprecate/newscorp-timeline.asp and http://la.indymedia.org/news/2003/04/47530.php
6   2007 --Murdock purchases Wall Street Journal.

making of the documentary.

Documentary Filmmakers use formats that do not manipulate or stage the events and subjects they explore. While many of the subjects covered may be topical the format should not emulate television news exploitation models. There are many inventive ways to approach nonfiction and documentary filmmaking that do not distort actuality.

How TV News Affects Documentary and Nonfiction Storytellers

Documentary Ethics

Because of the lack of credibility created by TV news there needs to be some principals and ethics used when documenting reality. While documentary filmmakers may not be reporting the news, they are looking at human realities that are actually happening or have happened so there is a certain amount of research and investigative journalism involved their work. There is a need to go beyond what is apparent and look at all sides of what it is being documented.

More than one side to every story.

Acknowledging that creating a documentary film with a particular point-of-view, is no different than someone writing a nonfiction book on the same subject is important. On what is this point-of-view based? What are some other views on this subject? What facts are known both pro and con on this subject? Is there a historical perspective that impacts the subject being discussed?

A documentary is an exploration of some aspect of human reality that has or is actually happening. Documentaries rely on non-invented situations and action i.e. actual events, and spontaneous interviews with real people about what they are doing. How do the opinions of the people interviewed compare with objective reality concepts? Can facts be found that confirm or contradict what has been said? Rather than 3rd party, voice over reporting use first-person accounts to tell the story.

Telling Actuality Based Stories

Observe and Measure

It might be interesting to borrow some ideas from science. It is said that; "Science observes and measures the natural world." Scientists accumulate information and use that data to deduce empirical laws that govern biological and physical systems in our universe.

But scientific explanations must be tested and proved by applying observations and by coming up with other observations that might disprove the explanation. This requirement is called making predictions falsifiable. This requirement rules out supernatural explanations which cannot be proved or disproved and would need to be accepted on conviction or faith.

You need to analyze all that is found against other information and sources; then share this process with the audience. So in serious documentary work why not try applying some regimens derived from scientific research or methods used for observational studies.

Begin with a point-of-view on a subject as a theory not a given, do the research and then tell the story including information that might be used to disprove the original point-of-view.

Of course not all the documentary stories are subject to any sort of scientific standards. A documentary made for a corporate entity about their corporation and its products may use a documentary style but its point-of-view is obviously corporate. Still it would be interesting for the viewer to feel that they are not accepting the message strictly on faith.

IN THE BEGINNING

Origins of Documentary Storytelling

The origins of nonfiction or documentary filmmaking begin with early photographic documentation and then with the Louis Lumiere invention of the *Cinematographe*, 1894 in France. In March of 1895 Lumiere shot a short film called *Workers Leaving the Lumiere Factory* as a test of his camera. He made many other short nonfiction film one of which, *Arrival of a Train*, when seen by the public, became widely known and is often considered his first documentary film. Lumiere leased his *Cinematograhe* in a franchise arrangement with filmmakers all over the world. It also could be used as a projector. For many years he would not sell it outright. Documentary or nonfiction films became popular all over the world and played in theaters. Audiences were anxious to see what was to them realities from other places in the world.

After awhile documentaries lost creditability as portions of the films were reenacted or "faked," to give audience information the filmmakers were unable to record. At this point documentaries faded in popularity until films like *Nanook of the North* made by Robert Flaherty emerged with, for the main part, actuality based footage. Controversial aspects of *Nanook* concern Flaherty's recreation of certain scenes, and emphasis on the subjects demonstrating traditional hunting and living even though in 1922 they were using more modern methods including hunting with rifles.

In the 1930's, documentary filmmaking in the US took on an advocacy posture with films sponsored or commissioned in some way by "New Deal" Government agencies. Government sponsored films had been made since 1908[7]as demonstration and other non-controversial internal projects that did not compete with the Hollywood film industry. *The Plow that Broke the Plains* made by Pare Lorenz previewed in 1936. It apparently had been financed in part by the Resettlement Agency (RA) and represented advocacy films that could play in theaters and compete with commercial films. In addition, since there was government involvement, they were considered to be propaganda by many people. Lorenz, and others did prove that well-made nonfiction films or advocacy documentaries did have commercial appeal.

Government Sponsored Documentaries

During the 1940's documentary filmmaking moved from advocacy to propaganda films for all the participant countries in World War 2. Actuality documentation was distorted to promote the cause of whoever shot and edited it. Frank Capra's *Why We Fight* series of films used captured German propaganda footage, re-edited to promote the cause of the allies against the Germans. Other documentarians tried to show realities around the world but faced government interference in the countries they visited.

In 1955 *Night and Fog*, a film directed by Alain Resnais, stands out as a post war documentary that broke new ground in that it documented Nazi atrocities by using black and white archival footage of the concentration camps and new color footage of the ruins of the camps in 1955. the documentary's point-of-view was that humankind should not ignore these crimes against humanity or let them happen again somewhere else.

Once again, for a wonderful, in-depth and informative history of the Documentary Genre, Erik Barouw's, *Documentary -- a History of the Nonfiction Film, Second Revised Edition*, is detailed informative and inspiring.

CONTEMPORARY DOCUMENTARY FILMMAKING

Contemporary documentary filmmaking evolved through the 1930's, 40's and 50's in to a journalistic style that suited itself to television. In particular, the work of Fred Friendly and Edward R Murrow typifies this new approach. The documentaries employed a host who was seen on camera, heard asking questions during interviews and did voice over narration. These programs included investigative documentaries

Television Documentary

7   Barnouw History of Nonfiction film pg 117

that looked into the Senate hearings conducted by Senator Joesph McCarthy in the 1950's.

Harvest of Shame, produced by David Lowe at CBS and narrated by Murrow was about migrant farm workers and was broadcast nationally in 1960. It was prevented from being distributed beyond its television broadcast because of its depiction of a problem in the United States.

Direct Cinema or Cinema Verite aided by the portability of film equipment that emerged after WWII.

At the same time during the '60's another type of documentary filmmaking emerged internationally. It may have been influenced by the work of early filmmakers like Dziga Vertov, a part of the early Russian Film-Truth philosophy -- "fragments of actuality" -- assembled for meaningful impact"[8] It was also connected with Lumiere's concepts of simply capturing reality or actuality with no editing at all initially. In the US it grew out of the work of Robert Drew who called his style a form of "reporting" based on a photographic and journalistic approach. Drew had worked for Life magazine which featured photo journalism and appears to have developed his approach to film documentary from that standpoint. Drew's documentary, *Primary*, is considered a Direct Cinema or Cinema Verite approach to "reality cinema" or documentary filmmaking.

Robert Drew

D.A. Pennybaker

Drew's associates including D.A. Pennybacker who made *Don't Look Back* is another example of the Cinema Verite style of documentary filmmaking. Made possible by the development of portable, mostly 16mm film cameras and equipment, the Cinema Verite style documentary attempts to record people and events with as little interference as possible, and no direct interviews. The camera merely observes the subjects interacting and going about their lives. Events are therefore covered from an observational perspective.

Today documentary filmmaking has established itself as a multifaceted method of telling all types of nonfiction stories for many different, often controversial, reasons. As was mentioned earlier a documentary may have a point-of-view in the same way a nonfiction book has a point-of-view. Everything written by a human being is a subjective interpretation of reality. "Fair and balanced" is as much a myth as "objective reporting."

There are documentary filmmakers who have an obvious position on a subject and set out to convey that position with what they consider to be reality, as they perceive it. If they include information that is

---

8   Barnouw, History of Nonfiction film pg. 55

factual (can be accepted as having some objective reality as a basis); that may or may not support their point-of-view it creates a more balanced view of the issues concerned.

A documentary may have a number of interviews with individuals who express an opinion but offer no objective reality proof to support their views; those views become suspect. Logic dictates that accepting an opinion requires it to be supported by facts.

Michael Moore is a contemporary documentary filmmaker who's work appears to have been inspired in part by the tenants of John Grierson, who believed that the sole purpose of documentary films was advocacy. Grierson believed in relentless advocacy when it came to humanistic subjects. There is no "fairness" or feigned objectivity allowed.

A look at the world around us indicates there are issues that certainly meet the criteria of being social or ethical problems. When a documentary filmmaker like Michael Moore looks around and sees that a large number of people in the United States are without adequate health care, he feels compelled to address this issue.

For Michael Moore, it's not a matter of "if" there should be Universal *Advocacy* Health Care in the United States, it is a major failing that needs to be corrected. Whatever it takes to get that point across is acceptable in this type of approach. Still, if there are no facts to back up the point-of-view it will not be accepted and the documentary deemed trivial or one person's opinion.

The trouble with the "advocacy - no holds barred approach" is that it is often such a one sided approach that it shows only one part of the story. For example in the documentary film *Sicko* Michael Moore focuses on how bad health care is in the US and how wonderful Universal Health care is in Canada, the UK and France, but fails to address, to any extent, any of the known problems with the Universal Health Care systems. By not including all the facts, his point-of-view appears biased, and becomes to some extent his opinion. It also gives the impression that some facts are being excluded or hidden.

Including both sides of a story is not really an attempt to be objective or fair. It may actually support a point-of-view by allowing the viewer to examine issues and make an informed choice. It also takes the wind out of extremist opponents of the topic who argue that all the facts were not included and who exaggerate minor issues.

In *Sicko* Moore humorously shows how Americans have been conditioned to react negatively to anything connected with "socialism," like "socialized medicine." It might have been a good idea to also show how certain reforms like Social Security, enacted by President Roosevelt (FDR) after the depression, actually helped Capitalism in the United States survive, possibly showing that there might be a best of both worlds solution to the problem.

Most people can accept this kind of advocacy even it they disagree with what the problem is or any solutions proposed. The subject that seems to get people riled up is when the documentary takes on a political point-of-view opposite to their own. Controversial subjects like government, war, social and ethnic equality, human rights, gender issues and religion all provoke emotional responses and lapses of reason.

In the United States some people seem to forget that there is freedom of speech, and the right to dissent as loyal, patriotic citizens. For some reason writing a book that supports or opposes some problem perceived in government does not evoke the same reaction that a documentary on the same subject does.

After Michael Moore's Fahrenheit 911 documentary that attacked President Bush and his administration on a number of fronts including the Iraq War, there developed a hate Michael Moore campaign that seems to equal the kind of response Islamic religious leaders mounted against Salmond Rushdie for his book *Satanic Versus*.

Michael Moore

Why this intense hatred of Moore personally? He's a filmmaker who makes films about the American way of life and topical issues. You may not like his style of storytelling or his mocking your favorite politician. But you can disagree with someone without attacking them personally. Did this film threaten someone's belief system? Did he present realities some people don't want to admit exist? Isn't it his right as an American citizen, a patriot, a member of the loyal opposition, to ask questions and to dissent? Is it possible that there are those in our culture who feel they can issue the American equivalent of a "fatwa" on someone who disagrees with them?

Documentary filmmakers should feel free to explore issues in every sphere without fear of character assassination for their views. Of course they are subject, as is everyone, to criticism aesthetically, factually and with opposing viewpoints.

DOCUMENTARY AND NONFICTION MEDIA

Documentaries may be produced in a number of ways using one or more mediums. The criteria remains the same.

Photographs: used alone, in a book, an exhibit, in a film, with or without audio, in a slide presentation, or in a magazine or newspaper. With tittles, written or voiced comments or without them. A classic documentary book of photographs is *Family of Man*. The *Family of Man* was originally a photography exhibit curated by Edward Steichen first shown in 1955 at the Museum of Modern Art in New York. According to Steichen, the exhibition represented the culmination of his career. The 503 photos were selected from almost 2 million pictures taken by 273 photographers, famous and unknown, in 68 countries, and offer a striking snapshot of the human experience which lingers on birth, love and joy, but also touches war, privation, illness and death. His intention was to prove visually the universality of human experience and photography's role in its documentation.

Documentary Photography

Family Of Man Documentary Photo Exhibit

The exhibit was turned into a book of the same name, containing an introduction by Carl Sandburg who was Steichen's brother-in-law. The book was reproduced in a variety of formats (most popularly a pocket-sized volume) in the 1950's, and reprinted in large format for its 40th anniversary. It has sold more than 4 million copies.

The exhibition later travelled in several versions to 38 countries. More than 9 million people viewed the exhibit. The only surviving edition was presented to Luxembourg, the country of Steichen's birth, and is on permanent display in Clervaux.

Paintings or drawings: depicting events witnessed by the artist singularly or as an exhibit.

Oral history accounts: verbally presented, or recorded, used alone or in conjunction with photographs or other documents or documentation that supports the account.

Plato's Cave

"See human beings as though they were in an underground cave-like-dwelling with its entrance, a long one, open to the light across the whole width of the cave. They are in it from childhood with their legs and necks in bonds so that they are fixed, seeing only in front of them unable because of the bonds to turn their heads all the way around..." --Plato The Republic.

Forced to face forward and unable to turn, humans see only the shadows of objects projected on the wall by the firelight from behind them. Objects are held up in front of the fire and humans think they see the object when they actually only see its shadow.

Documentaries explore the shadows in hopes of getting a glimpse of the objects true nature and identity.

Photo by J R Martin

Documentaries explore reality in the hope of revealing some truth. To do this they record or "document" actuality, that which is actually happening at the moment.

Documentary and Nonfiction Media (continued)

Interviews: edited or not edited.

Audio: documentaries using all non-visual media available to tell a nonfiction story. National Public Radio (NPR) radio does this style documentary. Narration, interviews, music and effects are used to produce the documentary.

First hand accounts: of events presented in person by individuals or groups.

Migrant Mother (1936), by Dorothea Lange while documenting migrant farm workers for the US Government's Farm Security Administration.

Home video, photograph albums: and other forms of recording people and events over the years. Painted and photographed family portraits, and older methods of recording reality.

Newspapers, magazines, and public records.

Literature: both nonfiction and fiction offer a glimpse into cultural and historical realities.

Mixed Media : film or video productions using all or some of the preceding media.

Nonfiction Presentations: A documentary style may be used for a Power Point® presentation to less formal types of reports.

This photograph has a POV that includes framing, angle, lens, and exposure, all conscious choices of the photographer.

Perspective depends on your point-of-view

Documentaries are like nonfiction books in that they have a point-of-view (POV). A POV is a subjective perspective.

Photo by J R Martin

DOCUMENTARY GENRES

There are many types of documentary films that look at various aspects of the human condition and the environment. A documentary may also be a discussion or exploration of a nonfiction reality that is social, political, anthropological, or other humanities or social science subject.

Documentaries explore topical subjects like travel, mountain climbing, boating, sports, medicine, finance and other nonfiction topics.

What follows is a look at current documentary genres, sub-genres, and traditional documentary and nonfiction subject areas.

Anthropological: Visual Anthropology, the exploration of indigenous cultures, customs, traditions and human activities in a social, historical, and ecological context.

Robert Flaherty Prospector and Documentary Filmmaker Circa 1916--Museum of Modern Art

"I am not going to make films about what the white man has made of primitive people."

Flaherty   Museum of Modern Art

Robert Flaherty was called "A Romantic" by John Grierson, because Flaherty tried to show the Eskimo's traditional way of life in *Nanook Of the North*. Flaherty spent many years among the Inuit people recording their way of life.

Nanook of the North is considered by film scholars as the first feature length documentary film. In 1916 this meant using real people doing the things they normally did, rather then hiring actors and writing a screenplay. There were no rules for nonfiction films.

Flaherty says he wanted to show how the Inuit people lived and hunted before they came into contact with European civilization. While their lives were changed in 1922, and there was no going back, they still had the hunting skills, and many of the basic life style traditions they had possessed for thousands of years.

Flaherty did not have any of the modern filmmaking tools, like lights and battery powered cameras. He developed all his own film on location with the help of the Inuit people. He seems to have felt that he needed a story built around a central character, which turned out to be someone he called Nanook.

Whatever it's faults, by modern documentary standards, it is difficult to dispute that it is a ground breaking work for its day and that it does preserve a glimpse of a people as they existed at one time. Documentary film scholars debate a number of issues regarding Flaherty's *Nanook of The North*. One of the primary debates seems to be if it is actually a "Documentary Film" at all.

The argument is that Flaherty basically had a script in mind when he went to shoot the film the second time; that he asked the Inuit to hunt in a traditional way that was dangerous (like the Walrus Hunt) even though they had long been hunting with rifles that they acquired by trading furs. In fact, according to Eric Barnouw, it was not Flaherty but Nanook who suggested they hunt in a traditional way.

It is also argued that many scenes were staged in that Flaherty asked them to do certain things at certain times and he set up shots. For example the scenes in the igloos where the family goes to bed and gets up were shot in an igloo shell with 3 sides and no roof.

They also point to the fact that Nyla was not actually Nanook's wife and the family was somehow artificially constructed for the documentary. They also contend that "Nanook" was not even the main characters real name.

Flaherty was criticized at the time by John Grierson, a filmmaker, who believed that Flaherty had simply romanticized the Inuit at a time they were facing increasing hardships due to the changes in their lives brought about by the Fur Trading Companies, that were sponsoring Flaherty's work.

Today there are guidelines as to what constitutes an anthropological documentary. Flaherty's work was not intended as an ethnographic or anthropological documentary, It was made to entertain and document the indigenous people of this region.

Despite all the controversy, this early documentary has a certain authenticity in that it did not seek to distort reality, simply to bring it to life in a way that captured what Flaherty felt was important to show to the public.

Documentary filmmakers today avoid creating artificial situations or scripting what the subjects will do. Making *Nanook of the North* with today's standards and equipment would create a different type of film, but the life style and traditional culture would still be a priority. Flaherty managed to convey the life style of the Inuit in 1922 with the resources at hand.

Fiction and Nonfiction films are able to distort or convey actual reality. A fiction story may lead you to discover some aspect of reality or a basic truth you did not previously consider. The difference is that nonfiction or documentary explores reality, that which already exists, in search of answers to issues using perceived reality as a starting point.

Ethnographic: Stories about various ethnic groups, their history traditions and customs. This type of research is included as a subdivision of Visual Anthropology.

Art: Documentary film, photographs and audio material used in an artistic fashion to produce the vision of the filmmaker/artist. An early example of this idea was a film called *Berlin Symphony of the City,* made in 1927 by Walther Rutman. It depicted Berlin from dawn to dusk, emphasizing the light, rhythms and patterns of the city. A symphonic score was composed for the film which was played in large city screenings.

Humanities and Social Sciences: Documentaries that look at issues and realities in these areas. Documentaries in this category have been funded by the National Endowment for the Humanities and local Humanities Councils including films by the author and other documentary filmmakers.

Environmental: Nature, the environment, the world around us, animals, and how our ecology works. How do humans fit in?

An Inconvenient Truth is a documentary that looks at the issue of Global Warming. It states its point of view, and then looks at the reasons and facts that support this premise in the tradition of nonfiction writing and advocacy documentaries.

Human Interest: Stories about how we live, the environment, unique people, and other issues. These documentaries take on aspects of other areas but may combine various themes or be more general.

Historical: Documentation based on historic photographs, film and other resources to visually represent history. These films are about events or individuals like *The Civil War*, by Ken Burns. In all of his documentaries including his most recent *The War*, about World War II, Burns has used photographs, documents, archival film footage, interviews with subjects, experts and actuality media to make his documentaries. *The Civil War* is primarily based on Civil War photographs and letters from people involved in the war read by voice over narrators. Burns uses camera moves over the photographs and sound effects to bring movement and action to the documentary.

Historical Documentary Topics -- The history of a town or neighborhood. The history of an event or individual.

Social Advocacy: John Grierson, perhaps the father of modern Social Advocacy Documentary Films, starting with *Drifters* (1929) and films like *Coal Face* (1936) about the problems of coal miners in Great Britain and *Housing Problems* (1935), called for the need for social and political reform. He was unapologetic about his point-of-view. He believed that documentaries were a tool to point out problems and solve social issues.

Social Documentary Topics -- People living below the poverty line, Human Rights, the workplace, and groups. Documentation of issues regarding the human condition and exploration social and political conditions. Ecological concerns.

The Plow That Broke the Plains, Directed by Pare Lorenz, Produced by the US Department of Agriculture.

A socially relevant documentary that played in theaters until it was deemed propaganda, because it was produced by a government agency.

Educational: Any topic that would aid in the study of any subject that one might encounter in the curriculum of all levels of education. Other subjects that may be of educational interest to the general public. Nonfiction issues that deal with education it self.

Mental Health: How people live with stress, disease, afflictions, handicaps and other psychological problems. Pharmaceutical drugs and addiction.

Medical Issues: Disease, drugs, nutrition, health, and related areas. Explore all medical issues facing civilization.

Public Service Sector: documentaries that focus on the occupations of fire fighters, police, canine corps, government and why people choose these careers? Also local events sponsored by local government agencies.

Family: Relationships, dysfunctional and functional, also family histories, oral histories and generational conflicts. Oral histories may be done with recorded interviews and photographs combined to make a documentary about a family or a community. These stories usually include psychologists, social workers and other experts on these subjects.

Sports: Documentaries about the world of sports competition and training. What they mean, why we participate or do not and stories about sports teams from little league and adult amateur to professional.

Nature: Nonfiction explorations of the environment and our relationship with it. Global Warming; does the man or woman in the street believe it? How do are activities in the environment affect our lives and all the other creatures with whom we share the planet. Many of these type productions may be seen on National Geographic, Discovery Channel, Learning Channel an other venues that make documentary style nonfiction programs.

Current Issues: Does anyone really care about high gasoline prices and why do they rise and fall at the drop of any crisis? Alternative energy sources. Urban life. Night life in the city. Local museums and places of interest. Apartment living. Personal stories.

Gender issues: Specific to women's rights, or life styles, and men's rights or life styles.

Religion: Secular and non-secular documentary exporation of religious and spiritual topics. The role religion plays in our lives? Religious groups and their customs. Spirituality. Separation of Church and State. The history of various religions.

Portraits: Portraits of or about the lives of various people successful, not so successful, old, young, what they do and or don't do.

Politics: Explorations of politics and various political subjects. Political Science subjects. Films like Michael Moore's *Fahrenheit 911 and Why we Fight* by Eugene Jarecki.   How people feel about government, politics and war?   States rights and the Constitution. Topical issues from any area of the political spectrum.

Note: At various times in US history political views have become extremely polarized to the extent that documentaries do away with any notion of searching for truth. The nonfiction context of documentaries is stretched, and in the name of "Advocacy" much of what is produced takes on a propagandist tone. Documentaries of lasting meaning should strive to examine and explore reality based on facts not distortions, character assassination and partisan political agendas.

Media: Documentaries that look at the role of Media in today's world. Films like *Orwell Rolls in His Grave*, Directed by Robert Kane Pappas. Also explorations of various media, their qualities and uses.

Entertainment: Documentaries about the arts, music and events like concerts. The kind of things people do for entertainment and how do unusual or new forms of entertainment fit into our culture.

Training: In sports and other areas including jobs and crafts. Military training videos. Corporate training films, videos and multimedia presentations.

Observer: Chronicle and observe events, subjects and various happenings of interest. This point-of-view allows for first person interpretation of reality. Direct Cinema an Cinema Verite formats bring the viewer in to the story as an observer.

Journalistic: Topical news stories in the tradition of Edward R. Murrow, Fred Friendly, 60 Minutes, Front Line, and cable channels like Discovery Channel. Network and local stories done in a documentary format.

Corporate: Internal documentaries about manufacturing, testing, training or product lines. At one time corporations sponsored documentaries about different subjects which were distributed to schools and often played in theaters as short subjects. Many of these films were shown in schools.

Informational: Public Service Announcement (PSA) documentaries usually provide some information about a not-for-profit, charity, or government agency to inform the general public on issues or concern.

Public Relations: Documentaries acquainting the public with a firm or corporation. Also sponsored films.

Docudrama

Obviously a documentary format may be used for many nonfiction films that do not strictly adhere to using actuality materials. One might make a nonfiction film about Athens, at it's peak during ancient Greek times. This might be a combination of scholarly research, surveys of ancient ruins and commentary combined with reenactments of certain events. As soon as we add the reenactments we move from a traditional educational documentary format to a partial nonfiction and fiction format since actors are being used to depict actions that we may only speculate on and which we do not have any visual evidence.

The often-used term "Based on a True Story," has to be categorized as fiction since it not only uses actors, but it is also made from a script based on hear-say or information that has been passed along to us. One such film that does a great job of "being based on a true story" is *The Thin Blue Line*, which is often thought of as a documentary film, but is actually a theatrical film using actors to reenact characters and events in this story. Interviews with subjects actually involved and dramatic recreations using actors to depict acutal events are used. This type of presentation is often called a "docudrama." This Academy Award Wining Film successfully blends actuality and theatrical speculation to reveal the story of a man convicted of a crime he did not commit.

There is a fine line between Fiction and Nonfiction films. There are times when it may be appropriate to include what amounts to a fictional component to a nonfiction documentary effort. For example, in many historical documentary style films and video productions short segments using actors and theatrical sets or locations, will be included. These scenes when tastefully done add a visual reality to the historical narrative. Since they are not "actuality" material they are someone's impression of what may have happened, scripted and acted out and therefore technically fiction.

Recorded Events

Recording an event like a football game without comment, editing or narration does not make it a documentary. the event is simply documented. If we interview players, coach and others combined with some of that documentation, editing it into a story about the game, we are making a documentary film.

Hybrid Documentaries

There are many documentaries that go beyond simply recording actuality. Filmmakers who, like Robert Flaherty, feel that there is something that involves real people and their lives that needs to be preserved or explored even though certain aspects of the story may need to be staged in someway. For example in *Nanook of The North* the Inuit had already started using rifles to hunt game and the family that Nanook was shown to be part of was not his family at all. What was staged was authentic but arranged by the filmmaker to take place. The actuality is authentic, in that the event and people involved are real and are involved in doing something they normally may do. The "fine line" between nonfiction and fiction may be an issue in this type of documentary.

Historical Documentaries

Documentaries with reenactments are a serious form of nonfiction storytelling used for educational, informational and entertainment purposes.

Historical Documentaries should not be confused with Historical Dramas or "Period" films that are fictional dramatic narratives based on historical events or set in the past. While some aspects of the story may be "based" on historical fact, the interpretation of that reality is by definition fiction.

Mocumentary

As the name implies these are satirical fictional, theatrical comedies, like *Best In Show* and *This is Spinal Tap,* that employ a faux documentary format. When done well they are great entertainment but obviously not documentaries or nonfiction.

Attackumentary

There are films and videos that call themselves "documentaries" that are nothing more than thinly disguised propaganda, personal attacks and character assassination vehicles. These videos do not attempt to discuss issues or explore reality. Instead they conjure up bogus conspiracy theories, unsubstantiated facts and out right lies to "attack" a person, institution, policy or politician to bring it into question and ultimately to destroy it. *Stolen Honor* was a character assassination attempt on Senator John Kerry who was running for President of the United States. It was totally fabricated using bogus interviews and footage edited in a documentary style. Many Attackumentary films are political and supported by political organizations that have an ideology and political agenda. They go beyond ordinary propaganda in that they specialize in personal attacks.

Many documentaries which are labeled "Advocacy" have a POV that advocates a position. While these films with their narrow POV's may border on propaganda, they usually have creditable sources and motives. They seek to find solutions to social and cultural problems. Advocacy documentaries are not "Attacking" anything, they are advocating ideas and causes. They look at what their point-of-view considers problems and offer solutions. There is a big difference between creating creditable nonfiction with an argument for or against an issue and creating a fictional story about an individual.

SUMMARY DOCUMENTARY GENRES

The word "Nonfiction," refers to everything that is not fiction, so this covers a myriad of different types of projects. The most well known type of nonfiction film or video is what everyone calls a documentary. A documentary film is a story composed of actuality material; this could be film, video, photographs, first person journals or interviews on audio. The main thing is that it actually occurred and that it was not staged or recreated. In other words it was recorded in some way when it actually happened.

In his documentary about the American *Civil War*, Ken Burns introduces letters and journals written by soldiers in both armies. These are offered as first hand accounts and recollections of those who were involved in the war. They have the perspectives of those individuals and it is their writing. This kind of offering is considered the same as if it were an interview or first person account and not used out of context.

Other nonfiction genres may not necessarily be completely based on actuality, but may be dealing with subject matter that is not fiction. Nature films, Travel, Corporate, Industrial, Sales, Educational and other topics fall into this category. They use a documentary style and incorporate actuality material and other more instructional or informational materials. These types of nonfiction films, videos and multimedia projects will have detailed scripts that show what action is needed.

"This above all, --to thine own self be true; and it must follow, as the night the day, thou canst not then be false to any man."

Hamlet, Prince of Denmark by William Shakespeare

" . . . it is very painful for me to be forced to speak the truth. It is the first time in my life that I have ever been reduced to such a painful position, and I am really quite inexperienced in doing anything of the kind."

The Importance of Being Ernest, by Oscar Wilde

5000 Year Old Mound
New Grange Mound Ireland

CHAPTER 2

PREPRODUCTION

PHASE ONE

DEVELOPING AND RESEARCHING

NONFICTION

AND

DOCUMENTARY PROJECTS

CHAPTER TWO

CHAPTER 2

Developing and Researching Documentary and Nonfiction Projects

"My aim as a filmmaker is to approximate some of the complexity of the real world, rather than to simplify it" - Frederick Wiseman

Considering and Selecting an Idea for a Documentary Project

When considering ideas for a documentary, think about the feasibility of doing the project and how it might be approached. What is the story? Is the idea something that can be accomplished with the resources available? How likely is the cooperation of the individuals, the institutions, government or officials involved?

It's one thing to have an idea for a documentary, it is another to conceptualize the idea and come up with an approach and a point-of-view on that subject. By taking certain steps in the process of developing an idea it is possible to see where the story might be and what areas to explore. A documentary story begins with an idea, notion, questions, problem or issue, that can be explored.

There are many ways to structure a story but all of them must be comprehensible to your audience. All stories have a beginning, middle and end whether they are fiction or nonfiction/documentary. Stories are a description of events, conversations, action, reaction and observations that include whatever conflict and tension that naturally occurs in the nonfiction material and whatever conflict and tension the storyteller builds into telling the tale. In a documentary context the storyteller may use existing conflict to tell the story but not distort the conflict to create false arguments or themes. As in all storytelling from a joke to an epic novel, timing, structure, pace and delivery are important.

The best stories engage the audience in a way that brings them into the process, allowing them to discover, ask questions (which at some point are answered) and that evokes emotion. Questions to consider about ideas are; will it shed any new light on the subject? How interesting is the subject and how much time will it take to present it. Is the subject large? If it is a large subject, on what area will it focus?

The approach and process depends in part on what the subject is

Start a project without firm preconceived notions of what you might find. Documentaries explore reality in a way that is conducive to bringing out basic understanding of those realities.

and the context of how the documentary will be used. An educational film on a given subject may be approached differently than a social advocacy documentary. However, there are some basic steps to at the beginning of the journey.

Audience

As difficult as it may be for the creative ego to accept; some ideas may not have universal appeal. In fact there may be only person interested in a particular notion. Therefor part of the research should be to see if anyone has any interest in the subject being considered for production.

Who is the audience for this subject?

Developing Questions for the Project

The first step in developing the story is to research the subject, either by preliminary talks with the people involved or by doing some research about the subject or topics being documented. Today much of this is as easy as going online.

Researching the subject helps develop an understanding of the subject and a focus for the story. Interview questions should be based on research. Go beyond what is known firsthand and find out what other sources say about the same subject. The easiest place to start researching most any subject or topic in the world is to go online and "Google" it. Read up on what information is available on the subject of the documentary.

Research the sub-ject.

Individuals who might be interviewed may have interesting histories or be well known for their achievements. A little research can give some insight into where they are coming from and topics with which to launch your interview.

Research Techniques

"Careful, systematic study and investigation into some field of knowledge."
--Webster New World Dictionary

There are many types of research done for different reasons. Documentary research varies depending on the type of film, video, slide presentation, or other nonfiction production.

Explore with an open mind.

There must be enough digging to begin the exploration with some idea of what the body of knowledge is pertaining to subject, positive and negative, new and old.

A social advocacy documentary may need to employ research techniques used by Social Scientists. A film looking into ecological issues in the Amazon or the impact of Killer Bee's on North America will require some field research before any shooting begins.

Where To Begin

Are there pre-con-ceived ideas about this subject?

What has been written, documented, said and discussed previously about the focus of your documentary? Start your research by reading books, articles and screening other documentary or nonfiction work on the subject. Go online and "Google" the subject.

Do some preliminary interviews with anyone knowledgeable or involved in the area of interest. Make notes about issues or subjects that might contribute to the story. Ask for other sources or experts that the interviewee thinks are important or that substantiate or dispute their views.

This process is similar to a journalist looking for facts and information to construct a story he is writing. In the case of a documentary this is most often a story that will, in part, be told by the people involved. The research provides information about what questions to ask and how to approach issues involved.

Exploring Reality

Documentaries are explorations of reality, not staged or manipulated situations. Do not go into the making of a documentary with the notion that the answers to the questions are already known or trying to push certain ideas. Perhaps a better way to explore reality is to ask questions like a child. Children learn by asking questions, sometimes unspoken as they explore the world growing up. Young children don't go out with pre-conceived notions of what they are going to find. They ask out of curiosity, with a genuine need to learn about the world and how they fit in.

Starting a documentary without firm pre-conceived ideas about someone or something facilitates discovery. It may be found that what was thought would happen, what was imagined about a subject or what a place might be like, was not the case at all. Not ever encountering or acknowledging new realities might indicate a problem in perception. There is a need to go beyond the superficial, contrived situations and seek to understand the realities that are being explored. Keep an inquisitive attitude while researching and making the documentary.

Narration and Third Party Commentary

Narration to explain what is seen is not always required. A documentary may reveal reality with out anyone having to explain it to the viewer. A subtitle graphic can add a fact without interpreting. Music may or may not be appropriate in some scenes depending on what music is *Use of Music.* supposed to accomplish Music makes a statement about the subject matter and helps or hinders the understanding of what we see. It may be considered a form of third party narration.

Find The Story

After all the research, it comes down to thinking about the most important aspect of the documentary effort, the story. Is there a *What is the story?* story here? What is that story and how will the story be told? A good way to start finding if there is a story is to create an outline of what is to be to covered or where it is thought the story might go. List the issues, individuals and other information uncovered in the research. Look for those elements, beginning, middle and end, that may form the basis for the story.

Consultants

It is a good idea during the research and writing stage to find consultants or experts who are knowledgeable about the issues involved in the documentary. These people may be academics who are expert in a related field. For example, a documentary about Immigration, might want to consult with a historian who has written about it, and a sociologist who understands that end of it. Also social workers and others who deal with immigrants could provide additional insight. The appropriate government agency will provide information on immigration policy.

After the initial research, the next step is to review all the research and refine your idea into a Concept and Treatment.

Writing a Concept and Treatment

Concept

The "concept" should sum up the idea in a sentence or two.

Treatment

Treatments should be short, about two pages for a 30 minute documentary. This is not a script. A treatment is a summary of how you intend to approach the subject, generally what the story is about (beginning, middle and end); what questions you would like to resolve; issues you want to explore and who the people are in the story. Someone reading the treatment should get a feeling you are focused on telling a particular story about a certain subject.

The following concept and treatment attempts to give the reader an idea where this documentary might go. It is not necessarily trying to sell anyone on the idea but a reader should feel that the subject is interesting enough that he would want to see the movie. The writer and/or filmmaker should feel they know where they want to begin telling the story; that you and that a script for the project could be written based on the treatment.

EXAMPLE: Research on an idea about a documentary exploring the impact of Killer Bees in North America is complete and a focus has been determined.

Example two page Concept and Treatment

"KILLER BEES IN NORTH AMERICA"
CONCEPT:

Killer Bees are spreading across the bottom half of North America. This documentary will look at the bee's impact on the indigenous bee population, honey production, humans and the environment.

TREATMENT

Over the last 40 years there has been much speculation over the spread of "Killer Bees," Africanized bees from South America spreading North. This documentary takes a look at the actual impact and what the situation is today.

Africanized bees, traveling about 200 miles per year have spread deep into North America over the last 40 years, into 9 states, including 22 counties in Florida.

Have they interbred with domestic bees and honey production in North America? Are they a threat to humans?

Killer Bees in North America will open with some of the commonly held perceptions, misconceptions, myths and facts about Africanized Bees, from Horror film scenarios like The Swarm, to scientific speculation.

Archival footage and graphics will be used to show how the Africanized bees in the western hemisphere descended from 26 Tanzanian queen bees (A. M. Scutellata) accidentally released in 1957 near Rio Claro, São Paulo State in the south of Brazil from hives operated by biologist Warwick E. Kerr, who had interbred honey bees from Europe and southern Africa. Hives containing these particular queens were noted to be especially defensive. Kerr was attempting to breed a strain of bees that would be better adapted to tropical conditions (i.e., more productive) than the European bees used in North America and southern South America. The African queens eventually mated with local drones, and their descendants have since spread throughout the American continent.

Footage and interviews with bee farmers looks at how Africanized hybrid bees have become the preferred type of bee for beekeeping in Central America and in tropical areas of South America because of improved productivity. However, in most areas the Africanized hybrid is initially feared because it tends to retain certain behavioral traits from its African ancestors that make it less desirable for domestic beekeeping. Specifically (as compared with the European bee types), the Africanized bee:

US Dept. Agriculture

- Tends to swarm more frequently.
- Is more likely to migrate as part of a seasonal response to lowered food supply.
- Is more likely to "abscond" - the entire colony leaves the hive and relocates - in response to repeated intrusions by the beekeeper.
- Has greater defensiveness when in a resting swarm.
- Lives more often in ground cavities than the European types.
- Guards the hive aggressively, with a larger alarm zone around the hive.
- Has a higher proportion of "guard" bees within the hive.
- Deploys in greater numbers for defense, and pursues perceived threats over much longer distances from the hive.
- Cannot survive extended periods of forage deprivation, preventing intrusion into areas with harsh Winters or extremely dry late Summers. (Source Wikapedia.com)

Does your treatment tell a story with a beginning middle and end?

Various experts on the issue will be interviewed including a spokesperson from the US Department of Agriculture, and others knowledgeable on the subject. Interviews with individuals who have had contact with the Africanized bee will be conducted including accounts of individuals attacked by the bees.

The documentary will attempt to separate fact from fiction and explore the realities facing Bee Keepers, and indigenous human populations as the Africanized bees spread and interbreed with the European Honey Bee throughout North America. The documentary concludes with what the future may hold for North America.

Treatments for longer documentary projects may be more than a couple of pages and discuss other concerns depending on who will read it. For example a treatment meant to "pitch" or sell the idea might include more information on why this is an important, topical subject and why it's important to make the film.

A concept and treatment grows out of an initial idea, research, an outline or break down of the subject areas. It forms the basis for the story, a script or shooting script. Sometimes a shooting script is more of a wish list but it does provide a framework for getting the coverage tell a story.

If the treatment gives a strong notion of the documentary story envisioned, it can be presented in a number of mediums including film, video, photographic exhibit, audio program or slide presentation. A well thought out concept and treatment not only provides a place to begin it lets others know what is envisioned. The treatment should convey the filmmaker's knowledge of the subject.

Story Check List.

Assessing An Idea For A Documentary Film.

- Who is the audience for this documentary?
- How will this idea or issue be turned it in to a story with a beginning, middle and end?
- What will be seen on the screen beside an interview?
- What questions will be asked?
- What kind of research has been conducted on this idea?
- Have there been other films on this subject? What did they cover? How will this film be different?
- What exactly will be documented?
- Using the concept, treatment and shooting script storyboard what type of coverage will be shot?
- What film festival featuring or accepting documentaries do you think would be interested in this film?
- What category or area would this documentary come under, social, historical, political, anthropologically etc?
- Will anyone beside a few friends want to view this if it was seen on You Tube, My Space page, or some other internet site?

Shooting Script Preparation

After the concept and treatment is finalized a shooting script can be written. Usually a shooting script is not written until the project is "green lighted" and a preliminary budget approved.

Shooting script based on Concept, Treatment and research.

Under most circumstances the shooting script is the basis for gathering the footage necessary to tell the intended story. The script does not detail what the subject will do or say; the shooting script details a plan for what to shoot to be able to tell the story that is proposed in the concept and treatment. *The shooting script is a plan for gathering footage to tell the story.* This plan may change depending or circumstances, however, it is a place to start rather the going out with a vague notion of shooting something or following someone around to see what happens. *Chapter Five* looks at the process in an actual case study.

The Shooting Script

A shooting script for a documentary does not script what the subject will do or say. It scripts what the filmmakers will shoot, the questions to ask and what the story is about. In some cases where there is a voice over narrator the script will show what the voice over will be and the picture that goes with it.

A shooting script for a documentary is a guide to shooting, a wish list, in some ways, for shots that fit the vision for that scene. Try to get all the shots scripted, however, some shots might may not be obtainable while other opportunities might present themselves as shooting progresses. The shooting script is basis for getting the coverage necessary to tell the story, equipment, crew, scheduling and budget considerations.

Nonfiction multi column scrpt format.

Scripts for nonfiction films and documentaries are different than formats used for theatrical fiction film screenplays. A basic two-column script with a column for the picture and a column for the audio is used. A column for the shot number and one for the approximate time of the shot to be added. This format may be used as a shooting script or an editing script. It some times has another major column in nonfiction production for a storyboard picture.

Since a documentary film is an exploration of reality, things that are actually happening, of which you have no control, it may not be practical to write a formal shooting script. However, a shooting script that shows what questions you are prepared to ask, shots and how you intend to structure the film is important. Sometimes a simple shot list and list of questions may be adequate to help insure getting adequate archival coverage of a one time event that will end up being part of a larger project. Other nonfiction film, video or multimedia projects do require a script since these stories are predictable. They may employ both nonfiction and fictional resources. In a pure documentary script describe the shots desired, who will interviewed, questions, photographs, quotes, and other footage required.

As was mentioned previously, documentary and other nonfiction projects use a multi-column script format (additional columns may be added if needed). This script details the action for picture and audio. This formatting is easy to do with the "Table" function in Microsoft Word®.

A story that combines actuality material or archival footage with dramatized recreations or anything that uses actors instead of the real people, falls into a gray area that is both nonfiction and fiction. If theatrical segments are used in a documentary they would be treated as a fictional scene and scripted in a screenplay format. In the case of a compilation documentary, that uses archival footage, photographs, interviews, and other actuality based material a multi-column script is appropriate.

When making an industrial, corporate, educational, sales, commercial or informational film, video or multimedia project a multi-column script that details everything is appropriate. Storyboards may also be used for these types of nonfiction projects. An additional column may be added for the storyboard frames.

Formatting a multi-column script in Microsoft Word®

Pick the number of columns needed and a number of rows to start out with, around ten would be plenty. More rows can always be added by tabbing on the last cell to add another row. Size your columns by dragging the lines to where you want them.

The great thing about the table is it keeps the cells in each row lined up so your picture and audio, stay opposite each other.

There are professional audio-visual script writing software programs like Final Draft® AV, Ver. 2 available, that tie in with budgeting and other Final Draft® software.

A MULTI-COLUMN DOCUMENTARY OR NONFICTION STYLE SCRIPT (with columns for shot numbers and shot duration time.)

Depending on the subject and the type of event a script for a documentary or nonfiction film may take a number of forms and be of varying degrees of detail. A shooting script can be written detailing may be ultimately seen on the screen. The more planning done for obtaining coverage of the subject the more options available in the editing process.

Shooting Script uses same format as Editing Script

SHOOTING SCRIPT

SHOT	PICTURE	TIME	AUDIO
1	CU Farmer's face	:05	Ambient Sound – VO from interview.
2	LS Farmer walking toward barn	:07	Ambient Sound – VO from interview
3	MS Farmer Bob Longwell standing next to row of Dairy Cows. (Super name lower 3rd)	:10	Interview continues: Answer to question – Why did you become a Dairy Farmer?
4	Misc. CU's, MS's and LS's of farm, equipment, barn, cows, and milking (action and "B" roll.)		Ambient sound.

Standard Abbreviations for Shots

Extreme Close-up -- ECU

Close-up -- CU

Medium Close-Up -- MCU

Medium Shot -- MS

Medium Long Shot -- MLS

Long Shot -- LS

Over-the-Shoulder -- OTS

Writing The Shooting Script

There are many approaches to writing for nonfiction projects. A shooting script for a documentary project shows what shots and questions are pre-visualized for telling the story. The script might say to get "coverage" of the event and interviews with whoever might be important to the event. It becomes the director's job to get the shots and interviews that can be edited together to depict the event. A documentary director needs to think about how the scene will be edited while shooting the scene. This means getting shots that cut together.

For example if a person important to the event is interviewed, it is necessary to try to get footage of what they're talking about ("B" roll) along with general coverage (action) of the event. It's the director's responsibility, but the camera operator should also be aware of the need for a variety of cut a ways and different size shots during an interview. The director and camera operator should discuss the kind of coverage the director is looking for and be thinking and listening to what is going on.

In preproduction, break down the shooting script in to which shots will be shot at each camera set up. For example, to save time questions may be asked in a different order than in the shooting script while at a particular camera set up. It is also necessary to shoot shots out of script order to avoid moving the camera and lights multiple times. This saves time and helps insure continuity in lighting and camera angles.

Finally the questions in the shooting script are a place to start, new questions will come to mind as you listen to the interviewee.
Follow-up on these questions because they can be more revealing than the ones you came up with before the shoot. Listen to your interviewee's answers.

One of the main ideas of creating a shooting script is to insure adequate coverage for editing. Whenever possible visit the location before writing the shooting script.

Fair Use

As early as the scripting stage some thought should be given to possible copyright issues. Copyright laws give the owner of the copyright exclusive use of the work. Anyone wishing to use any portion of that work must have the permission of the copyright holder. There are no exceptions. However over time there has grown a grey area that is called "fair use." Fair use covers certain situations or circumstances where using protected work may be permitted.

But there are no fair use laws. The concept of fair use is as a defense; that something owned by someone else is being used without obtaining permission because it doesn't infringe on the other person's copyright, trademark or likeness in a way that violates the spirit of copyright protection. Since there are no fair use laws, one can only make a case for the notion that the using the protected work in a particular way does not infringe on the copyright. Some "rules of thumb" may be used to gage fair use.

What is Fair Use of Copyrighted Material?

The following list is not intended as legal advice. It is only offered as a layman's guide to the grey area known as "Fair Use." Legal council should be consulted.

Fair Use "Rule of Thumb" Guide.

Rules of Thumb to consider before using copyrighted material.

Is the work protected? Since 1989 absence of a copyright notice does not necessarily mean the work is not protected.

Is the work original (a compilation like the phone book)

Is the work in public domain? Generally work published before December 31, 1922 is considered public domain.

Was the work created by the US Government? If so, it may be used by USA citizens.

Ideas, processes, methods, and systems described in copyrighted work. An idea cannot be copyrighted.

The use of quotes or short segments from copyrighted work in scholarly publications, newspaper articles, books, documentary films, educational work, critical reviews and satirical parodies is usually considered fair use.

Highly recommended for a detailed discussion of intellectual property law is, *The Pocket Lawyer for Filmmakers by Thomas A. Crowell, Esq. Focal Press, 2007.* According to Mr. Crowell there are a number of factors a court considers when determining fair use. These factors include; *"the purpose and character of the use," "the nature of the copyrighted work," "the amount of the portion of copyrighted work used,"* and *"how the use of the work influences the potential market or value of the copyrighted work."* While these are valid factors to consider before using copyrighted material they are no guarantee that there will not be other considerations.

There are a number of fair use areas that apply to educational applications by teachers and students, as long as the use is academic and not commercial in anyway. It should be noted, however, that whether or not a profit is made does not determine fair use.

The use of archival photographs, film or video clips in documentary films follows the same guidelines as those for print. Stock footage libraries base their rates on educational, commercial and theatrical uses.

Preproduction is the first stage in making a documentary film. It includes hiring production personnel, developing the concept and treatment, research, scheduling the shoot and budgeting for the entire project.

CHAPTER 3

PREPRODUCTION PHASE 2

*PREPRODUCTION FOR DOCUMENTARIES,
NONFICTION FILMS,
VIDEOS AND MULTIMEDIA PROJECTS*

CHAPTER THREE

Preproduction

Once a project becomes "Green Lighted," given the go ahead, development work continues in the next phase of preproduction. Preproduction is getting ready to do the project. It produces a map, a blueprint, a master plan and a means to achieving the goal of completing the project on time, on budget and as intended. The shooting script is the starting point for a number of areas in this phase of preproduction.

Preproduction For Nonfiction Films, Videos and Multimedia Projects

Preproduction is usually managed by the producer of the project who is the person who also handles the budget and hiring of key "above-the-line" staff like the director. Many times the producer, director and writer in a documentary project are the same person. If so some assistance is needed to help in these areas. Associate producer or assistant producer, first assistant director and perhaps another writer depending on the scope of the project.

Work on a documentary or some other type of nonfiction project, follows much the same pattern as for a fiction film. The first step is to break down the shooting script so that what needs to be done may be seen, estimate how long it will take, crew and equipment required among other things.

Script Breakdown

Breaking down a shooting script is finding locations, groups of unique scenes and shots at those locations that will be shot from the same camera setup. It's done scene by scene and shot by shot to determine in what order and how best to shoot the project. This process facilitates an estimate of how long it will take to shoot and the equipment and crew needed.

The first thing to do when breaking down a documentary shooting script is to look at locations. Next, what needs to be shot at each location, how many days it will take, what size crew, what equipment and other resources are required. At each location how many camera setups will be required? Schedule all the shots included in the script, wherever in the script they occur, at the same time. It's necessary to determine how many camera setups will be needed because it will take time to set up and light each time the camera is moved.

Making a documentary film is a collaborative process.

Making a documentary is:

65%   Preproduction

25%   Production

60%   Postproduction

150%   Total Effort!

Next look at transportation requirements. Some documentaries may require going back to the same location a number of times. Is this a one-time event being covered or are there a series of one-time events that will be part of this documentary? If so what over what period of time will they occur.

Particularly important to documentary filmmaking, are firm agreements from anyone who is going to be interviewed. This may be verbal or written. A talent release is signed before the interview takes place. This release gives he production permission to use the interview in the film. There are standard release forms available.

Two areas to consider when breaking down the shooting script are the Directors needs and logistical considerations.

Location releases are signed by the owner of the property where shooting occurs. Some property owners will require liability insurance to cover any damage that might happen. Production companies carry workman's compensation and liability insurance. Film and video production rental houses also require insurance to rent equipment.

Deciding whether to use film, various forms of analog or digital video formats is extremely important and is based on a number of factors. Usually the number one considerations are quality and money. Is this project for the big screen, television screen or the internet? Will this project be available to the high definition (HD) market? What resources are available? Is it better to rent or buy certain equipment? What in-house digital video or film equipment is available? In the case of a corporate multimedia project is this going to end up a CD, DVD or online? Each one of these areas has their own set of requirements that need to be examined in order to come up with a plan and budget.

After breaking down the script and estimating the number of days and locations it is time to look at crew and equipment needs. At this time the producer gets together with the director and the director of photography (DP) to go over the shooting script, breakdown and location schedule. The DP assess the shots the director wants to do and makes suggestions as to what equipment and lights will be required.

The producer or an assistant makes calls to confirm locations and get agreements from the subjects of the documentary. The director and the DP scout locations. The director will also do what ever research they believe needs to be done in order to come up with questions for the interviewee. Under certain circumstances the producer may hire a research team and a writer who will work with the director.

In some instances the director will not be doing the interviewing. In that case the director's responsibility is to direct talent and camera to obtain the needed coverage.

Hiring The Crew And Determining What Crew Is Required

HIRING PRACTICES

The producer hires the director and other "above the line staff," including the producer's assistants. The producer usually confers with the director on the choice of a DP and script supervisor since these people work closely with the director. Most directors have certain people they like to work with, in particular the DP, first assistant directors. Production managers usually come with the producer, as the are involved in pre-production.

Most Directors of Photography (DP) request crew members they know or have worked with before for their crews. These positions include a first assistant, a camera operator (if the DP is not doing it himself) a second assistant or loader (if shooting film), a gaffer (lighting) and grips. Audio crew may be on recommendation of the DP or hired separately. Production assistants as required are hired by the producer as well as other positions.

An inhouse producer draws from staff and hires free lancers for any positions not available inhouse. Some television stations, hire independent producers for a specific project and include some staff and/or offices.

Documentary and Nonfiction Crew Positions & Responsibilities

Not all of the following crew positions are required or recommended on a nonfiction or documentary project. Many positions will be combined or eliminated depending on budget and the scope of the project.

Producer

PRODUCING

The producer may generate original concepts or may purchase, adapt, or handle existing concepts and scripts from other sources. Producers puts the production together from inception and see it through to distribution. There are a number of different types of producers. An executive producer is usually someone associated with the financing of the project or head of the production company. A producer may be someone who is part of a production company or hired as an independent producer for a specific project. Independent producers also may originate projects independently and find financing for those projects. A line producer is someone who works for another producer. The line producer supervises projects in the same way the producer does.

Producers secure financing and make production, distribution, and exhibition deals for the project as well as hiring the director and other crew members may also be part of the producer's responsibility. His staff oversees location scouting, scheduling, budgeting, travel arrangements for crew, talent (if any), and interviewees. In some case the producer may also be the writer, director, interviewer, and/or editor in a traditional documentary effort by an individual filmmaker.

FINANCING

It should be noted that there are many types of projects that fall under the nonfiction category that are not traditional actuality based documentary efforts. These nonfiction projects include training films, historical reenactments, docudramas, educational, scientific, and many kinds of so called "reality based," television programming. The producer's role will vary depending on the type of project.

Other members of the producer's category are the unit production manager or a production manager both of whom help coordinate a project and report to the producer.

Director

The director's role in making a documentary film varies depending on the type of nonfiction or documentary project. The director of a traditional documentary is usually the person doing the interviewing, working with the DP/camera operator, editor and other key crew members.

The director is responsible for the look and feel of the project. If a producer is involved they hire the director because they feel this is the right person to direct the production. Whether it's a traditional documentary or other nonfiction story, the director researches the concept of the documentary and comes up with a treatment and/or shooting script for the subject. If it's not an actuality based project the director takes the script and develops a look and feel. At this point, as in fiction productions, the producer will sign off on what the director has decided to do.

CREATIVE CONTROL

The usual prerogatives and responsibilities of the director apply as to the selection of certain key crew positions like the cinematographer and to staying within budget. Depending on the type of project the director will consult and work with the producer to develop a shooting schedule; work with the director of photography to plan compositions, camera moves, and lighting plots. The director scouts locations often with the DP. The director works closely with the editor to choose usable footage including stills and stock footage. In an actuality based documentary he usually does the interviewing.

Writer

The writer in a documentary production may be the same person as the director and/or the producer. A writer may be employed in a nonfiction production for an educational film, corporate training film or for a television style documentary production. Depending on the needs of the production they may be asked to research and/or find archival and historical records to develop a script for narration. Writers may be asked to work with the producer and director to maintain historical accuracy with regards to events and dialogue.

First Assistant Director (AD)

The AD carries out a number of administrative duties for the director, including scheduling shooting, arranging logistics, calling personnel to the proper location for shooting; maintaining order on the set or location; checking budgets; and communicating with department heads. They insure that all proposed or planned shots are covered. In small crews the first AD position and script supervisor position are often combined.

Second Unit Director

The second unit director is used when a documentary entails gathering coverage that either goes beyond the main location shooting area or is in some remote location that does not warrant the director and total crew going there. At an event such as a concert, a second unit director would be assigned the task of shooting pick-up shots and "B" roll footage. This might be additional footage that the director cannot cover for some reason.

Director of Photography (DP)

The director of photography on a documentary film works closely with the director, often as collaborator, and camera operator. The DP is responsible for lighting or complementing the lighting of a given location in order to clearly see subject matter (priority) and possibly invoke mood. The DP may operate portable lighting devices during shooting; oversee the general composition of the scene; the colors of the images; the choice of cameras, lenses, filters, and media; camera settings and movements and the integration of any special effects, animation, or opticals. Depending on the size of the production the camera crew may include a gaffer to oversee lighting.

When film is the medium used the DP is involved in the decision-making concerning film printing, answer print correction and often works closely with film processing labs. Working with the Director he strives to keep the look and feel of the film consistent with the Directors vision and overall continuity. The DP is usually involved in the planning stages of the project and must be aware of locations and weather conditions to plan shots. The DP is in charge of the gaffer, camera operator, and grips and in small crews may assume all of these positions.

Camera Operator

The camera operator works under the director of photography and is directly responsible for managing the camera during shooting. They view the scene through the viewfinder, making certain that the image is correct and adjust settings and camera positioning. The camera operator performs in-camera movements, as well as static compositions and should be familiar with locations prior to the shoot as much a possible. Experience with handheld work, camera-assist units (e.g., steadicam, jibs), and ENG style are important. This position may be combined with director of photography.

First Assistant Camera Person (AC)

The first AC is directly responsible to the Director of Photography and/or Camera Operator for the proper and prompt selection, set-up, and maintenance of the camera) and related camera accessories. Changes lenses as necessary, sets lens stops, and pulls focus for all takes. He insures that the appropriate film or tape stock is loaded and labeled and he maintains an accurate record of shots, takes, and expended footage, as well as camera settings. The first AC inventories camera equipment.

Second Assistant Camera Person (second AC)

The second AC is responsible to the first assistant cameraman for loading and unloading magazines with the appropriate film stock, as well as accurately labeling said magazines. He also marks the slate and claps the sticks of the clapboard before each take, calling out the appropriate indexing information. They keep count of the amount of footage used and remaining each day. Generally not used in documentary filmmaking; because half of these responsibilities will fall to the camera operator or DP and the other half to the Script Supervisor or Sound Mixer.

Video Assist Technician

The video assist technician sets up, maintains, and monitors any video tape devices attached to film cameras or VTR's used for the recording of taped projects. They calibrate external monitors for correct color, brightness and contrast, and alters vector scope and waveform monitor settings to obtain the best possible color and contrast thresholds. The video technician logs and replays footage and may perform assemble edits of video dailies. In certain instances the Script Supervisor may handle this position.

Gaffer

The gaffer is responsible for supplying, placing, operating, and maintaining the required lights, as well as their power sources, for illumination in both studio and location environments. He oversees general power requirements for all equipment, including the all-important battery supplies. With the DP he may be asked to scout locations to determine power requirements, existing lighting availability and location weather conditions. The best boy is an assistant to the Gaffer. A best boy helps rig lighting and keep track of lighting costs.

Grips

Grips perform an assortment of duties, including transporting and setting up equipment, especially with regards to lighting accessories; moving and placing props and scenery; setting dolly tracks; and operating dollies. He answers to the art director, director of photography, or camera operator and may double as boom operators. Said by some to be named, grip, because of their need to maintain a firm "grip" while carrying objects or pushing/pulling the dolly. This position is usually shared by all other positions on smaller crews.

Production Assistants (PA)

PA's generally work under specific department heads and perform a variety of important tasks for the production, including distribution and posting of printed materials, preparation for shooting, crowd control, office duties (making copies and answering phones), and running general errands ("go for" food or last-minute supplies). This position is usually shared by all other positions on smaller crews.

Script Supervisor

Script supervisors are responsible for maintaining a record of individual takes and their details, including the beginning and end of takes; their durations; the properties appearing in the shot; the camera's position and movement; and an example or synopsis of the dialogue recorded.

They helps bridge complementary ideas and images from scene to scene and ensure that all proposed or planned shots are covered and that all impromptu ones are logged. The script supervisor can absorb some of the second assistant camera person's responsibilities as far as helping with logs. In some situations they may also serve as the video assist technician/VTR and/or first assistant director.

Sound Mixer

Sound mixers are responsible for recording sound and mixing levels during shooting in a manner that is clear, accurate and balanced and does not obstruct shooting. They must be familiar with a wide array of recording instruments, their unique polar patterns and construction, as well as with area acoustics and local ambience. The sound mixer maintains recording equipment, records sound logs/reports and notes any necessary sound effects or ambience and supervises this position or may also be the boom operator.

Boom Operator

The boom operator maintains the boom pole or fish pole in a manner in which the attached microphone is always pointed at the appropriate subject to pick up the best recording consistent with said microphone's particular polar pattern. A boom operator strives not to interfere with the visual aspects of the production, in other words keeps the boom out of the shot! The boom operator wears a head set to monitor the microphone on the boom pole.

Editor

The editor shapes and arranges shots, scenes, and sequences, while also modulating and integrating sound and music, in order to bring rhythm, mood, tone, emphasis and story to the final impact of the piece. The editor incorporates graphics, on-screen titles, animated sequences, stills and stock footage where appropriate. The editor works closely with the Director to create the pacing and feel desired by the Director. In the early days of motion pictures in Hollywood, the directors job was finished after shooting. The producer or studio oversaw the editing. This is no longer the case and now the Director supervises the first cut of the film as it is the director's vision that is being edited.

Assistant Editor

Assistant editors maintain a record of all editable elements in a production and may oversee or assist with the logging, capturing, digitizing, or transferring or recorded material from one medium to another. They assist in synchronically relating image and sound and splicing together or grouping varying pieces of footage and are responsible for maintaining editing equipment.

Composer/Sound Designer

The composer develops the score for the project. As in fiction filmmaking, this generally happens after the fine cut is done but may be commissioned earlier to facilitate editing. The composer may be involved in the sound design for the entire project and work with the director and sound editors.

Art Director/Set Designer

Depending on the requirements of the production an art director may be employed in set or location design. An art director may also be involved in designing graphic elements used in the documentary including, credits, titles, lower third graphics, archival photograph recording and DVD art.

PREPRODUCTION CHECK LIST

Approach resolved.

Concept and Treatment written and approved.

Research on subject and topics conducted.

Agreements and Releases signed.

Financing source secured.

Shooting Script written.

Locations visited if possible.

Shooting Script Break down.

Crew Hired.

Equipment needed checked.

Budget finalized.

Shooting Days set.

Location meals and Per Diem arranged.

Call times set for crew.

Final confirmation interviews or contacts regarding time of arrival.

Release Forms and other forms for shoot.

Film stock, video tape or digital media storage packed for travel.

A budget for a documentary project is an educated estimate of what it will cost to make the film. The contingency fund covers anticipated and not anticipated events and needs.

BUDGET SUMMARY

| PROJECT NAME: |
| PRODUCTION COMPANY: |
| ADDRESS: |
| TELEPHONE NUMBER: |
| PRODUCER/DIRECTOR: |

NUMBER OF EPISODES:	BUDGET DATE:
LENGTH OF EPISODE:	REVISION:
PRE-PRODUCTION DAYS:	
SHOOTING DAYS:	LOCATION WEEKS:
POST-PRODUCTION WEEKS:	

SUMMARY OF PRODUCTION COSTS:	ACCOUNT		Total Cost
A. Story	100	Sub-total A:	$0.00
B. Production Staff & Talent	200	Sub-total B:	$0.00
C. General & Administration Costs	300	Sub-total C:	$0.00
D. Pre-production Expenses	400	Sub-total D:	$0.00
E. Production Crew	500	Sub-total E:	$0.00
F. Location & Travel Expenses	525	Sub-total F:	$0.00
G. Equipment Expenses	550	Sub-total G:	$0.00
H. Videotape Expenses	575	Sub-total H:	$0.00
I. Post-Production Editorial	600	Sub-total I:	$0.00
J. Music and Score	650	Sub-total J:	$0.00
K. Distribtion	700	Sub-total K:	$0.00
L. Insurance & Legal	800	Sub-total L:	$0.00
M. Publicity & Promotion	900	Sub-total M:	$0.00
		TOTAL:	$0.00
N. Contingency/Weather	925	Sub-total N:	$0.00
		GRAND TOTAL:	$0.00

| COMMENTS: |
| |

CHAPTER 4
BUDGETING

Chapter Highlights

Above the Line and Below the Line

Budgeting for Each Department

Budgeting for Preproduction

Budgeting for Production

Budgeting for Postproduction

Sample Budget

Budget Check List

CHAPTER FOUR

BUDGETING

Once you have a script breakdown, a schedule, equipment and crew requirements you're ready to work on a budget.

1. The first step in making a budget for any project is to determine the amount of time it's going to take to do the project. How many days for pre-production, production and postproduction?

2. The second factor is how many days will be needed for production and shooting? There may be more production days than actual shooting days since production includes travel and set-up days.

3. Third, estimate how long the edited version of the project might be and what medium is to be used i.e. film (35mm or 16mm) , video, DV, slides, etc? As far as estimating the length of script, there are guidelines that are used for budgeting theatrical screenplays, like approximately one minute per page, but they like most "rules of thumb" in production are adjustable by all kinds of other factors.

In nonfiction and documentary production it is not unusual to aim for a particular length. Review the Concept, Treatment and Shooting Script to determine if the subject is being adequately addressed with in the time allotted, whether it be seven minutes, 30 minutes or feature length at 90 minutes or longer.

4. After you choose the medium and estimate how long the film will be, you should determine a shooting ratio (the ratio of footage shot to what is used in the final film). Most documentaries have a high shooting ratio.   A student project budget might limit itself to 15 to 1. National Geographic, the BBC or Home Box office might be 50 to 1.

5. Finally, how much time is needed for postproduction? This includes editing and all aspects of finishing the project.

Once all these factors are known use them to determine the budget. A budget is an estimate of what it will cost to do the project. Try to be conservative in all calculations, in other words, do not underestimate or greatly over-estimate.

What follows is a basic list of the categories and a brief description of categories, jobs and responsibilities for nonfiction or documentary production. Not all of the following crew positions are required or recommended on a nonfiction or documentary project. Many positions will be combined or eliminated depending on budget and the scope of the project. For a complete description of the duties of each position see Chapter 3.

Producer

The budget should reflect whatever compensation the producer is getting or taking for producing the project as well as all the other personnel in that department. In very small projects the producer may do many of the jobs in that department.

Please note that there are many types of projects that fall under the nonfiction category that are not traditional actuality based documentary efforts. These nonfiction projects include training films, historical reenactments, docudramas, educational, scientific, and many kinds of so called "reality based," television programming. The Producer's role and compensation will vary depending on they type of project.

Above-The-Line -- Production and Talent

Above-the-line expenses in a film budget refers to contractual costs that are fixed and agreed on before production actually starts. These areas include the producer, writer, director, and pre-production expenses.

Writer

A writer, when necessary, either to write a shooting script, editing script or to write narration for the film or video.

Director

The director usually begins work during pre-production, works during production and in postproduction supervises the editing of the project. The director's salary is negotiated in advance for a certain number of weeks or months.

Consultants

Documentary projects of all kinds employ academic consultants, and others with expertise in the area the documentary is covering. Compensation may be based on a daily or flat rate. In some case an honorarium may be awarded.

Narrator

In films using a 3rd party voice over narrator. Daily or flat rate is used.

Below-the-line

Below-the-line expenses in the budget include all costs anticipated once production has started. It may also include salaries not determined before production began.

Production Personnel (Below the line)

1st Assistant Director

In large projects a second assistant director my be budgeted.

Camera Department

Director of Photography (DP)
Camera Operator
1st Assistant Camera person
2nd Assistant or Loader
Gaffer
Grips

When budgeting for a nonfiction or documentary project the size of the camera department depends on the scope of the project. A DP is someone who knows all the jobs in that department. On small shoots they may operate, light, and do other jobs as needed. On small projects it is not unusual to have a DP/operator and a first assistant camera person who, with the help of a grip, handle all camera department responsibilities.

A still photographer is often used in a documentary film for photographs to be used in the documentary and production stills.

Rates for the Camera Department will vary depending on the size and scope of the project, if it is union or non-union and where shooting is taking place. In any event compensation is usually based on union scale and the length of the working day. Non-union rates are competitive with union rates in certain markets. Non-union "days" are often longer than union "days." In a "right-to-work" state like Florida, non-union "days" are usually 10 hours as opposed to eight hour union "days." This difference enters into the computation of overtime calculation. In other States there is no difference between union and non-union "days."

Travel & Location Expenses

Expenses should be budgeted as required. If the production needs to travel to locations away from home overnight, a per diem stipend is paid for each day on location. This is above and beyond providing a hotel room, air fares or other transportation, and meals while shooting.

1. Air fares all personnel.
2. Per diem.
3. Local transportation
4. Hotel
5. Crew meals
6. Location fees
7. Petty cash
8. Gratuities
9. Car rentals
10. Gas & tolls

Equipment

Requirements for each shoot will vary depending on the scope and needs of the project. Most equipment may be rented for days, weeks or months. Rates change and usually are negotiable depending on the length of time equipment is rented. A week's rental may be based on four days. A months rental on three weeks. Basic equipment categories include:

1. Camera
2. Lenses
3. Camera supplies
4. Walkie talkies
5. Sound package
6. Lighting
7. Grip equipment
8. Misc. sound

Video Tape, Film (Raw Stock) or Other Media

Not all of the line items are needed. Shooting on film, 16mm or 35mm, requires film stock and other items not needed in a video shoot. Shooting documentaries on film today is not as common as using videotape because of a number of factors. Film is usually more expensive and requires more equipment and crew. Video is usually less expensive, more portable and suited for documentary style shooting. Quality once a major issue in choosing between film and video is less an issue now. The bottom line in choosing is how the final product will be viewed.

A major documentary meant for theatrical release in theaters would strongly consider film, either super 16mm or 35mm. However, there are certain digital formats that can be "blown-up" and transferred to film for theatrical release. A documentary made for television would consider high definition or other high end digital video formats.

Tape – DV, DVC-PRO, and other formats may be purchased online at competitive rates.

Film

1. Negative 16mm or 35mm -- Best purchased directly from Kodak
2. Developing prices vary from Lab to Lab
3. Work print – prices vary from Lab to Lab
4. Transfer to video or digital (non-linear edit)
5. Sound recording tape (for double system film shooting) or audio interviews --Newer recorders use hard drives no tape required.
6. Magnetic stock for sound transfers (if film work print is ordered)
7. Magnetic transfers

Narration and Recording

1. Studio rental
2. Audio tape

Sound and Music

1. Music rights
2. Transfers
3. Audio stock
4. Mixing

Titles, Graphic and Optical's

1. Art
2. Shooting (if film)

Editing and Finishing

1. Editor
2. Assistant editor
3. Syncing dailies (if film)
4. Editing supplies (if film)
5. Flex files if editing non-linear and finishing in film
6. Editing facilities (film or non-linear)
7. Editing equipment rental (flat bed editor for film)

8. Non-linear editing software and computer (DV)
9. Off-line editing facility (video tape)
10. On-line editing facility (video tape)

Finishing in Film

1. Magnetic stock
2. Transfers
3. Negative cutting
4. Optical effects
5. Answer prints
6. Internegative
7. Release prints
8. Video dubs
9. DVD dubs

Overhead

1. Office rent
2. Telephone
3. Transportation
4. Shipping
5. Copying
6. Postage
7. Office supplies
8. Office equipment
9. Legal fees
10. Accounting fees
11. Insurance
12. Office personnel

If you take a good look at the budget form, you will see all the items that need to be resolved in pre-production. All your planning and scheduling is, of course, subject to change! So don't forget a contingency fund that should equal about 10% - 15% of the total below-the-line budget. Add it on after the subtotal, before the grand total. No one ever has money left in the contingency fund after the production is complete. There will always be unplanned events, like a rainy day or special equipment that uses up that fund.

Shooting, editing and finishing your documentary from start to finish using any number of digital formats like DV, DVC-Pro, DVC HD, or HD is a common practice today. Consider how your documentary will be released when choosing a format. It would not make much sense to shoot using film for something that will be seen exclusively on the Internet.

Budget Considerations

Once there is a shooting script and an idea how the documentary will be shot determine if it's for TV, video, the big screen, DVD, or the web? Budget for the highest quality you can afford that meets the release requirements.

At one time most documentary shooting was done on 16mm film because the use of video on location was not practical and the quality of film was far superior. In the late 70's almost all production outside of TV Studio was done on film, 16mm or 35mm; 16mm being the most popular format because equipment was more portable, requiring smaller crews and the cost of film stock and processing was cheaper.

Today, many documentaries are shot in some type of digital format. HD is probably the best format for a documentary that is meant for television or DVD release since having it as a Master, allows you to transfer it to media with less resolution. Some HD can even make the trip (bumped up) to film with good quality. Film these days is reserved for high-end projects with larger budgets that anticipate a possible theatrical release.

A budget is based on the best information and estimates available at the time. If the budget is for a project that is more than a few months away prices may change. If it takes a year for the project to begin the budget may need to be updated to reflect current costs.

Prices with individuals and suppliers may be negotiated. For example, equipment rental houses list a daily rate for he rental of most equipment. If the equipment is going to be rented for a week or more this rate is negotiable.

Shop around for prices on everything including hotel accommodations and catering.

A production always needs workmen's compensation and liability insurance.

Budgeting for Post Production

Most production companies these days have their own non-linear-editing (NLE) resources. A rental rate for these facilities should be included in the budget along with the cost of the editor and assistant editor as required.

If the services of any of the production personnel, such as the DP or audio engineer, a day rate for these people should be included in the postproduction budget.

Estimate the time to edit the project based on how long it took to shoot, how much footage is available, how tight the editing script is and past experience with the editor and director of the project.

The services of a writer may be needed to write voice over narration or help in the writing of an editing script.

In some projects there may be a need for animation, graphics and other illustrations. Titles and credits also need to be produced.

If the project is to be released on DVD for previews or festival entries a DVD designer should be budgeted.

Working with Union Personnel

Members of various unions and guilds associated with the film industry are among the best skilled and talented people in the business. Many of the unions and guilds understand the limited budgets and resources for documentary projects both theatrical and non-theatrical. For example the Writers Guild of America (WGA) has a special contract designed to meet the needs of documentary filmmakers. In one instance it allows deferred payments when there is a writer-producer or in other situations.

The Directors Guild of America (DGA) has rates for documentary and non fiction projects.

It is best to check with local chapters of each union for rates and contract terms when working on the budget. In some states, like Florida, there are so called "Right to Work" laws that allow productions to hire both union and non-union personnel. Productions may use union crew in one area and not another.

BUDGET CHECK LIST

- What kind of budget is available for this project?

- How long is the documentary?

- Who is the audience?

- How will the documentary be distributed?

- How quickly will production need to proceed?

- What medium will be used (film, video, photographs, Power point or Keynote presentation, print)?

- How long might pre-production, production and postproduction take?

- Review the concept, treatment and shooting script.

- Consult with the director and DP regarding shooting script and equipment requirements.

- Break down the shooting script.

- Finalize all above the line expenses.

- Estimate how many days are needed for shooting.

- Consult DP regarding crew and equipment requirements.

- Determine crew requirements.

- Get prices on all equipment required.

- Determine Transportation, meals and per diem costs.

- Estimate all postproduction expenses.

- Estimate music and any 3rd party narration or consulting fees.

- Include insurance, publicity, and distribution costs.

- Estimate contingency fund 10% to 20% depending on variables like weather, location and subject.

Each category in the Budget Detail is linked with the Budget Summary. Each item in a category has its own account code. When money is spent it is applied to the appropriate category, line and account.

BUDGET SUMMARY

PROJECT NAME:
PRODUCTION COMPANY:
ADDRESS:
TELEPHONE NUMBER:
PRODUCER/DIRECTOR:

NUMBER OF EPISODES:	BUDGET DATE:
LENGTH OF EPISODE:	REVISION:
PRE-PRODUCTION DAYS:	
SHOOTING DAYS:	LOCATION WEEKS:
POST-PRODUCTION WEEKS:	

	SUMMARY OF PRODUCTION COSTS:	ACCOUNT		Total Cost
A.	Story	100	Sub-total A:	$0.00
B.	Production Staff & Talent	200	Sub-total B:	$0.00
C.	General & Administration Costs	300	Sub-total C:	$0.00
D.	Pre-production Expenses	400	Sub-total D:	$0.00
E.	Production Crew	500	Sub-total E:	$0.00
F.	Location & Travel Expenses	525	Sub-total F:	$0.00
G.	Equipment Expenses	550	Sub-total G:	$0.00
H.	Videotape Expenses	575	Sub-total H:	$0.00
I.	Post-Production Editorial	600	Sub-total I:	$0.00
J.	Music and Score	650	Sub-total J:	$0.00
K.	Distribtion	700	Sub-total K:	$0.00
L.	Insurance & Legal	800	Sub-total L:	$0.00
M.	Publicity & Promotion	900	Sub-total M:	$0.00

	TOTAL:	$0.00

N.	Contingency/Weather	925	Sub-total N:	$0.00

GRAND TOTAL:	$0.00

COMMENTS:

Above The Line

Category A (Story): Includes all writing and script costs.

Category B (Production & Talent): Pension & Welfare for on Camera Talent included.

Category C (G & A) Based on a percentage of of Categories E through J.

Category D (Pre-production)

Below the Line

Categories E through J (Production Crew, Equipment, Tape, Post -Production, Music)

Category K (Distribution)

Category L (Insurance & Legal)

Category M (Publicity)

Category N (Contingency)

BUDGET DETAIL

A. STORY	No.	Fee	Cost
101 Treatments			
102 Screenplay			
103 Shooting Scripts			
104 Editing Script			
		Sub-total A:	$0.00

Depending on the project categories A thru D in this budget are "Above the Line," expenses. Pre-production may be excluded in some budgets.

B. Production & Talent	Weeks	Fee	Cost
201 Producer			$0.00
202 Director			$0.00
203 Host			$0.00
204 Co-Host			$0.00
205 Guests			$0.00
206 Associate Producer			$0.00
207 Assistant Director/location Coordinator			$0.00
208 Production Secretary			$0.00
209 Script Supervisor			$0.00
210 Consultants			$0.00
211 Pension/Welfare			$0.00
		Sub-total B:	$0.00

C. General & Administration Costs	Rate %	Total	Cost
301 G & A			$0.00
302 Office			
		Sub-total C:	$0.00

D. Pre-production Expenses	No.	Days	Rate	Cost
401 Research and Development				
402 Travel Expenses				
403 Air Fare				
404 Accomodations				
405 Ground Transportation				
406 Phone, Duplication, Etc.				
			Sub-total D:	$0.00

Below the line covers production expenses and other variable expense categories.

E. Production Crew	Days	Rate	Cost
501 Dir. Photo./Camera Operator	0		$0.00
502 Video Technician	0		$0.00
503 Sound Mixer	0		$0.00
504 Production Assistant	0		$0.00
505 Grip/Driver/PA	0		$0.00
506 Editor	0		$0.00
		Sub-total E:	$0.00

F. Location and Travel Expenses	No.	Days	Rate	Cost
526 Location Fees				
527 Permits				
528 Van Rental				
529 Boat Rentals				
530 Boat Driver/Operator				
531 Parking / Tolls				
532 Accomodations				
533 Mobile Telephone				
534 Telephone / Duplication / Misc.				
535 Lunch				
536 Per Diems				
537 Air Fare				
538 Air Freight / Excess Baggage				
539 Cabs and other Transportation				
540 Gratuities & Tips				
			Sub-total F:	$0.00

G. Equipment Expenses	No.	Weeks	Rate	Cost
551 Camera Package Rental				$0.00
552 Camera Support / Tripod				$0.00
553 Camera Mounts / Steadicam				$0.00
554 Playback Adapter / VTR				$0.00
555 Video Monitor / WFM				$0.00
556 Wireless Microphones				$0.00
557 Lavalier/Shotgun Microphones				$0.00
558 Microphone Mixer				$0.00
559 Audio / Video Cables				$0.00
560 Grip / Lighting Rental				$0.00
561 Walkie Talkies / Bullhorn				$0.00
562 Batteries / Other Accessories				$0.00
563 Supplies & Expendables				$0.00
Editing Equipment				$0.00
564 Still Photo / Film & Processing				$0.00
			Sub-total G:	$0.00

H. Film &/or Videotape	No.	Rate	Cost
576 Videotape Stock			$0.00
577 Transfers to NLE System			$0.00
578 Dubs			$0.00
579 Film Stock			$0.00
580 Processing Film	feet		$0.00
581 Transfers	hours		$0.00
582 Complimentary Dubs			$0.00
		Sub-total H:	$0.00

Budgeting is a skill that grows with experience.

I. Post-Production Editorial	No.	Days	Rate	Cost
601 Footage Logging				
602 Time-coded Dubs				
603 Transcriptions				
604 NLE System				
605 NLE Edit				
606 Sound Sweetening Effects Editing				
607 Voice Over and Narration				
608 Sound Mix				
609 Edit of Promo Spots				
			Sub-total I:	$0.00

J. Music and Score	Rate	Cost
651 Score Composition		
652 Studio Recording & Mixing		
	Sub-total J:	$0.00

K. Distribution Expenses	Length	No.	Rate	Cost
701 Design DVD Package				
702 Transfer to DVD Master				
703 Screening copies				
704 Release copies				
705				
			Sub-total K:	$0.00

L. Insurance & Legal Expenses	Fee	Cost
801 General Production Liability		
802 Equipment Floater/Faulty Stock		
803 Talent Insurance		
804 Crew / Workmens Comp.		
805 Third Party Property Damage		
806 Legal Fees		
	Sub-total L:	$0.00

M. Publicity & Promotion	Rate	Cost
901 Publicity & Promotion		
	Sub-total M:	$0.00

Important: See Notes on Next Page.

Renting or Buying Equipment

Budgets for clients do not usually include equipment purchases. Budgets for clients include rentals and expendable items with no residual value or that will be used up during the shooting. You may wish to purchase equipment for your company that will enable you to do projects and charge each project a fair price for the use of that equipment. The idea is that you have enough business to warrant owning equipment (tools) that you need for each project. This saves you and the client money.

Equipment you purchase may be depreciated over a period of time for tax purposes. Generally equipment that becomes obsolete in a year or software does not need to be depreciated.

Owning a state-of-the-art professional level camcorder may seem advantageous, however, "state-of-the-art" is a temporary thing these days.

The case study of Studio A - Profile of A Disc Jockey covered in the next three chapters applies the information in preceding chapters as a practical example of the principals involved in the making of a short educational documentary film from the birth of the idea through all phases of production.

Crew inside Studio A - WLS Chicago

CHAPTER 5

CASE STUDY -- EDUCATIONAL DOCUMENTARY

THE MAKING OF STUDIO A -- PROFILE OF A DISC JOCKEY

Thirty Minute Educational Documentary Film

Examining the making of this documentary provides a look at all the steps involved in the production, from idea to screen and distribution.

Chapter Highlights

How The Project Came About

Rationale

Approach

Financing & Reality Check

Participation

Research

Writing A Concept & Treatment

Writing Shooting Script

CHAPTER 5

The Making of Studio A – Profile of a Disc Jockey
Educational Documentary Film

How The Project Came About

John Landecker was a very popular AM radio DJ on WLS Chicago. At this time in the 70's WLS was the top rated AM station in the country, 50,000 watts of top 40 Rock. John Records Landecker was rated number one DJ, in the country by Billboard that year.

Rationale

Because of his popularity and national presence it was thought that making a documentary about Landecker and his job might be

interesting. The idea was to bring the audience into studio to visit with a disc jockey while he was on the air. In 1977 there were no radio personalities on TV like Imus, or Howard Stern, so few people had any idea what goes on behind the scenes at a top 40 AM radio station or even what most of the people behind "the voice" coming out of the box, looked like.

Approach

Bring the viewer into the studio.

The idea was to focus on John while he was on the air, look at his job and his personality. What kind of person can sit in a small room and talk to millions of people he can't see? What does it take to do the job and what does the job entail? What seemed to be emerging at this point was an educational documentary about one aspect of the broadcasting industry.

Financing and Reality Check

Before you put your own money or other peoples money into any film production project, it's a good idea to look into what the distribution realities might be. Many filmmakers and investors have learned the hard way that no matter how excited they might be about a concept, they need to take a hard look at whom, if anyone might want to see the movie.

In this case research was done into what educational films existed about radio broadcasting and being a "disc jockey." There wasn't much out there on the subject. It was speculated that this documentary might find an audience in colleges and universities where radio broadcasting was taught.

The project had a celebrity of sorts, since John Landecker was heard all over the country. He was on the air in the evening and WLS was a 50,000 watt clear channel AM station, which meant that no other station, was on that frequency in the United States. AM radio waves, unlike FM radio waves, do not travel in straight lines. They go up and bounce around off clouds or whatever. On any given night, John might have a huge audience.

Remember this was before the shock jocks and TV views of radio personalities on the air; people might want to see the man behind the voice. Two educational film companies were contacted to see if they might be interested in a film about a Disc Jockey, and they said they would be interested in screening it, after it was made. Unless you have an ongoing relationship with a distribution company, as an independent producer, this type of reaction is about the most you can expect.

This was the filmmakers first independent educational documentary project. Distributors will not invest money or even give a distribution commitment; there are too many risks associated with doing that. So, technically, the film was made "on spec." Distributors have no way of judging if what you make will be appropriate for the educational film market. Giving you a letter or some form of written or verbal support or promise of distribution could be used to help raise money from investors. If the project fails the "promise of distribution" or even possible distribution might be considered the reason investors backed the film and therefore the investors might sue the distributors to get their money back if the film fails for any reason.

John Landecker and WLS Participation

The next step was to negotiate an agreement with John Landecker and the radio station owners. Landecker agreed to the terms for making the documentary, which did not include any money, only a copy of the finished film and the right to show it. WLS also agreed to let him do the documentary and agreed that the producers would own the copyright. A short written agreement was composed and everyone signed it.

Distribution of this type of documentary today might be done through an educational film distributor or in a self-distribution online manner. (see Chapter 7)

Distributors will usually take a wait and see position unless they are familiar with your work.

WLS agreed to allow the documentary to be made for promotional purposes. Arrangements with WLS were worked out for three, four-hour sessions in the studio with John Landecker to shoot the film (three consecutive days while he was on the air). The film crew had to be

John Records Landecker

in and out in four hours because there were other DJ's on the air before and after. More sessions were possible but the budget would have been higher. The script breakdown indicated that 12 hours of shooting would produce enough coverage to make the documentary.

Research

Most documentary projects require some research, and study of the subject to come up with an informed concept and treatment. Personal knowledge of the subject is helpful, however, there's no substitute for actual research into what a top 40 AM Radio station was and generally how such a station might function.

Spending two nights visiting with John in the studio, hanging out in a chair nearby, observing and asking a few questions provided an opportunity to learn a lot about the subject. Visiting the studio was important research showing what the routine there was each evening from 6 p.m. to 10 p.m.

Research included visiting the location and sitting in on the broadcast prior to formulating questions and writing shooting script.

This type of research helps the filmmaker write a concept, treatment, a shooting script and determine other logistical requirements regarding the shooting schedule and location.

There were a number of issues that needed to be addressed in this documentary that gave it credibility as an educational film for broadcasting curriculum. The documentary needed to show the technical side of John's job and the role of the engineer. Questions on these subjects were planned as well as visual coverage of what Landecker does as part of his job every night.

Concept and Treatment

A **Concept** is a short description or idea for a documentary story.

A **Treatment** is a short narrative description of what the story is about and how you will approach it.

Concept and Treatment

The Concept for this film was quite simple; it is a profile or portrait of a disc jockey working in a major market on a top 40, radio station. There's a long tradition in documentary of doing portraits or profiles of individuals from all walks of live. Some take the form of biographies, compilation projects (these usually after someone has passed away), or portraits for a series of people in one profession.

The Treatment for a documentary film is essentially a summary (Not to be confused with a synopsis.) of what the documentary is about, its purpose and the approach telling the story.

Documentary filmmaking should not make things happen, the filmmakers record what's out there. Researching the subject or observing helps come to up with an idea of how to "treat," "visualize" or "approach" the subject. *Most important the research should determine what questions will be asked, what the issues are and the focus of the documentary.*

Go into the process with questions and an open mind. Making a documentary is not trying to prove what is already suspected. If you are convinced all the answers are known it will probably turn out that nothing new will be discovered.

The Treatment gives an idea of how the story will be told and what the purpose of telling it is. It also describes who or what this story is about. The best treatments are good reading and tell a story themselves. The reader should feel that they have an idea of the beginning, middle and end of the story and how you are approaching it.

CONCEPT

Profile or portrait of a Disc Jockey working on a top rated station in a major city. Chicago.

TREATMENT

Capture the flavor of Studio A, WLS Chicago and visit with Disc Jockey, Radio Personality – John Records Landecker.

Filming to be accomplished while John is actually on the air. A casual conversation develops between an unseen guest (interviewer) in the studio and John. The audience has the POV of the guest. The result brings the viewer into Studio A, a virtual fish bowl, modern, super slick radio studio with glass all around. John talks to the guest, not to the camera. He incorporates the questions in his answers, so that we do not hear the interviewer ask questions.

Example: Interviewer: When did you come to Chicago? John: "I came to Chicago…"

Because John must go on the air or take care of other tasks that are part of his job our conversation is often interrupted. John doesn't miss a beat and picks up conversations exactly where he left off.

Inside his studio space John is, to a great extent, separated from the outside world for four hours while he is on the air. Even his contact with the engineer is limited. He can see the engineer through the glass window where she sits, and, via a one-way link gives her instructions. John is isolated and insolated, but still on view, as his back faces another large window to which the public has access. For a while we enter the fish bowl, where we gain access to what until now, was a voice without a face.

The telephone is John's link with the outside world and his listeners. He gets calls, requests, conducts contests and special segments like the "Boogie Check."

The film opens with a series of shots that establish the boundaries of the fish bowl. John remains somewhat anonymous for a short time. Finally, inside with him we begin to see and hear more of what he looks like. First a mouth speaking into a microphone, hand on a switch, writing in a logbook or back of the head. This is not an attempt to create mystery. It's a reminder of the fact that, up to this point, the audience may have only heard this person's voice. Until now the only frame of reference has been a disembodied voice coming out of a box. He enters the story faceless, a disembodied voice. The audience visits what is usually his private space and discover the person behind the voice.

Having been introduced, a conversation begins. You visit and speak with John Records Landecker while he works. He tells you some things about himself, his job, how he got started, where he's from originally, where he's worked, how he feels about his job, how he got started, and what he thinks the future will bring.

All the time he continues to do his job. He goes on the air, gets on the phone and casually returns to the conversation. You get to see not only what his job entails, but also how well he does it. Doing his job includes knowing when to break the conversation, making entries in the log, reading commercials, talking to listeners on the phone, which has many lines all constantly blinking, and a multitude of other tasks in addition to announcing the name of the next record. As the film progresses you learn what the job is about and what Mr. Landecker, the "radio personality" is about.

This documentary gives the audience insight into what it's like to be on the air. The POV is from the inside out. Because of time and budget constraints, there are scripted shots to cover the 12 hours of shooting with John Landecker. There are a large number of questions to ask. John will not know what the questions are beforehand. His performance is spontaneous.

_____

The Concept and Treatment gives the reader an idea what the story, approach and point-of-view is for the project.

Writing The Shooting Script for Studio A
Profile of a Disc Jockey

Documentary Shooting Script details the shots and coverage we want to get to tell the story.

There are many approaches to writing for nonfiction projects. A shooting script for a documentary project includes shots and questions to form the basis for telling the story.

The script might call for "coverage" of an event and interviews with whoever might be important to the event. It becomes the director's

Documentary Coverage

Action - The actual event, activity or subject of the documentary.

Interviews

"B" roll - footage that supports the action and interviews being shot.

Director's vision for how the story will be told must include how each shot in that story will connect in each sequence.

job to get the shots and interviews that can be edited together to depict the event. A documentary director thinks about how the scene will be edited while shooting the scene. This means getting shots that cut together. In addition how to keep the look and feel of each segment consistent.

For example if a person important to the event is interviewed, it is necessary to try to get footage of what they're talking about ("B" roll) along with general coverage (action) of the event. It's the director's responsibility, but the camera operator should also be aware of the need for a variety of cut a ways and different size shots during an interview. The director and camera operator should discuss the kind of coverage the director is looking for and be thinking and listening to what is going on.

In writing the shooting script for Disc Jockey there were a number of issues to consider. First the location was in a small studio with glass windows on two sides. On one side was the engineer and on the other side a hallway where the elevators arrived for this upper floor in a high-rise office building in Chicago. Second, shooting was limited to four hours to get in and out each of the three days allotted to shoot. Lighting needed to be unseen and limited. A disc jockey does not get up and move around; he sits and talks with a microphone in front of him, so there was a "talking head" to deal with.

A talking head is not cinematic and can be tedious after a short time. A director looks to find ways to creatively overcome this type of problem. There needs to be enough additional coverage, action footage, cut-a-ways and a diversity of shots, to work around the talking head in editing. As was mentioned previously the shooting script is about what will be shot, not necessarily what the subject will do. The shooting script is written to make sure there is a plan to get enough footage to tell the story.

John talks to an engineer who sits on the other side of a glass partition. This relationship is something that is important in establishing that he does work with other people to be on the air. Otherwise he talks to people on the phone and 5 million people out there somewhere! Cut-a-ways show various lights and buttons John uses in doing his job. Writing in the log was an activity he did to comply with FCC regulations and station policy that provided an informative cut-a-way that was integral to his doing his job.

To allow maximum flexibility in the editing John was asked to wear the same clothing for each of the three shooting days. This would give the editor the ability to use inserts and cut-a-ways, where any part of John's body was included, anywhere in the film.

There were a number of topics in this documentary that would give it credibility as an educational film for broadcasting curriculum, including showing the technical side of John's job and the role of the engineer. Questions were planned on these subjects as well as visual coverage.

In preproduction you break down the shooting script in to what shots you can shoot in a practical way. For example, to save time questions may be asked in a different order than in the shooting script. Questions from anywhere in the script are asked while at a particular camera set up. It is also necessary to shoot shots out of script order to avoid moving the camera and lights multiple times. This saves time and helps insure continuity in lighting and camera angles.

Finally the questions in the shooting script are a place to start, new questions will come to mind as you listen to the interviewee. Follow-up on these questions because they can be more revealing than the ones you came up with before the shoot. Listen to your interviewee's answers.

One of the main ideas of creating a shooting script is to insure adequate coverage for editing. Visiting Landecker in the studio, as research provided ideas on what to include in the script.

CU's used as inserts and cutaways should be relevant to the action taking place in the scene.

CU's from left to right-- Flashing lights, buttons, engineer, writing in log, and digital counter.

Opening Shots

Usually you only hear a radio personality as you listen to the radio. The idea was to introduce Landecker by bringing the viewer into the studio from outside. Shots were scripted that would convey this idea on the screen. *(See facing page)*

*Standard Abbreviations
for Shots*

Extreme Close-up -- ECU
Close-up -- CU
Medium Close-Up -- MCU
Medium Shot -- MS
Medium Long Shot -- MLS
Long Shot -- LS
Over-the-Shoulder -- OTS

| 1 | 2 | 3 |

4

Starting from outside
the studio *(1)* we push in
through the glass *(2 & 3)*
where we see Landecker
from the back *(4).*

| 5 | 6 | 7 | 8 |

Inside from a CU of the VU
meter *(5)* we cut to a LS from
OTS of the Engineer *(6).* The
next shot is an ECU of part of
Landecker's face *(7)* and next a
cut to a side view of Landecker
at the Console *(8).*

Nonfiction multi column script format.

SHOT	PICTURE	TIME	AUDIO
1.	Super open Titles and Credits over out of focus shot of Studio A window.		Voice over of John Landecker on the air.
1A.	Pull focus on entire frame filled with window to studio. Lettering on widow reads: "STUDIO A." Pull focus as title credits end until letters are sharp. Studio behind letters is softly lit and still soft focus. As we zoom-in and focus becomes a little sharper, we begin a dolly toward window.		Voice over continues.
2.	ECU - profile lips and mouth speaking into microphone.		Sync voice continues.
3.	ECU - Yellow warning light blinks on.		Voice over continues.
4.	ECU - fingers on switch.		Voice over continues.
5.	CU - Four digital clocks that count off seconds or minutes since last top 4 records were played.		Voice over continues or commercial whatever is happening.
6.	MS - From behind Landecker, his back is in focus, raises hand to cue and engineer who can be seen, softly through and on the other side of a pane of glass. Rack focus to the engineer as he give her the signal.		Landecker is on the air talking over some music or whatever.
7.	Engineer's hand, finger pushing a button, raising volume		Landecker Voice Over continues.
8.	MS - Match pull out (over the shoulder of engineer) from finger to reveal console. Tilt up to show Landecker talking to engineer through window.		Landecker giving instructions to Engineer.

8. Cont'd	Pull back to FS of Engineers booth, Engineer from behind silhouetted against with Landecker in background Dissolve To		Landecker on air sync or doing other activities.
9.	CU Landecker's hand writing in Log.		Commercial or other programming in the background.
10.	CU Yellow Warning Light		Commercial or other programming in the background
11.	CU Landecker speaking into Microphone.		Landecker on the Air. Introduces next record.
12.	MS Landecker at console, pushes a button, shuffles papers etc. Turns toward unseen interviewer who is sitting next to the camera and starts to talk in answer to a question that will not be heard in final cut of film. NOTE: The finished version of this film will not include shot's of the interviewer or his questions. Landecker will speak to the interviewer as if he is a guest in the studio, sitting there watching him do his show. Landecker will not talk to the camera, but to the guest (audience viewer) who will now feel as though they are in the room with Landecker. Landecker continues talking to us and doing is job. Landecker will phrase is answers to include the questions.		Example question and answer. Q: How much time do you spend in this studio? Is this a heavy schedule? Are you comfortable here? A: I'm on the air... (See Interview questions at the end of the script that will be asked as we progress.)
13.	MCU Landecker continues talking to us, glances at console...		Landecker talking. Questions: Where did you go to school? Studied what? Did you always want to be on the radio? Where did you get your start? What was your first paying job?

Shooting Script uses same formatting as Editing Script

Shots in the Shooting Script were not **shot** in script order. The script is broken down by camera positions and other factors.

Times have been omitted in this script since there was
no way to determine how long most shots would be.

14.	ECU Warning light.		Landecker talking.
15.	MCU Landecker prepares to go on the air, puts headset back on. He goes on the air.		Landecker talking.
16.	CU Landecker holding copy for a commercial. He reads copy.		Landecker reading copy.
17.	MCU Engineers putting tape in machine.		We hear Landecker over PA in Engineers booth, which is a live feed of what is going out over the air.
18.	MS Over the shoulder of engineer as she fades up tape.		Commercial Jingle
19.	MCU Landecker at Console. He gives hand signal to engineer and...		Landecker talking.
20.	MS from POV guest as Landecker finishes up after jingle, takes off headset and resumes talking to us.		On air music heard in background mostly as bleed from Landecker's headset.
20 A	Cutaway people looking in widow of studio, behind Landecker.		Conversation resumes. Question: When did you come to Chicago? How did it happen?
21.	MLS Landecker is still speaking to us, however, he continues to work, making log entries, looking for the next commercial script and giving instructions to engineer. (Note: the engineer rarely responds verbally.)		How long at WLS? How does this new studio compare with old studio? Talk about working in Chicago. How far does this station reach? How does it feel to be talking to a couple million people?
22.	CU Landecker's fingers on Microphone switch		Landecker talking.
23.	MCU - Over the shoulder of Landecker we see engineer through the glass. Landecker goes on the air. Camera dolly to the opposite side of Landecker to almost in front of him by console.		Landecker on the air.
			Finishing up...

Scripted for a 30 minute or less documentary.

24.	MCU hand signal to engineer.	
25.	CU Landecker continues conversation after giving a few more instructions to engineer. He speaks to us for a while...	Landecker Play number 12 and number 4 Questions: What do you like and dislike about your Job? Do you ever feel isolated?
26.	CU shots of each of the clocks as Landecker explains there function	Talk about top four digital clocks. What are these clocks for? How often do you have to play the top four songs?
27.	CU section of the console.	What is the state of AM radio today?
28.	CU section of the console.	Describe various parts of console.
29.	CU section of the console.	What are all the buttons for? Which button is for the engineer?
30.	MCU - Landecker pushes 7-second delay button.	What do you do if you get an obscene call?
31.	CU - Phones that are all lit up. They are blinking away.	Why do people call in? What types of interaction i.e. contests, promotions, "Boogie Checks?"
32.	MCU - 45 degrees from previous POV. Landecker is back on the air.	Landecker On Air
33.	ECU - Red Warning Light	Landecker On Air
34.	MCU Landecker profile on the air. He finishes up, goes off the air, and starts to talk to us again, even as he prepares for next on air segment.	Landecker On Air

35.	CU - Landecker talking to us. Digital clock popping of elapsed seconds.		Continues, "What's the strangest call you ever had? How do feel about making personal appearances? Does it interfere with home life? Talk about wife and children.
36.	MCU Landecker continuing conversation		How do you feel about the top forty music you play? Has it changed? Are there some songs you really hate? Why do you still play them?
37.	MS Landecker turns pages in commercial binder, continues to talk. Landecker going on the air may interrupt conversation in during a shot. He usually comes back and resumes conversation.		What is the difference between AM and FM formats in Chicago? What is the difference between you and other DJ's on this station, in this market? What kind of listeners do you have in Chicago, what do they want to hear?
38.	MLS - Landecker conversation - Pick-up CU's for inserts of what he is doing.		What would you change about your program if it were up to you? Do you feel AM radio can be improved? Who, if anyone, is or was your favorite radio personality?
39.	CU - Landecker		What do you know about the Payola scandals?
40.	MLS - high angle, wide, looking down over shoulder of John Landecker as he continues. We want to see as much of his workspace as possible.		As a radio personality what kind of image should you have? Does the public have the wrong image?
41.	MCU - Microphone fro over the shoulder includes shoulder and part of face in shot. Red light on in background may be visible.		Landecker does weather, promo's, contest, gives instructions to engineer, reaches for phone.

42.	CU Landecker hand comes into shot of phone with all the lights blinking, picks up phone.		
43.	CU as in 42, but Landecker is now pushes the buttons on the phone as he counts.		You're number 1, number 2, number 3, number 4 until he reaches some number he has in mind for picking the contestant.
44.	MCU Landecker on the Phone.		Number 15 you're the winner. Have you won anything from us in the last 7 days? What's your name? Wait a minute didn't you just win an album yesterday?
44A.	Hangs up the phone reaches to push another blinking button. CU Blinking button pushed.		Hello you're the winner
45.	MS Landecker taking information from winner.		I think some of these people just live to call in for the contests
46.	CU- Lights on the Console.		Landecker announcing winner.
47.	CU - Engineer thru glass watching waiting...		Landecker VO announcing next record.
48.	CU Landecker cueing engineer.		Music starts
49.	MS - Landecker from front. POV engineer. Finishes cue, then fills out log, etc. Starts conversation.		Do people ever recognize you on the street?
50.	MCU Landecker talking.		Did you ever wonder if anyone was listening?
51.	CU Landecker.		Get into hobbies and interests, etc.
52.	Telephones blinking as Landecker continues conversation.		WLS station promo jingle.
53.	CU Hand of engineer putting cart in machine.		K-Tel commercial or equivalent. Hit machine.

54.	ECU - Landecker at microphone.		A few beats of music from record.
55.	CU - Entry in log.		Music in background.
56.	CU - Clocks		Music in background.
57.	CU - Red Warning Lights		Music in background
58.	CU - Telephones flashing. Landecker preparing for "Boogie Check" segments.		Promo for Boogie Check
59.	MCU Landecker (as much to the front as possible.		Landecker on the air.
60.	MS Landecker doing "Boogie Check" segment.		Landecker on the air.
61.	MCU -Landecker pushing button on phone to talk to the first caller. Note: There will be several callers talked to. Size of shot may change at times between callers. 61A. Insert shots pushing button for each caller.		Landecker talking to each caller.
62.	CU - Landecker as he tells someone they are tonight's winner. Pull out to wide shot as segment ends and he cues engineer.		Landecker - Announcing winner.
63.	CU - Digital clock		Landecker VO
64.	MCU Landecker - takes off head set starts conversation with us again.		What is your interest in film? Is it just another career goal, or does it hold a special interest?
65.	CU Landecker talking		Where do you go from here? Would you be content to stay in this job?
66	MS Landecker talking		Discuss possibilities of a career in Radio.

67.	CU Engineer working.		Landecker VO
68.	CU Red Light - Landecker stops conversation - gets ready to go on air.		Are your day's numbered is there an age limit for someone in this time slot? What are you doing about it?
69.	ECU Microphone - Landecker comes into shot and talks on air.		Landecker on the air.
70.	CU copy Landecker is holding and reading on the air.		Landecker on the air.
71.	MCU Full Face Landecker and microphone. Focus starts to go soft, slowly match cut with		Landecker on the air.
72.	Full Shot of Landecker, thru the glass, over the shoulder of engineer. Focus will continue to go soft.		Landecker on the air.
73.	High angle from behind, looking down on Landecker at console.		His Voice dissolves into promos.
74.	MS - Landecker from behind at console - Pull focus and zoom back through glass, to reveal lettering on outside of window. Credits appear above Studio Window.		Landecker on the air talking to a listener.

Lumier's Arrival of Train - Early Documentary seen by the Public in 1895. Filmed at La Ciotat in Southern France.

Arrival of the Train at La Ciotat (1895)

Arrival of a Train was filmed with Lumier's *Cinematographe* Camera in one stationary shot of about a minute. The camera was placed at one end of the platform close the tracks and the train was seen coming toward the camera from long shot to close-up.

John Records Landecker in Studio A Profile of a Disc Jockey

CHAPTER 6

PRODUCTION

CHAPTER SIX

CHAPTER 6

Production

A shooting script was written for the Disc Jockey documentary after visiting John at work in Studio A. Because John would be doing predictable things, sitting at a microphone etc, it was possible to script how this film would be shot. This would guarantee that adequate coverage was obtained. The shooting script indicated how the story would be told but it did not script what John Landecker would do or say.

Script Breakdown

A shooting script is broken down into what is logistically expedient to shoot based on camera setup, lighting, and other factors and not necessarily shot in script order.

Once the shooting script was finished it was broken down as to what would be shot on each day, from each camera position. This meant that the documentary would not be shot in script order. On any given day certain shots wherever they were in the script would be shot from each camera position.

The interview questions were worked into the schedule so that a conversational atmosphere was created between the audience and the disc jockey. The biggest factor regarding the order of shooting was the fact that the crew had to be in and out of the studio in four hours -- no setting up or striking before or after the four hour block. With approximately 80 shots in the shooting script this meant that about 25 to 30 shots needed to be done each session.

Crew in Studio A WLS Chicago

Crew size in the studio was limited to the director, DP/camera operator, first assistant camera and sound recordist. The rest of the crew, a film magazine loader, 1st assistant director/script supervisor/continuity/PA

and lighting grip persons stayed outside on call to move camera, change magazines, or move lights. Talent releases were obtained from WLS, John Landecker, and the Engineer before shooting began.

The crew had to work in a harmonious way to deal with the short shooting schedule and cramped space. Actually work days were eight or more hours per day. First meeting and picking up all the gear, driving to the location and arriving at least two hours earlier than the shooting time, to get everything ready to move in to the studio. During this time the camera team checked out the camera and loaded enough magazines to get us started. Each magazine holds 400' of 16mm film that lasts for approximately 10 minutes of shooting, so the loader was constantly loading and unloading three magazines outside the studio space.

After the shooting another two hours was spent "wrapping," putting all the gear away and then getting back to our office and unloading. The first AC, got the film ready for the lab each day and took it to the lab for processing. The next morning we had a camera report, which told us how, our footage looked and a work print was made. When shooting film it is critical to know that the film shot previously is okay since you cannot see it until it is developed.

Location Shooting

Shooting this documentary today, in a high end digital format like High Definition (HD), would have saved time and money. Tape stock is cheaper than buying film stock, processing it and making a work print. Using a system that records video to a hard drive or flash cards, including Panasonic's P2 cards, would also be practical, however, work time for the crew is about the same since there are still things to do before and after the shoot. Also There would need to be time for changing tapes or transferring from recording media to storage drives.

Camera positions were changed in a limited way due to the small space. This was made more difficult because of reflections in the glass between the studio, hall and engineer booth.

Shooting went on for the three days with the crew getting in and out of the studio in four hours. There were a number of sources for audio recorded to get what went on the air, what was said in the studio, and what was coming in on the phone.

Eight four hundred foot rolls of film were expose per night. That's about 80 minutes of usable footage per night for a total of 240 minutes. This works out to a shooting ratio of about 8 to 1. Based on a projected thirty minute film. The shoot was budgeted for a 10 to 1 ratio, so it came in under budget as far as film stock used.

In this documentary and in most documentary situations only one camera is used. Film was and still is an expensive commodity to purchase, process and work print. Even when shooting video the expense of a second camera crew makes it impractical to use two cameras. It is therefore necessary to understand that there is a technique to working with one camera to cover an interview, event or other situation. It is not only possible to get adequate coverage with one camera it may be preferable in many cases.

Most documentary production is done on location, in someone's office, home, place of business, on the street, or at an event of some kind. Documentary filmmakers shooting film or video work quickly, bringing as little attention to themselves as possible. Most of the time working with a single camera is an advantage

Shooting in the field is much different than shooting on a sound stage. Both are different than shooting in a television studio. A television studio primarily used for talk shows, the news, and other multi-camera situations using video cameras. Cameramen get instructions on head sets from a Director who is sitting in a control room. Sporting events work basically the same way and because of the on-going action and the need to spontaneously cover the event and send it out over the air these are multi-camera shoots.

Major television programming may be shot on film using more one or more cameras. It is transferred to video and edited before being broadcast. Other programming, like the "soaps" are shot on video using multiple cameras. Most of the editing done as the show is recorded, however, each camera is also recording the action to tape for possible later use.

Theatrical production on a sound stage takes advantage of the ability to light and move sets, and stop and start. Scripts are broken down and shot in the order most convenient. For most situations one camera is adequate. On location the same conditions exist including the limitation of space to use more than one camera. Scenes where it would cost more to recreate an event like an explosion or major car crash, would use more than one camera.

Equipment

Equipment needs are based on the format being used. Shooting a project on film that will only be seen on the internet sounds like overkill. It would be cheaper and more practical to shoot the project in a reasonable video format. Audio equipment for any project should be of a professional quality since even streaming audio online can be CD quality. Lighting is usually fairly basic for documentary projects, however, productions involving events or large venues might require more elaborate lighting requirements.

The crew for a short documentary is usually small, some jobs may be combined. Director, 1st assistant Director/Script Supervisor, Director of Photography/Camera Operator, an assistant camera person who also helps with lighting, Audio recordist/mixer/boom operator, one Gaffer/Key Grip. Documentary shoots are on location and the logistics of moving a small crew around are less difficult and expensive than a large crew.

Production days are based on the script or requirements of getting the coverage needed to tell the story.

In this documentary there were limited angles and positions from which to shoot the interview because of the size of the studio and placement of lights and camera. From this position we could get various size shots like this MCU.

MCU LANDECKER AT CONSOLE

There were limited places to set up the camera for a frontal view, because of the placement of the console where Landecker worked.

This MS is from another camera position slightly over the shoulder (OTS) of Landecker as he sits at the console. Care had to be taken to avoid reflections in the glass separating him from the Engineer and keeping our lighting and crew out of the shot.

3/4 OTS MS AT CONSOLE

This reverse angle from OTS of the Engineer was the only full front shot of Landecker possible because of the console. It is also scripted to open up the feel of being in the small space with a talking head.

LS OTS ENGINEER -- LANDECKER

This OTS shot of Landecker writing in a log, required by station and FCC regulations, was scripted. But an opportunity for a match cut with an unscripted shot from another angle and camera position was discovered.

OTS CU LOG ENTRY

The script called for a CU of Landecker writing in the log. By letting his hand come out of the frame it could be matched with a reverse angle of Landecker doing the same action. This allowed for a match cut on the action in both shots.

Often while getting the shots scripted a director will notice other shots or angles that will allow for continuity editing and possible match cutting. Other times good coverage may lead to editorial discoveries while editing that add to the production value.

Production Audio

Audio in any production is an important part of telling your story. Good clean recording that is not over or under modulated is a given. However adequate audio coverage in a documentary is as important as the visual coverage.

In the case of Studio A - Profile of a Disc Jockey elaborate methods were needed. After all this is radio! It was necessary to be able to record the interview, then what was going out over the air and also what was coming in via the telephone.

It was arranged with the engineer to record what was going out over the air and telephone calls coming in, before they were broadcast. In addition, a copy of the archival recordings of the entire broadcast which is made for the FCC was obtained.

There were a few choices of microphones available to record the interview (possibilities included a boom, handheld, or lavaliere). the choice in this case was a lavaliere, out of site, taped to Landecker's chest. This microphone recorded his voice well on or off the air. Some background noise and audio bleed from his ear phones was picked up and provided ambience while he was being interviewed.

Radio stations have a seven second delay on what a telephone caller says and when it actually goes out on the air. This allows the DJ to stop obscene language from going out on air and being heard by the listeners. By having all the audio sources covered, we had the recordings of callers phoning in before the delay and after. This gave us the ability to edit the conversation uncensored.

Audio packages for most documentaries include at least a two channel mixer, wireless and line lavalieres, a boom pole microphone, a shotgun microphone and a handheld omni directional microphone. Most camcorders have either a built in microphone or accommodations for a camera mounted microphone. In certain instances these microphones can be a valuable resource, providing they are set to manual by the camera operator. Automatic gain settings should not be used as they will boost the gain during quiet pauses as they search for a signal thereby recording noise until someone speaks again.

Getting good Audio

Often overlooked is how important the audio part of the story is to the final product. It is extremely important to get dialog and ambient sound that are sharp and clear. Distorted audio is equivalent to an out-of-focus picture. Over-modulated audio in an interview cannot be fixed in post. Audio with all sorts of noise and crackling cannot be used. There is little prospect of doing Automatic Dialog Replacement (ADR) for a spontaneous interview that was done on the street. The lighting and cinematography might be brilliant but if the audio isn't clear and/or you can't understand what someone is saying, the footage is damaged and may not be usable.

Getting clean audio even when no one is speaking is important for use in editing. Shoot all "B" roll with audio. Without the audio the shot loses a dimension that will be needed even if someone ultimately is speaking over the shot. Room tone and location ambience should also be recorded for possible use by the editor.

One important basic approach when recording is to make sure that the signal (what you're recording) to noise (everything else) ratio is such that the signal is strong and the noise weak; a high signal to noise ratio.

On a windy day or in a noisy room the shotgun microphone would be put into a windscreen to cut down any wind noise. A "shotgun" is a directional microphone and has a very narrow range of reception. It is a versatile addition to a documentary audio package.

SHOOTING AND EDITING

A comparison of the shooting script for Studio A - Profile of a Disc Jockey to the final screen version, shows that the screen version does not exactly match the shooting script. There are many reasons for this.

One reason is that the scripted shot was not obtained or it was not used for some reason; perhaps a better shot was found while shooting.

In editing, it may have been found that a scripted shot could not be used because it didn't cut to the next shot smoothly or because of time constraints, it could not be included.

Many documentaries create a narrative from the interview footage and cut between the interviewee speaking on camera and with the interviewee's voice over (VO) other footage. This may change the order of scripted shots.

In the case of Disc Jockey, the shooting script was followed generally and with revisions based on the footage available. The shooting script evolved into an editing script.

A major consideration in the editing of this documentary was how to get away from 30 minutes worth of a "talking head." All of the footage that showed John Landecker's actions, features of the console in front of him or the engineer, became very important.

CHAPTER 7

EDITING POSTPRODUCTION AND DISTRIBUTION

CHAPTER SEVEN

CHAPTER 7

Post Production

Postproduction for documentary films and videos takes much the same process as editing for other projects. Its main purpose is the editing and finishing of the film or video. One of the first things that get done when shooting in digital video formats is to capture the footage into whatever Non Linear Editing (NLE) editing program you are using. (Other programs like Adobe's After Effects and a specialized audio editing program are also useful. Today Final Cut and Avid offer "Studio" versions of their NLE programs that include specialized applications for all advanced aspects of digital editing.)

Editing Process

Editing is a creative process involving the construction of a visual story or narrative. Review all the footage, make written transcriptions of all the interviews in-order to create a paper edit or editing script. Log all the action and "B" roll footage so that it is easy to find.

The director and the editor review the footage and transcriptions looking for the best action, interviews, and "B" roll. The also review the original concept, treatment, and shooting script. After the review an editing scrip or "paper edit" is written by the director or a writer might be brought in to shape the narrative based on the interviews. A writer may write narration to edit the documentary around but more often narration is written once the film has taken shape.

A shooting script and editing script for a documentary or nonfiction project look pretty much the same. They both use a multi-column format beginning with two columns, one for picture and one for audio. Additional columns may be added for story boarding or other information. In the example a column for shot number and another for time has been added.

The major difference is that the editing script is based on the footage shot and actual dialog or interviews obtained. The original shooting script is a starting point but may be modified based on new information or new ideas for telling the story.

SHOOTING SCRIPT EXAMPLE (Chapter 6)'

SHOT	PICTURE	TIME	AUDIO
1	CU Farmer's face	:05	Ambient Sound – VO from interview.
2	LS Farmer walking toward barn	:07	Ambient Sound – VO from interview
3	MS Farmer Bob Longwell standing next to row of Dairy Cows. (super name lower 3rd)	:10	Interview continues: Answer to question – Why did you become a Dairy Farmer?

EDITING SCRIPT

SHOT	PICTURE	TIME	AUDIO
1	CU Farmer's face	:05	Ambient Sound – VO from interview. "Well I never really thought about it, my Father was a Dairy Farmer and so was his Father..."
2	LS Farmer walking toward barn	:07	Ambient Sound – VO from interview. ...I guess it just runs in the family.
2A	CU of Tractor	:03	Ambient sound Farmer walking
2B	CU Farmer opening gate	:04	Ambient sound gate opening
3	MS Farmer Bob Longwell standing next to row of Dairy Cows. (super name lower 3rd)	:10	Interview continues: Answer to question – Why did you become a Dairy Farmer? ...we have 100 cows at this time...

An editing script based on the actual footage acquired and other factors is written. For example "B" roll might be added to supplement a shot like the farmer walking toward the barn.

The first edit of the film based on the editing script is called a rough cut. Once a rough cut is edited it should be reviewed to see how the cuts and pacing are working and generally how the story is playing. The rough cut should be watched on a large screen monitor or projected on a screen. The rough cut is what the word "rough" implies. It may be that there are missing shots, only the dialog tracks, no effects and partially still an assembly of takes. It should be a rough edit of the entire story; not just a couple of scenes, although on longer films rough cuts of certain segments may be screened.

Getting a real feeling for the edit at this point is not possible on a small editing monitor. In addition, seeing the film on a large screen magnifies all the cuts. Audio heard over larger speakers helps hearing things that might be missed on the smaller NLE system speakers. It is also a good idea to bring in a consultant, trusted advisor or someone who has not worked on the film for a reaction at this time.

This is also a good time to think about music and effects for the film. If original music is required, the composer should be invited to the rough cut screening. Additional screenings as the edit proceeds are a good idea too.

Fine Cut

After screening the rough cut it's time to start evolving a fine cut, creating effects and music tracks in addition to the two dialog tracks already created.

Audio

Audio is an important part of the editing and plays a large part in telling the story. Audio for films and videos falls into three areas; dialog, effects (FX) and music. At the start of editing, begin with two dialog tracks so that you can inventively edit dialog as you go along. Some editors might jam all the dialog onto one track "butt splicing" it all together, later, they break it up into multiple tracks. This is not very practical and sets up the possibility of mistakes and bad audio cuts. With NLE software having multiple audio available splitting tracks from the start is a good idea.

It is much better to start out with two audio tracks so that later the process of equalizing, cross fading or pulling up the sound for "J" cuts is facilitated. There is nothing worse than getting to the point where you want to do a cross fade between tracks only to find that you don't have the additional frames available.

Ultimately, at least two dialog tracks are needed because each person's voice will require some tweaking even if is was recorded in the same room, not to mention cutting between interviewees in various locations. Ambience and room tone will be different depending on time of day, the weather and the number of people in a room.

After dialog, work on effects tracks and music tracks. There are situations when it is necessary or desired to cut dialog or action to music when a certain pacing of shots is desired. Even when music is added to a fine cut there may be some tweaking needed to help the rhythm of the editing. There also needs to be at least two music tracks, to facilitate cross fading the music or to let it fade out under some action in the next scene. If the final music track isn't available something with the same beat might be substituted so that the rhythm of cutting can be established.

Dialog, FX, Music

Documentary films may need effects edited in to the story. Multiple tracks may also be needed for those effects. Effects include everything from room tone and location ambience. Location ambient sound is needed to bring a still photograph to life. Effects, like a bird chirping, can bring a photographic landscape to life.

Keep your dialog, effects and music tracks in separate groups that can be pre-mixed into the three respective categories. They will be mixed into a final 3 track recording in a final mix.

As the fine cut of the documentary evolves tighten up scenes and change or eliminate those that do not seem to work. Using a non linear editing program facilitates being able to revert to a previously saved version, so do not be afraid to experiment.

During the editing process you may want to bring in associates and a friend or two to get reactions. Bring in a cross section of people who's reactions to certain things might be predictable. For example another editor might pick up editorial problems. An expert in a certain area that the documentary deals with will be thinking about the subject matter more than how the film is cut.

Even when a director is working with an editor there is a tendency for self-indulgence, in that both individuals become committed to ideas that might have some problems. Bring in the DP to give you feedback on color correction; audio engineer to listen to the sound and the script supervisor who may pick-up something that has been missed or may remember an alternative shot that solves an editorial problem.

Test Screenings

Disc Jockey was tested when it was finished by showing it to a live audience composed of some students and faculty in the film department at Columbia College in Chicago. The reaction was mixed with various students and faculty reacting according to their own social or political point-of-view rather than if the film told a story.

For example, one group following the tenants of John Grierson that all documentaries needed to have a social advocacy purpose, felt the film should have dealt with the social implications of a being a "Radio Personality."

Disc Jockey had no political or social agenda and it did not try to "rip off" a top 40 Disc Jockey as some sort egotistical purveyor of pop music to teenagers. The film did not have any social agenda. It was meant to be educational, informative and entertaining.

Some critics may just be plain envious. There are times when screening work will produce constructive opinions and there are other times when the work will be attacked. Know where the attendees are coming from and judge their reactions accordingly. It is also important to know what the film is trying to say or do. The whole point of the test screening is to get reactions and find the strengths and weaknesses of the film so that they can be dealt with. Does the audience react in the way anticipated? Do they laugh or cry in the right places?

Distribution

Disc Jockey was offered to a Chicago based educational film company. They turned it down for reasons that had nothing to do with the quality or relevance of the film. Perhaps it did not fit their catalog or they did not see the potential of a documentary about a local DJ in a national market. They may not have liked the format of the film or had some other personal reason for not picking it up even though the producer/director had a previous working relationship with the company.

It was subsequently offered to Learning Corporation of America (LCA) who liked it. They offered a distribution contract with an advance and a 20% royalty based on the gross revenue of the film. This meant that every time a print was sold, 20% of the sale, went to the producer, after the advance was paid back. LCA got 80% of the revenue but had to pay, out of their percentage, for the cost of making prints, advertising, festival fees, shipping and catalogs. The contract called for accounting statements and payment of royalties monthly for the first two years followed by quarterly statements and payments thereafter.

The film was put it into The American Film Festival where it won awards, and was one of the top ten finalists at the festival. LCA distributed it successfully for over 10 years.

Disc Jockey did well. During the next ten years many university libraries bought the film and it also ran on Nickelodeon. The initial investment was returned and reasonable profit made over that period. There will always be a market for well-made educational documentary films and videos.

The secret is to make a documentary that has relevance in a particular area. *Disc Jockey* successfully showed a man doing his job and how he felt about doing it. John Landecker, the disc jockey, came across as professional and passionate about what he did. The audience was able to determine what the job entailed, and how one personality handled the job and the celebrity.

Copyright

In addition to displaying copyright notices on your work you must register your copyright with the Library of Congress in a timely fashion. Forms are available online from the US Government copyright office. http://www.copyright.gov/register/

Music Rights

The music rights in *Disc Jockey* were cleared by WLS, the radio station doing the broadcasting. ASCAP and BMI are two sources where you can find the copyright holders for music and song lyrics. Copyright holders should be contacted for permission to use copyrighted music on lyrics in your documentary production. They can be found on the Internet.

ASCAP
http://www.ascap.com/ace/search.cfm?mode=search__

BMI
http://www.bmi.com/search/__

"Men occasionally stumble over the truth, but most of them pick themselves up and hurry on as if nothing had happened."

- Winston Churchill

Mayoral candidate Richard Daly being interviewed for Wrapped In Steel documentary at a union hall on the SE side of Chicago. In 1983 Daly lost his bid for Mayor in the primary election.

CHAPTER 8

INTERVIEWING FOR DOCUMENTARY AND NONFICTION FILM PROJECTS

Interviewing techniques used in making documentary and other types of nonfiction films, videos and multimedia projects.

Chapter Highlights

CHAPTER EIGHT

CHAPTER 8

INTERVIEWING FOR NONFICTION FILMS AND DOCUMENTARIES

Construct a Narrative for a Documentary or Nonfiction Film

When the subject tells his own story it is considered first person.

"I like to go for walks because it relaxes me."

When a narrator tells us the story it is considered third person and by default has a subjective POV.

"He likes to go walking because it relaxes him."

A narrative may be constructed by removing the questions asked by the interviewer and editing the answers with actuality footage to tell the story in a first person context. A voice over narrator may also be incorporated, as well as other third party comment in the form of graphics or subtitles that furnish factual information regarding what is seen or heard. Third party comment is factual information (objective reality facts). Presenting factual information offers the opportunity for a non-judgmental point-of-view or a "view from the inside looking out." This is not to say that it offers an objective or impartial point-of-view. A purely objective point-of-view, by a human being does not appear to be possible; however, subjective realities may be presented in a contrasting fashion. In addition certain facts or information that constitute an "objective reality," may help us gain insight into the situation.

A third party voice over style employs a narrator who tells us what we are seeing, explains it, or puts it into a context. This style uses visual material that is actuality footage and may be based on interviews conducted. Interviews with individuals involved and others who have an opinion regarding the subject being documented are also used.

A narrative may be constructed visually with no third party voice over or interviews. The documentary would rely on visual actuality material or footage. Music and/or effects and ambient sound might accompany the visual material. Interviews and/or third party narration are not prerequisites for a documentary. The story in a documentary film should, ideally, be conveyed visually with action not talking heads.

A style, often used for television, is to have an on camera host or interviewer who interviews subjects involved in the documentary. The interviewer interacts with the interviewee. Both questions and answers are heard.120

Each of the above examples have variations and may be combined in one documentary or nonfiction film. The common factor among most approaches is to conduct interviews with those involved creating a first person narrative based on interviews and actuality footage (film, video, photographs, recordings). An editing scrip based on the original script and coverage obtained is written before editing of the documentary begins.

Conducting an interview for a documentary has some roots in journalistic interviewing, and uses some of those techniques. But it goes farther because of the need to create a narrative from the answers that allows the interviewee to tell his or her own story in the first person. A journalist retells the story in his own words, (third person) usually with quotes from the interviewee, but it is still the journalist who is reporting the story. A journalist may try to be "objective" in what can only be a subjective interpretation of what was said..

Second person is most often seen in print.

"You should go for a walk"

Interviewing Styles

An interviewer may interact with the interviewee using different approaches.

Confrontational – interview sounds like an interrogation rather than a conversation and does not always get the cooperation of the interviewee. The interviewer tries to intimidate the interviewee. This style typified by TV journalists like Mike Wallace who takes on an argumentative, judgmental or accusatory tone of voice.

Conversational – creates a dialog where the interviewee feels comfortable talking and answering questions. Talk show hosts like John Stewart on the Daily Show use this form when interviewing guests on his show.

Argumentative interviewers create arguments.

Observational – creates an atmosphere where the interviewer is attempting to learn more about a process or ongoing event. The interviewee becomes a guide, helping us to understand what is happening.

One key factor in the above interviewing styles is not only having questions but also listening closely to what the interviewee is saying. In conversational and observational interviews a neutral or unbiased approach works best. Questions should not be seen as being critical or judgemental. Let the interviewee speak; avoid interrupting the interviewee in the middle of a sentence or thought.

There are sensitive situations where there has been a recent death or other traumatic events. These circumstances need to be handled with care and thoughtfulness for the subject's anxiety or grief without getting too emotional. If in doubt about a topic ask if it would be okay to bring it up. There is a certain amount of psychology involved in conducting an interview.

At the end of an interview thank the person and if time permits, after the camera stops rolling, continue the conversation briefly. Showing interest and politeness is important and may help to more easily do a follow-up interview or call the person back for clarification of something they said.

Coming Up With Questions

The best way to approach an interview is to come up with questions based on research. Knowledge of the person being interviewed and the subject is important. Seek more than one source when doing research to find divergent opinions on the subject. Before finalizing the questions determine what needs to be learned the interviewee.

Listen to your interviewee and you will know what your next question should be.

To be fully prepared and focused for an interview, a list of questions needs to be prepared. Questions should instill some confidence in the interviewee that the interviewer knows something about the subject. Asking obvious questions demonstrates minimal knowledgeable on the subject. Even though there is a list of questions, listen carefully to the answers to these questions. Those answers may lead to more questions and insightful answers. At some point in the interview ask the interviewee if there is anything that wasn't covered or if they would like to add something to what has been said.

It's okay to come back to a question or answer for further clarification or to follow-up on some thought that occurred while listening to the interviewee. Ask the interviewee in a very casual way if they "think of it, to incorporate the question in their answer." This gives the editor a little more latitude when removing the questions during editing.

It's good to be knowledgeable on the subject being discussed . however, the interview is not about the expertise of the interviewer, it's about the interviewee's point-of-view or ideas. Prefacing questions with long monologues expressing opinions or knowledge might make the interviewee wonder why he's there. Limit framing the question to a brief sentence or two.

It is considered unethical to do an interview with someone under false pretences under most situations. Let the subject know what will be discussed.

Leading questions frame the boundaries of the response.

Leading questions are questions that attempt to push the interviewee to answer in a particular way. They most often "frame" the question and elicit a biased response. Children who often want to please an adult interviewer are more easily led into a particular response by this type of questioning.

Examples: "What kind of problems do you see in your relationship with your family?" The question infers that this person might have problems with their family.

"How fast was the speed boat going when it hit the sail boat?" Implies that the speedboat was going fast and that it hit the sailboat.

"Why did your sister make bad faces at you?" Leads the child to a conclusion.

Questions may be **Open-ended or Closed-ended**. A closed-ended question gets a short, often one word answer.

Example: Q: "Do you live in Ohio?" A: "Yes."

An Open-ended question inspires the interviewee to respond in more depth. The might begin with"Who, What, When, Where, Why or How."

Example: Q: What's it like living in Ohio? A: "Well, I grew up in Cleveland so Ohio is home to me." Q: What are some of the things that make Ohio "home?" – might be a follow-up question, even though there was something else next on your list.

WHO: Tell me a little about who you met at the party.

WHAT: What kind of music was the band playing?

WHEN: When you and your friends arrived what was happening?

WHERE: Where did you hear about this party?

WHY: So why do you think you got involved in the argument between Sharon and Dinella?

HOW: How did you feel while all this was going on?
Asking someone how they feel about something or what they believe may be used to evoke more of an emotional response.

Who, What, When, Where, Why and How are used to begin Open-ended questions.

Conducting an Interview

To start, the interviewer introduces themselves and tries to relax the interviewee. This sets the tone for the conversation. Casual conversation about a neutral subject as mundane as the weather is okay.

The camera starts rolling and the first question is asked. After that there's an important thing that must done by the interviewer for the balance of the interview. *The interviewer must listen.* Inexperienced listeners concentrate on what they have to say not what the other person is saying.

Everyone has experienced talking to someone and realized that they are not really listening. How does it make someone feel to think that they could say almost anything and the other person would not hear it? Would that make anyone feel like really opening up about what's being discussed or a personal issue?

Listen to the person you're interviewing and focus on what they are saying. Keep eye contact.

In an interview situation it's important to listen to what the other person is saying verbally and non-verbally. Listening isn't as easy as it may sound. Some people let their own emotions, biases or other filters cloud what they hear to the point that it distorts what they think the other person is saying.

Head cocked to one side may indicate individual is trying to understand question or answer.

Listening to Verbal and Non-Verbal Responses

Be motivated. Decide what needs to be learned from the person who is being interviewed. Ask questions when speaking. Listen with a goal in mind. Know the purpose of the interview. Don't be distracted and don't interrupt unnecessarily. Look for nonverbal clues. People send messages with their bodies, facial expressions and gestures. Keep non-confrontational eye contact.

Make notes or have someone else take notes as they check the list of questions to see if everything has been covered. By listening, the interviewer will often hear many of the questions being answered before they asked, or hear places where a question on the list seems appropriate to ask at that point.

React to what is said not the person. Don't let personal feelings about the other person filter what is heard.
Be patient. Don't rush to ask the next question, sometimes the

interviewee will fill in the pause with additional information. Remember it's difficult, if not impossible, to listen and speak at the same time.

Know what you would like to learn from the interviewee.

Responding

Clarify - Ask for more detail or information on a particular issue.

Confirm - Paraphrase the interviewee's words. "...So if I understand you're saying..."

Empathize -- Understanding and perceiving another person's feelings and often unexpressed meanings and reflecting on them. This is not the same thing as being sympathetic or taking on the other person's feelings as your own.

Follow-up -- Ask questions that are non-judgmental or non-opinionated.

Re-Phrase -- Repeat or re-phrase answers and statements the interviewee makes.

Respond -- Use few definitive responses and more non-committal statements or questions.

Non-Verbal Communication

Everyone communicates non-verbally using body language. There is a vocabulary of gestures, postures, head movements, hand movements and other actions that all communicate certain things. Some non-verbal communication is unconscious and some may not be. Imagine going to visit someone and being greeted at the door by someone standing with their arms folded across their chest and no smile, at the same time they are saying "glad you could come." Which would have more impact, their words or their body language?

Respond to what the interviewee is telling you. Acknowledge what they are saying so that they know you ar e listening.

Non confrontational eye contact.

Recognizing Non-verbal Messages

Learn to manage personal non-verbal signals. Be aware of yourself and your own non-verbal communication. How are you sitting? Are you in a receptive posture? Are you maintaining eye contact? Are you slouching or looking bored? Do you have your arms folded in front of you?

Body Language

Signals

Be aware of the other person's posture. Are they speaking with arms folded or legs crossed? Do they maintain eye contact? If so what kind of eye contact? Do they blink a lot or touch parts of their body repeatedly? Body language and signals may give you information about whether someone is being honest or evasive.

Two Levels of Conversation

It's as if two conversations going on at the same time, one verbal and the other non-verbal. Be aware of the other person's non-verbal signals and adapt. For example, it's noticed that an interviewee is getting upset, a signal that shows interest and receptivity, sitting forward on the chair and maintaining eye contact may help.

Eye Contact

Messages from the Face and Head

Broken eye contact and blinking repeatedly might mean someone is being less than truthful. Looking past someone may show boredom or distraction. Hard eye contact may show anger. Steady eye contact generally indicates sincerity. Head

Looking down, no eye contact may indicate anger, embarrassment or distraction.

Body Language

turned or cocked slightly shows evaluation of what you are asking. Squinting may also show evaluation or not understanding. Tilting of the head slightly shows uncertainty about what is being said. Nodding usually indicates agreement. Smiling, generally shows agreement, confidence or accord. Never looking at the other person, may signal dishonesty.

Messages In Movements

Gestures often come in groups. Single gestures can be misleading or inconclusive. For example, someone may have an itch and scratch it once. But if the same person scratches an itch, rubs their nose and touches another part of their body it could signal nervousness, anger and/or being untruthful.

Hands are at the center of most gestures. For example, someone might lean back in their chair and clasp their hands behind their head in an attempt to dominate or act superior. They also might put their feet up on the table or desk at the same time trying to show they are in charge. As the interviewer you would not think of this posture unless you were a lawyer deposing someone and were trying to intimidate them. Touching the fingers of one hand to the other in the form of a steeple could also be an attempt to dominate the conversation or show authority.

Open palms gestures are usually a positive signal showing openness and no hidden agenda. Ringing of the hands shows a lack of confidence or fear. Touching of one's self nervously on the nose, pulling an ear, touching the chin, head and hair, or pulling at one's clothing may show someone is not being sincere.

Gestures

Picture a party, a couple are sitting on the sofa, they each have their legs crossed in such a way that their legs form a barrier to those outside. This sends us a non-verbal message that this couple is close and that they are together, shutting out others. A couple not getting along or two strangers sitting on the same sofa would probably cross their legs in opposite directions and sit further apart. Interviewing someone, legs crossed would not instill trust in the interviewee because it sets up a non-verbal barrier. Leaning forward slightly with an open, legs not crossed, feet flat on the floor posture is more likely to send a positive message. At the same time be aware of the interviewee's posture; what message are they sending?

Complicating the subject of non-verbal communication is that signals may vary from country to country and culture to culture. In certain cultures in the Middle East and Europe conversations are held in close proximity, where as in others like the United States, a bigger distance between speakers is maintained. Gestures have different meanings depending on where one is. A smile may mean different things depending on the situation. "Flipping someone off" in England requires a different gesture than in the U.S.

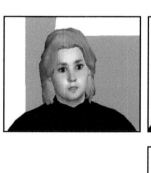 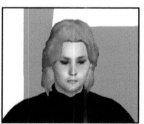 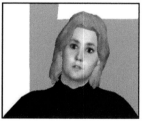

Interview Situations and Non-verbal Messages

1. The interviewee is leaning forward in their chair, they blink more rapidly when answering a question and scratch their head and touch their hair. Occasionally they sit back in the chair and cross on leg over the other. What non-verbal messages are they sending?

It seems in this case the interviewee is trying to look sincere but their blinking, scratching and hair touching betray a certain amount of untrustworthiness. Sitting back in the chair and crossing one leg over the other is a defensive posture as if they are trying to gain control of the interview or because they are nervous, control of themselves.

The interviewer might pause for moment, smile ask the person if they are comfortable or would they like some water. Also chat a bit about the weather or other mundane topic before you get started.

2. An interview is scheduled in the office of a corporate executive about his company and the fact that they have sustained some financial losses. He shakes the interviewer's hand palm down, sits down in his high back executive chair, leans back in and places his hands behind his head, and puts his feet up on the desk as the interviewer sits down opposite him on the other side of the desk.

This person is trying to establish himself as superior and in charge. He will try to dominate the conversation. It could be that he is somewhat insecure about his company's finances.

Instead of asking confrontational questions regarding the company's finances immediately the interviewer might try asking empathetic questions, perhaps about the general economy of the country or region and the difficulties in his industry.

3. After an interviewee is asked a couple of questions they begin staring at the interviewer intently and getting red in the face. The interviewee pulls her handbag up in front of her chest and frowns.

This person is obviously angry and defensive. She is protecting herself with the purse. She does not approve of the questions or is not being truthful.

4. The interviewer is interviewing someone and fails to make eye contact. They take off their glasses and clean them while the other person is speaking. They also repeatedly look over at their assistant taking notes and check their watch. At other times the interviewer leans back in their chair and scratches their nose or points at the interviewee when asking a question.

The interviewee will notice the inattention and failure to make eye contact and will not trust the interviewer. Looking at a watch, the assistant and cleaning glasses are all signs of boredom. Scratching the nose could mean someone may be asking a misleading question. Pointing at interviewee may be interpreted as trying to intimidate.

The interviewer is sending negative unprofessional messages.

5. The interviewer sits a bit forward in their seat with arms open and palms up as they ask a question or listen. Any movement is in sync with the interviewee. The interviewer maintains friendly eye contact and smiles or nods while listening to the other person.

The interviewee will feel comfortable and believe that the interviewer is acting in a friendly manner. Sitting or leaning forward a bit and maintaining eye contact show that the interviewer is listening to what interviewee is saying. Friendly smiles or face movements, or tilting of the head show that one is trying to understand what is being said and that the interviewer may want to ask a clarifying question.

The interviewer is sending positive professional messages.

Interview Crew Responsibilities

In a documentary interview situation there must be a synergy between the director/interviewer, the camera operator and sound person. All three people are involved in listening to the interviewee. The director has discussed how the interview should be shot with the camera operator. For example, whether to use more CU's or MS's. Also the director often gives the camera operator some latitude in when to change the shot. For example, if the plan is to cut out the questions, the camera operator knows that he can change the size of the shot or pan over to someone reacting while the director/interview is asking a question. The sound mixer must decide how to "mic" the interviewee depending on how many people are being interviewed at that time.

Interviewing On Location

Here are some basic guidelines for conducting interviews in all types of circumstances. Practical considerations often make it difficult to do certain things so a number of situations are examined.

AT A HOME OR PLACE OF BUSINESS – Make sure they know you're coming. Respect the home or place of business. Work quietly setting up and striking. Try to find a room or out of the-way place to put your equipment.

Interview with Ms Wilson in her Kitchen

Pick someplace in the house that the interviewee will feel comfortable sitting in. In a place of business where shooting must take place in an office try to avoid the backlighting from windows. Draw the blinds or drapes, if available, and light the subject.. If there is

no way to eliminate the light from the window try to use the window light as the main source of lighting (key light). This may necessitate having the subject face in another direction. When appropriate use a conference room or place that you can light and have a quiet ambience.

Camera and Interviewer level with the Mulac's sitting on their living room sofa.

ON A SET – Use a neutral backdrop, avoid props or colors that will distract the viewer from the interviewee. Light the set in a high key style unless a low key mood is appropriate. A high key mood will be more neutral. (See glossary for definition of High Key and Low Key)

In A Crowded Room -- When working around a room getting interviews, try to keep eye lines and balance in the coverage. An establishing shot of the crowded room, party or other gathering helps set up the space. The next part is to make the viewer feel that they are in the space with the interviewee.

Interview at political rally with Harold Washington, Mayor of Chicago

ON THE STREET AND OUTDOORS – Try not to shoot with the sun behind the interviewee. Use a Flex-Fill (reflector or bounce board) to fill in shadows. Keep the microphone as close to the person being interviewed as possible and out of the frame.

Man on the street interviews should be brief, a couple of questions. Don't spend a lot of time qualifying a prospective interviewee. People on the street are usually going someplace, so don't waste their time. Tell them who you are after you ask the question.

EXAMPLE: Hi, how do you feel about the Gators beating Ohio State in two major confrontations?

Consult the Glossary for definitions of unfamiliar terms or equipment.

Interview on the street

AT AN EVENT – Stay out of the way of what is going on at the event. Blend in with other media, don't block anyone else. At the same time be assertive about getting shots or asking questions when appropriate.

Bounce some light in to a set-up with a flex fill rather than a camera mounted light. Getting someone to put a lavaliere microphone on is not always practical so a shotgun or boom is useful. A shotgun microphone has a narrow angle range, so your audio person should stay close to the camera and point the shotgun microphone at the person's mouth. This will help keep out crowd sounds.

Shooting 16MM film with minimal bounce light.

In A Moving Vehicle, Train, Plane, Bus, Limo or Car

Interview in a limousine

Find a comfortable position for both the interviewee and the camera operator. Find a way you can steady the camera for handheld shooting. Using a lavaliere may not be practical so an onboard camera microphone or shotgun may be best. Lighting may be a problem, in a small place. Plugging in lights may not be possible, so using available light from windows and/or bouncing some light from portable lights may help.

MISCELLANEOUS EXTERIOR LOCATIONS – Scout locations when possible to see what conditions exist. Exterior night shooting may need special planning and portable lights. In most urban environments there are street lights and other ambient light sources that can be used. Remember to white balance in all lighting situations, always, everywhere.

Locations

Getting interviews and covering events to make a documentary or series of short documentaries means moving quickly, and having a basic plan on how to cover various aspects of the event. One approach is to show anyone being interviewed in front of what they are talking about. In the interview (bottom right) with a veteran Corvette enthusiast the sky occupying half the frame during the interview feels appropriate. It creates an ambiance that complements the interviewee.

Consult the Glossary for definitions of unfamiliar terms or equipment .

In the first shot (right) the interview takes place with enough of the background to give the feel of the National Corvette Restorers Society NCRS event. The interview with an exhibitor is part of a series of short 5 or 6 minute documentary looks at what goes on at the event. Graphics identify the interviewee.

Note the interviewee is facing the interviewer not the camera.

When he talks about his product line he is asked to stand by a display with those products.

National Corvette Restorers Society (NCRS) meeting in Florida.

All Photographs
©J R Martin

Award wining 1955 Corvette Owner J. Anderson in short documentary for Lyndale Island

Coverage, "B" roll and setting up the Interview

In this interview with the owner of a restored DC3 shots of the plane exterior, the engines starting and other shots were obtained to set the context for the interview and to use as "B" roll.

"B" roll--Any foot-age that supports the action, interviews or continuity of the story.

By starting out with shots of the plane a sense fo where we are going is established..

Interior shots included the cabin, cockpit, pilots, instruments, interviews and shots looking outside as the plane took off.

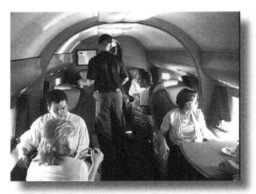

All Photographs
©J R Martin

(right) In this interview situation the Interviewer (middle) is part of the conversation and picture. The camera can shoot from the front or move around to get CU's (close-up) and reaction shots.

This shot can go (push-in) from an Over-The-Shoulder (OTS) shot to a CU.

This interview begins with establishing shot (above) and voice over from the interviewee (right)). As he continues there are cut a ways (lower right) to shots of what he's talking about.

Frames from interview with the Captain of The Bounty, a replica used originally in the Mutiny On The Bounty film and now used as a training vessel and for other films. - LyndaleIsland.com

Shooting Interviews

There are a number of ways to approach shooting interviews for documentary films. The most common set up is to have the person being interviewed talk to an unseen interviewer sitting or standing next to the camera.

The interviewee looks at the interviewer not the camera.

Interviewer sitting on the left side of camera which is level with person being interviewed.

The Camera is shooting on the right side and over the shoulder of the interviewer directly in front of the interviewee. The camera operator can easily zoom in for a tighter shot.

MCU Interviewee as she would appear in the above interview setup.

The interviewee may be framed anywhere in the frame depending on other compositional factors. Eye line remains the same.

Interviewer sitting on the right side of the camera. Interviewee looking toward interviewer.

Consult the glossary for definitions of unfamiliar terms or equipment .

(Left) CU Interviewee with Interviewer on right side of camera.

(Below) Interviewee looking directly into camera.

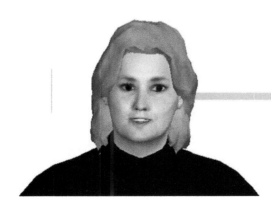

"B" Roll -- Action/Reaction and Cut a ways

Shooting additional footage that can be used to supplement the interview, show the environment, or add complementary action is know as "B" roll in television. Basically it is footage we need in addition to our interview and coverage of the action. In some instances action scenes are the main focus and the interview is used as voice over to narrate the scene. Cutaway shots are shots that cut away from the main action in a scene to show something else.

In the case of a documentary film "B" roll is more than a few cut a ways to help in editing. It should add to the narrative of the story and be used in part to highlight or bring clarity to what the narrative or interviewee is talking about. Whenever possible "B" roll should be shot with ambient sound.

The main action footage incorporated into the story is the "A" roll. "B" roll is both unused Action footage and additional footage shot to support the main action.

Guidelines For Editing Interviews

Once the interview is shot it needs to be transcribed so that it can be used to create a first person narrative to be used in the documentary. All of the questions will be cut and only the interviewee's answers will be heard. A transcription is usually a written word for word copy of the interview. This copy is read and the passages or sentences to be used are highlighted. The highlighted areas are numbered and cut & pasted into an editing script.

After transcribing the interview it is read to find the most succinct answers to questions and the best way to create a narrative of what the interviewee said. Sometimes this requires using portions of the interview in a different order than they were spoken so that a beginning, middle and end to the interview is created. During this editing process it is important not to distort what was said or use it out of context. This is unethical and usually transparent to the viewer.

Once it is decided what is to used an editing script is written placing the everything in the order it will be seen. At this point we're not to worried about the picture as we will use "B" Roll footage and other material to help cover the cuts. If there is an idea for the picture, put it in the script. The editing script is a guide to start editing with as it may be that there are problems with connecting the shots as scripted. Breaking up sentences might be difficult because of speech patterns, breathing, movement to and away from the microphone, different ambience in the background or connecting the segments together. This is where adequate coverage and a good selection of shots are critical. A simple technique like the camera operator changing the size of each shot while the Director/Interviewer is asking questions gives the editor a chance to make match cuts between segments.

Editing should create a smooth, seamless narrative that tells the story. Cut a ways are used to add to the visual information and should be relevant to what we're talking about. If someone is talking about his or her life and we cut to a clock on the wall to cover a bad cut, it will confuse the viewer. What does the clock have to do with his or her life? But if we cut to some pictures of the interviewee when he or she was a child, while the subject is was growing up, it will complement what we are talking about. Talking heads rapidly become tiresome if we leave them on the screen to long. Cutting and coming back to the person talking when they are making a strong or emotional point makes for good story telling.

Match cut: A cut from one shot to the next where the action or subject in both shots is matched.

There are times when an interview can layered over action scenes in order to explain what is happening. At the end of the segment, cut to the interviewee for a few final words.

Are there multiple interviews with different people that are being editing in parallel? A visual link can be established that helps establish a transition between two or more interviewees. Example: a group of people are at conference table. The first shot establishes everyone at the table. There are then CU's of people speaking seen. Then a cut to someone listening as the other person's voice is heard. At that point the person listening responds or there is a cut to someone else responding.

It's a good idea to show what the interviewee is talking about not just a talking head.

Editing is a creative process and therefore a problem solving process. Piecing together a story based on actuality footage, interviews, archival footage, photographs, and "B" roll, is like putting together a puzzle. Each time a new piece of the puzzle finds a link it is very rewarding.

Transcribing interviews to create an editing script is a great help in finding the answers that tell the story. Reading "hard copy," helps to find the underlying thoughts among the interviewee's sometimes-lengthy answers to questions.

Narration

Interviews may be used in a number of ways; as narration that is in juxtaposition with action to create a new notion; to describe what is being seen and to describe something that is not seen or heard. It can be first person narration or third person narration.

SAMPLE TRANSCRIPTION

In the example below different colors and numbering are used to show the lines in the interview to be used. When working with actual paper transcripts a highlighter could be used.

TRANSCRIPTION TAPE 3 -- INTERVIEW SHANILLE

EXT. MS Shanille sitting on park bench being interviewed.

Q: How did your family react to you going to study film?

Shanille: Well let me think... I guess my family was supportive, but at first my Mother was worried. I was involved in all the shows in high school and she thought I'd become an actor and starve in L.A. or something, but then I told her I was going to Orlando and she thought I was going to work at Disney and become a mouse or something, but then I talked it over with my Dad and explained that I wanted to be an editor and basically what an editor did. So in the end my family was very supportive and they are very happy for me.

The choice to edit the interview in this way was not to distort what was said but to condense it or use the most succinct part. It may be that due to speech patterns we cannot edit this exactly as hoped for. Work-a- rounds are found in editing.

Using the transcript go through the answers and highlight sentences or parts to work with in the editing script. Number clips or sentences to indicate the order to use them if desired.

At his point don't worry about the picture or how it will visually cut together. Try to create a succinct answer to the question. If it ends up that there are odd cuts, after it's all strung together, it may be possible to use "B" roll to cover the cuts.

A basic two column script format is used to assemble the editing script. Use the "Table" function in "Word," to create four columns and a dozen or so rows, then size them. All cells expand with text across each row. (See page , Chapter 5.

Editing Script (uses same basic two column format as a shooting script). An editing script is based on transcripts of interviews and other available footage.

No.	PICTURE	TIME	AUDIO
1	MS Shanille	:03	...in the end my family was very supportive and they are happy for me.
1a	MS Shanille	;01	Mother was worried
2	MS Shanille (Archival footage or photographs silent film starlet looking hungry.)	:04	I was involved in all the shows in high school and she thought I'd d become an actor and starve i L.A., but then I told her I was going to Orlando and then she thought I was going to work at Disney and become a cast member, mouse, or something.
3	MS Shanille (B Roll Shanille in class)	:03	But then I talked it over with my Dad and explained that...
4	MS Shanille	:03	...I wanted to be an Editor and what an Editor did.

Sample editing script based on interview transcripts.

There are a number of excellent digital camcorders made by Panasonic, Sony, Canon and JVC that will provide broadcast quality video for documentaries.

There are pro's and con's to each type of system ranging from camcorders with built in hard drives, tape systems, and dual tape and storage card systems.

Going tape-less may seem a great advantage in situations where dumping the digital information is convenient and archival priorities low. It must be remembered that once footage is downloaded to a non-linear editing system it could be lost and not retrievable if an archive has not been established. With tape it can always be recaptured if a crash occurs. Tape may also be stored indefinitely for future use.

Digital Single Lens Reflex Cameras (DSLR's) are currently being used in documentary production. They furnish high quality still photographs as well has HD video. Sync Sound can be recorded with the video in the camera on flash memory cards or, for better quality, recorded separately.

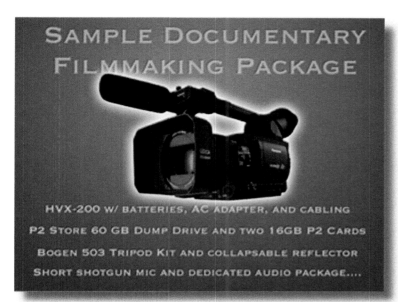

SAMPLE DOCUMENTARY FILMMAKING PACKAGE

HVX-200 w/ BATTERIES, AC ADAPTER, AND CABLING

P2 STORE 60 GB DUMP DRIVE AND TWO 16GB P2 CARDS

BOGEN 503 TRIPOD KIT AND COLLAPSABLE REFLECTOR

SHORT SHOTGUN MIC AND DEDICATED AUDIO PACKAGE....

CHAPTER 9

DIGITAL PRODUCTION SHOOTING AND EDITING FILM AND DIGITAL VIDEO

CHAPTER NINE

CHAPTER 9
Shooting and Editing Film and Digital Media for Documentary and Nonfiction Projects

Shooting a documentary today using film and editing film is expensive and increasingly not being done. For high end television productions High Definition formats (HD) is great to look at, easier in many ways to work with and less expensive.

In many applications that are not for television, like the internet or distribution on DVD, standard definition (SD) format, digital video (DV) is more than adequate. Even if a project is shot on film it is likely it will be edited on a non-linear editing (NLE) system like Final Cut, Avid, or Adobe's Premiere among many other possible digital editing systems available for both Mac and PC.

Film Stock

There are a number of considerations and choices available when shooting film either for transfer to a digital format or for finishing in film. Film stock comes in many configurations and types; from film that is balanced to be exposed in daylight to film that is balanced for tungsten lighting. Film comes with a number of different levels of sensitivity to light (International Standards Organization (ISO)[1]. The lower the ISO number the less sensitive to light. The range is from about 25 to 1600 ISO. A high ISO rated film is said to be a "faster" film stock. The lower the ISO of the film, the finer the grain. A 200 ISO film stock would have a finer grain than a 400 ISO stock. Grain technically is the silver halide crystals used in film emulsions. The larger the grain the more it can be seen on the screen. Sort of like seeing enlarged pixels in the digital realm. So there is a trade off in using a higher ISO film stock, in that the higher the ISO the more grain the film will have. With the current line of film stocks the differences are not as noticeable between ISO 100 and 250 as they once were.

Some digital still cameras allow you to adjust the camera's sensitivity by changing a digital ISO. In a digital context, boosting the ISO will cause more "noise" in the video image. It is equivalent to "pushing" the ISO in film, rating the ISO higher than specified and then over-developing the negative.

------

1 At one time ISO's, Film Exposure Index, was known as ASA (American Standards Association -Index)

Types of Film Stock

Film stock comes as negative and reversal (positive image). Most filming uses negative image film stock, from which positive prints can be made directly to a positive film stock. Available from Kodak, are a few reversal film stocks that, much like slide film, render a positive image when developed. This film stock can be projected.

Film stock is available in black and white and in color. Both also have all the variations mentioned above.

Film comes in various sizes for professional applications, 16mm, Super 16mm, 35mm and 65mm. Most theatrical motion pictures are shot in 35mm. There are a number of 35mm formats, with different size image areas.

Super 16mm Film Stock

Super 16mm has an image size that can be "blown-up" to fit a 35mm wide screen ratio losing only about 25% of its image area. It also fits a high definition (HD) format well. While HD is better than any SD digital format it still does not have the look and feel of film. This can be seen in the contrast ratios, detail in the shadow areas and the ability to control depth-of-field.

Super 16mm film may be blown up to a 35mm wide screen format or transferred to a wide screen digital format like HD. A project shot in super 16mm could be transferred to a digital format for editing. When the film is finished editing the digital edit will be used to conform the super 16mm negative. Only the shots actually used in the film would be blown up to 35mm.

Major theatrical documentaries meant to be screened in theaters usually shoot in 35mm. Super 16mm is an option, however, the cost of blowing up the image to 35mm may out-weigh the savings of using the smaller format. One advantage of Super 16mm is smaller crew sizes and lighter equipment. Shooting a concert for theatrical release is probably best filmed in 35mm because of the static location of the event. A project with many locations might be less expensive to do in Super 16mm.

Some early documentary films were shot and edited using standard 16mm color reversal film. Color reversal (the same stock and process used for slides) was finer grain, at the time, than negative film and readily available. It was used by many television stations and actually developed at many TV stations in time for the 11 P.M. newscast ("film at eleven"). The film stock is still available at this time.

Reversal stocks provide a camera original or master that could actually be projected and in some instances, like television news, it was edited, put on a telecine chain and broadcast. When video cameras became portable TV switched to video. When new and better negative film stocks became available, most 16mm production started using negative instead of reversal film stock.

Today negative is transferred to a digital format and then captured into a Non Linear Editing (NLE) program where it is edited. After editing the film, using Flex-files created when the film was transferred to a digital format, an Edit Decision List (EDL) is made which is linked to the original negative and that is conformed to the NLE cut. Flex-files connect the original film frame to the digital frame. It is important to let the film lab developing and transferring the film to a digital format, know the intention to finish the project on film after editing on a NLE system. The lab will make the flex-files needed.

To edit the film in the traditional way, a duplicate of the camera negative is made for editing, which is called a work print. After the work print is fine cut it will be matched or conformed to the original camera negative. The conformed negative and mixed sound are used to make a print known as an answer print. It is the first release print and must be perfectly color corrected and "answer" to all the specifications requested by the filmmakers. After this an internegative or interpositive is made from the conformed negative and used to make large numbers of release prints. The conformed negative might also be transferred to a digital format to make DVD's,

In 16mm it is necessary to conform the camera original into "A" and "B" rolls to be able to make the splices invisible in the finished print. 35mm film projects are usually shot using negative film and do not require "A" and "B" rolls to make splices invisible because there is enough room between frames to make a cement splice.

Film editing on analog equipment is a process of physically splicing film (shots) together. This can be done in a number of ways using basic film editing equipment; rewinds mounted on a table with a device called a Picture Synchronizer (Pic Sync) in the middle. The picture was synced with the sound, the footage logged, projected on a double system 16mm Siemens projector for review. Based on that screening an editing script is written. The first cut can be an assemblage or a rough cut. If there is an editing script start with a rough cut. It is better to edit with two sound tracks and the picture to start with to facilitate mixing sound later. Editing film can be accomplished using a number of different methods using various editing devises.

The Acme Pic Sync (Left) is a motorized devise that combines a picture head and three sound heads synchronously. It can handle up to 3 sound tracks and one picture at any time. Combined with rewinds it provides a good film editing platform. Trim bins are used to hang clips in as editing proceeds. A tape splicer is used when working with a work print copy of the negative.

Non-Linear Editing Programs Emulate Film Editing

Editing may also be accomplished using a flatbed-editing machine like a *Steenbeck Flat Bed Editor (below)*.

Steenbeck 8-Plate 16mm Film Editing Machine

The great thing about editing with a Non-Linear Editing programs like Avid or Final Cut is that they emulate traditional film editing both are a non-destructive editing process. They both have multiple audio tracks and multiple video tracks. Non-linear editing on a computer work station, is a non-destructive editing process in that you can change anything at anytime without destroying your original or the current edit. Mechanical film editing is also nondestructive because tape splices can be undone. A project edited on a NLE system may be finished as a video and transferred directly to a DVD.

Ideal formats to transfer film to video depend on bandwidth, detail and amount of movement. Two recommended formats are 720p 24 and 1080p 24.

The choice to shoot film or video depends on how it will be used and to budget. Film still has some advantages over any type of video recording. For example some film stocks have higher resolution per frame, better contrast and detail in the shadow areas of the scene.

Shooting Digital and High Definition Video

Camcorders these days run the gamut from consumer level, prosumer and industrial to professional production cameras. There are a number of formats and configurations also available. Most of the time the first thing to consider is how the final product will be distributed. Cinematographers should be familiar with all the digital video advantages and disadvantages when shooting digital instead of film.

At this time the first choice is whether to shoot in Standard Definition (SD) or High Definition (HD). At this time SD is still the universal standard and most homes and offices do not benefit from HD, although HD is becoming more prevalent. Shooting in HD uses up a lot more space on tape, a hard drive or P2 card than shooting SD.

High definition television (HDTV) resolution is either 720 or 1080 scan lines. Digital, standard definition, NTSC television (DTV) is 480 visible scan lines out of 525 scan lines. PAL and SECAM DTV have 576 visible scan lines out of 625 scan lines and are used in Europe. Only Blu-ray Disc has HD quality images. Standard DVD does not.

There are two types of scanning, progressive (p) and interlaced (i). Interlaced scanning draws the image twice for each frame, first the odd numbered lines than the even numbered lines. Progressive scanning redraws all its lines each time it refreshes the frame. Interlaced scanning creates greater screen resolution but does not deal with moving objects as well as progressive scanning. In progressive scanning the image is called a frame. Interlaced scanning deals with fields because it creates two fields for each frame.

The screen aspect ratio for HDTV is 16:9 (1.78:1) SDTV has a 4:3 (1.33:1) aspect ratio. HDTV requires an HD television to view it.

High Definition Video Frame Sizes

FRAME SIZE	VIDEO	PIXELS	TYPE SCANNING
1280 x 720	720p	921,600	Progressive (p)
1920 x 1080	1080p	2,073,600	Progressive (p)
1920 x 1080	1080i	1,036,800	Interlaced (i)
2048 x 1536	2K	3,145,728	Progressive (p)
4096 x 3072	4K	12,528,912	Progressive (p)
3840 x 2160	2160p	8,294,400	Progressive (p)
4520 x 2540	2540p	11,480,800	Progressive (p)
7680x4320	4320p	33,177,600	Progressive (p)

Frame and Field Rates

Frame or field rates may be indicated without an apparent resolution. 24p is 24 progressive scan frames per second. 50i is 25 interlaced fps (50 interlaced fields). Some confusion exists in HD production and post-production because in NTSC 30 fps is actually 29.97 video or 23.98 if converted from film by using 2:3 pull-down. 60 fps is actually 59.94 fps.

In HD production there are standards for 23.98, 24, 29.97, 30, 59.94 and 60. So in production and post-production there needs to be compatibility with the standard chosen. For example it is important that when working with NTSC that we realize that 60i is a designation that is not compatible. When used in the US it actually represents 59.94i which is compatible.

Compatibility of HD Frame Rates and NTSC

There is a need for backward compatibility in down-conversion of HD video to SD for broadcast and SD DVD's. The key to compatibility is the frame rate not if it is interlaced or progressive scanning. Shooting with an NTSC compatible frame rate facilitates conversion. Compatible frame rates are 23.98 (24), 29.97(30) and 59.94(60) in 720 or 1080 interlaced or progressive.

24p (23.98): This frame rate exists in both HDTV and SDTV standards. In most cases in the United States 24p is actually the rounding off of 23.98 (which is itself actually 23.976). This rate is down converted using a system known as "2:3 pull-down" This system also is the standard for converting film shot at 24 fps to 30 fps (29.97 fps).

30 (29.97): standard rate for NTSC television and video in the United States and other countries. 60i (59.94): 30 (29.97) fps interlaced fields per second.

In the United States, all HD broadcast video must be mastered so that it has NTSC compatible frame rates, even if it is intended for HD broadcast. In countries that use the PAL system HD things are more straight forward since no "pull-down" is needed because PAL runs at 25 fps. So the frame rates are 25p, 50i and 50p.

When working with 720 or 1080 make sure all the possible compatibility issues are resolved.

HD Aspect Ratios -- 16x9 HD video is either squeezed (anamorphic) or full raster (full frame). Most HD formats do not display a full raster 16x9 frame. There are two square pixel, full raster 16x9 frames. They are 1920x1080 and 1280x720.

Digital Camcorders

There are three levels of camcorders, professional, "prosumer," and consumer. Prices vary according to level and features.

High end professional cameras include heavy non portable studio cameras and ENG/EFP portable cameras that produce broadcast quality signals and have features required for professional production. So called "prosumer" camcorders range from cameras with features that rival professional ENG/EFP portable and industrial equipment to high end consumer models. These camcorders are available in a price range that documentary, industrial and small video production companies can afford. Quality runs from high to minimal broadcast images. Formats may be switched between Standard Definition (SD) and High Definition (HD) and a 3 CCD chip is standard.

Consumer level cameras vary in quality and features and are available at competitive prices for home or amateur use.

Major manufacturers including, Sony, Panasonic, Canon, and JVC make the most popular camcorders for documentary and industrial video production. Every six months or so, they come out with camcorders that are smaller, higher in quality, and with more features than previous models.

Before buying a camcorder it is important to compare brands and models and look for features that fit the type of production anticipated.

Digital Single Lens Reflex Cameras

Still photographs are an important aspect of telling documentary stories both on their own and used in film or video documentaries. Up until recently shooting using negative film, developing and printing were the only way to get quality prints. Today digital single lens reflex (DSLR) cameras with high mega pixel ratings can record high quality images for prints, presentation slides or for use in film or video. All of the DSLR's have interchangeable lenses and function like the original SLR cameras that used film stock.

One of the latest DSLR's is the Canon® EOS 7D an 18-megapixel superior image quality DSLR. This camera also shoots full HD video at 1080p or 720p. Audio can be recorded while shooting video but the quality may vary depending on the situation. The built in microphone may pick up camera noise, however, an external microphone may be plugged into the camera. The camera records excellent quality HD, 1280 x 720 at 60 fps (actual 59.94 NTSC and 50 fps PAL). Full HD at 1920 x 1080p at 30 fps (NTSC actual 29.97, PAL 25 fps) or 24 fps (actual 23.976). With a 32 gig compact flash card quite a bit of video can be recorded in maximum 4 gig clips. Most of the features of the camera can be incorporated into video recording. While this camera is not a substitute for a full featured HD camcorder it is an excellent adjunct tool.

One of the main features of this camera is the ability to shoot photographs in RAW or JPEG formats. RAW images have little processing and are not compressed. JPEG images have more

Canon® EOS 7D Digital SLR

processing of information relating to the photograph and are compressed. The 7D uses an APS-C size CMOS sensor which is slightly smaller than a 35mm frame. The camera has automatic and manual exposure with control of f-stop, shutter speed and ISO settings. The Canon EOS 5D is similar, but with 21-megapixel, 24mm x 36mm full frame, 35mm equivalent size, CMOS sensor. The EOS 5D is more expensive and heavier in weight.

Audio

Nonfiction and documentary films, videos and presentations benefit from high quality audio recording, editing and mixing. Hearing is second only to seeing when it applies to our senses. Good audio adds depth, texture and reality to what we see.

The first step to achieving high-end audio in the final product is to start by recording excellent audio. There are a number of basic ways to achieve this depending on what it is being recorded.

Signal to Noise Ratio

The "signal" is whatever needs to be recorded. "*Noise,*" is just about everything else, background sounds, room tone, and other extraneous sounds like a car passing by, an airplane flying over or people talking nearby. The idea is to keep the signal in front (high) and the noise behind, low and often below the threshold of hearing if possible. This is known as a *"high signal to noise ratio."*

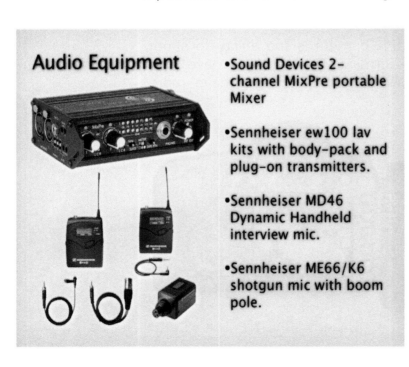

Audio Equipment

- Sound Devices 2-channel MixPre portable Mixer

- Sennheiser ew100 lav kits with body-pack and plug-on transmitters.

- Sennheiser MD46 Dynamic Handheld interview mic.

- Sennheiser ME66/K6 shotgun mic with boom pole.

To achieve a signal to noise ratio that produces a strong signal and a weak background *(a high signal to noise ratio)* it's important to get the microphone close to the source of the signal. There are a number of microphones that can be used depending on the situation and what it is you are recording. The use of an automatic volume control for recording is not recommended at any time. One big problem with automatic control of volume is that whenever things get quiet for any reason the automatic control tries to find where the sound is by raising the volume. This results in it recording whatever noise is out there when there is the slightest pause in the signal.

Microphones most used in Documentary Production

Lavalieres – built to be worn by a person being interviewed. It should be attached somewhere below the neckline on the chest about six inches below the mouth. Lavalieres should be clipped to clothing in such a way as to not rub against anything the person is wearing. Lavalieres are available in wireless or wired versions. *"Lavs"* are omnidirectional and can be used in situations where a very small microphone is needed, however they are balanced to be worn on the chest.

Omnidirectional – Usually used as a handheld microphone or on a table or desk facing the person. This microphone can be mounted on a stand and used to pick up other sounds including musical instruments. It is able to pick up sound from all directions.

Shotgun – Handheld or on a pole, this directional microphone is useful in many documentary situations. Available as a camera mounted microphone in many instances.

Unidirectional microphones pick up sounds better from the front than from the sides.

Fish pole Boom Microphone – A shotgun microphone attached to an extendible pole and held so that it is either pointed at, held above or below and in front of the person speaking or other sound source. The operator wears headphones so that the sound or voice of the speaker can be heard.

Mixer – A two channel or four channel mixer is a valuable tool in recording sound for documentaries in a number of ways, but is important when there is more than one source to record. The operator wears headphones and may feed a signal to the boom operator so that they both can hear the sound.

In a documentary film most interviewing is done on location not in a recording studio sound booth. Location situations vary and each may require a different approach and microphone. Sometimes improvisation is required to get the best sound available under the circumstances, keeping in mind that the priority is to hear the speaker clearly separated from the background noise.

35mm, Super 16mm Film or HD for Theatrical Release

The choice to use HD or film for a documentary that will be theatrically released, has a number of factors to be examined. The first is where will it be shown? There are a few options available if distribution begins with a release in festivals and theaters.

Use of 35mm film, shooting in 1:85 wide screen format is certainly an option if money is available and portability of equipment is not a problem. Theaters are all able to screen this wide-screen format.

The 1:85 film format uses standard 35mm film. The shot is framed in a wide screen aspect ratio resulting in the loss of part of the top and bottom of the standard 1.33 35mm frame. A high quality standard definition, wide-screen and HD version could be produced for DVD distribution.

Super 16 mm film is a viable alternative to 35mm production. Super 16 "blows-up" to 35 with a minimal loss of quality. It affords more portable equipment and smaller crews. Super 16 may be transferred directly to high definition digital formats.

Digital Production

Making documentaries using digital production resources has become the standard for the majority of documentary production. Equipment is lite weight and portable. The latest version of Digital Camcorders rival film resolution. Crews can be kept small and are able to move quickly. Spontaneous coverage of events with multiple cameras is economically viable if needed.

Before deciding whether to use a digital format or film as the recording medium, there should be a careful analysis of many factors including the distribution requirements and budget. Each medium has its advantages and disadvantages.

Film makes sense in certain situations where theatrical distribution internationally is anticipated. Certain festivals require an entry to be shot in film and to be screened at the festival from a release print. In this case film leaves all options open and the film can still be edited in a digital NLE system.

Shooting a documentary in a digital format is usually less expensive, in every way than shooting film. Documentaries tend to have shooting ratios in most situations. It is not unusual for a major documentary effort to shoot 50 minutes for every minute (50-1 shooting ratio) used in the film. That's a lot of film stock, development and transfer expense, not to mention other post production expenses.

A documentary can be shot in high end HD digital formats, with high shooting ratios economically. The footage that ends up in the final version can then be processed and a film version produced. There are high charges, per frame, transfer digital video to film. In addition these per frame rates come in megabyte resolutions, each with a unique rate, from one megabyte to four megabytes. The higher the megabytes the higher the resolution. The frame rate applies to the number of frames in each foot of the film which in 35mm is 16 frames per foot. In 16mm there are forty frames per foot of film.

Double System Digital Production

Many documentary filmmakers are using DSLR's with external digital sound recorders like the Zoom H4n. This recorder has both built in microphones, and accepts two XLR inputs. Camera and Audio are recorded separately. This is similar to shooting "double system" in traditional productions using 16mm or 35mm film. When working double system it is a good idea to slate each scene to aid in syncing up picture and sound in postproduction.

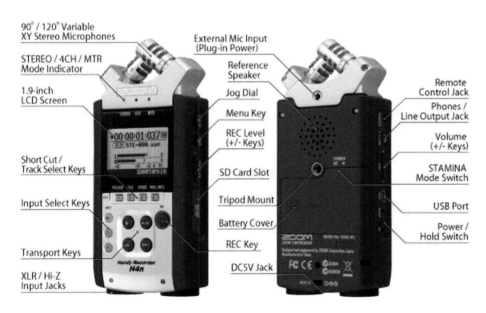

Zoom H4n Handy Recorder © ZOOM Corporation

The director of a documentary project is someone who benefits by having insight into all aspects of production and technical crafts involved.

"The most beautiful thing we can experience is the mysterious. It is the source of all true art and all science, He to whom this emotion is a stranger, who can no longer pause to wonder and stand rapt in awe, is as good as dead: his eyes are closed." Albert Einstein

...umentary
...ction there is
...biotic rela-
...ip between
...rector and
...a Person

CHAPTER 10

THE FILMMAKER/DIRECTOR
AND
NONFICTION PRODUCTIONS

Basic Realities and Production Techniques
For Directing and Making Documentaries

Chapter Highlights

Types of Scenes

Lenses

Framing

Real People

Locations

Lighting

Crews

DIRECTING DOCUMENTARY PRODUCTIONS

Director's Responsibilities

Determine the overall look and feel of the film.

Consult with DP about lighting, type, size and lens used for each shot.

Interview subjects with prepared and researched questions. Questions may be researched by others.

Direct camera and crew.

Obtain coverage adequate for editing.

Work with editor during post-production.

There is a major difference between directing a documentary production and directing television news gathering methods (Electronic News Gathering (ENG).

ENG production relies mainly on handheld shots of newscasters in the field, panoramic views of events and few attempts at visual story telling. Available lighting is the standard with the occasional camera mounted light applied to pierce the darkness.

Documentary film story telling is based on cinematic story telling conventions and methods employing composition of shots, lenses, lighting and editing styles found in most fiction films. The introduction of electronic recording devices, analog video and digital video, does not change the methodology; it only changes the recording medium. This is not to say that recording images electronically rather than on film does not change the look and feel of what is shot. On the contrary it greatly changes what is seen and felt.

The images seen on film are different from the electronic images seen on a television. Film is considered a "hot" medium, television a "cool" medium. Film, to start with, is a solid picture or frame of something. When it is projected, the light shines through the film producing a warm image up on a big screen. It engages the viewer. Other hot media are paper and money which also present a solid image that engages us.

Television with its electronically produced image is considered a "cool" medium. Essentially an electronic tube, LCD or plasma device on which are projected lines and fields with electronic coolness. It does not evoke the kind of emotional reaction that a film in a theater does because it lacks detail. Television is not the image but points of light that form an illusion of an image that is constantly changing.

Creating a documentary for theatrical release is different than making a documentary for television. Television needs more close-ups and action than a film to tell story. Cutting is generally faster. Shooting film, for ultimate showing on television, must take into consideration that the images will be seen on a much smaller screen than in most theaters. Also when shooting wide screen or HD formats you need to consider that not everyone has a wide screen television and that most action needs to happen within standard TV safe areas.

When writing a shooting script or putting together a shot list there are a number of factors to consider. What kind of shots are necessary to provide adequate coverage of the event, action or interview? There are three types of scenes a director may encounter 1) action with no dialog, 2) dialog with no action and 3) action and dialog. Each type of scene requires a different type of coverage.

Types of Scenes

ACTION NO DIALOG – A parade is all action and no dialog. It would be good to shoot a master shot, fairly wide, of the parade coming toward us. Additionally some close-ups of the individual band members or marchers as insert shots to be used with the master shot. Also needed are some MS's and CU's of the people watching the parade. Are there floats? Maybe LS of the floats and CU's of people on the floats. Audio of the band and ambience of the scene is also recorded. Another aspect of coverage is the screen direction of the parade. Moving from left to right on the screen implies the parade is moving away from us. Moving from right to the left implies it's moving toward us. Screen direction continuity is important so as not to confuse he viewer.

DIALOG NO ACTION - Also known as "a talking head." Coverage here needs camera movement and different size shots to provide something to edit and ways to cut out the questions being asked. A scene might start out with a Full Shot (FS) of the interviewee standing or sitting. The interviewer asks the interviewee to introduce themselves. The camera operator frames a MS to cover this dialog. While the interviewer is asking the next question, the camera operator pushes in and frames a CU. Each time a question is asked the camera operator changes the size of the shot. This gives the editor some choices and is a lot better than the camera locked off in a static MS for the entire interview. Also an alert camera operator might find times when pushing in or pulling back during the answer gives the shot some impact.

ACTION AND DIALOG - A political rally situation has both action and dialog and requires an assortment of shots of people moving around, signs and posters and shots of speakers. This might start out as all action and end up as action and dialog if interviews with the people attending the rally are included. Additionally there is a need to consider movement of people in the scene, at the location, and who should be covered. For example, should the POV be internal, from inside the rally or externally as an outside observer?

Focal Length of the Lens

Whatever type of scene being shot, the focal length lens being used is an important. A wide angle lens will give increased depth-of-field. A telephoto lens will decrease the depth-of-field. Where the camera is positioned and its height are important factors in recording the event. A neutral POV is established by bringing the camera level with the subject, neither looking up or down on this person and by using an appropriate lens for a MS.

Framing

Where is the subject in the frame? On the left, middle or right? Sitting or standing? Are they looking toward the center or speaking off camera? Is there a reason for where they are in the frame and if so what is it? Does it make sense for continuity? What else will be seen in the frame? Will all of this coverage be able to be edited with some continuity?

Shooting

Real People

Shooting a documentary film is different in many ways from shooting a theatrical film. The "actors" in the story are real people in real life situations doing something being documented. There are no sets, only locations that were not built to make films in, although in some nonfiction films and other situations, a set might be built to do an interview or facilitate some environment that isn't available.

Locations

Shooting in someone's home or office requires a number of considerations. The footage should provide the look and feel of the location; but good exposures and places to set up the camera for the best composition of shots is also important. Most homes will have 15 amp or 20 amp circuit breakers which limits the amount of watts (Approximately 1500 watts and 2000 watts[1]) of power that may be pulled on each line.

Offices may have higher amp lines but there may be office equipment on those lines that might be crashed if a circuit is blown. Usually a homeowner can identify the best place to plug lights into. Office buildings usually have an electrician or building supervisor who can help. (In many instances it is not unusual to offer this person a gratuity for their assistance; it should be in the budget.)

If it's not possible to scout a location in advance some extra time should be allowed to check things out on arrival. When interviewing someone in their home look for the place where they will be comfortable and that offers the best light. Often all that can be done in a room is to bounce some light off the ceiling for fill light and bring

---

1 Ohms Law: Amps x Volts = Watts

up the overall lighting for a good exposure.

Offices are full of fluorescent lighting which isn't as much of a problem for good digital camcorders as it is for film. White balance the camcorder under the fluorescent light and the color balance should look natural. Any additional light used should be filtered to match the fluorescent.

Lighting

When shooting film other methods are necessary. One method used is to shoot daylight balanced film under fluorescent light with some filters on the lens to help the color. In big budget situations there are other methods such as swapping out all daylight balanced tubes for tungsten-balanced (3200ºK) fluorescent or just turning them all off and lighting the space. Gels, which balance the fluorescent tubes for tungsten light may also be used in the fixture housing.

Documentary film crews are usually small and mobile, able to work in tight spaces and environments where other events are taking place as shooting continues. Available light is often all that can be accommodated, although when possible it is desirable to light or augment the available light. In exterior situations "Flexfills" or other reflective methods can be used to bounce fill light into shadows on faces or scenes.

Crew Size

It's important for documentary crews to work quietly and as inconspicuously as possible for a number of reasons, including not interfering with what is being documented. By working quietly and blending into the environment the subjects can relax more and be themselves. On outdoor locations or big events it is good to have a second AD or PA who can quietly do crowd control to give the camera operator and director some space in which to work.

If possible, locations should be checked out in advance to see what is required. In some cases such as public parks and city streets, location releases or permits may be required. However, in many cities, documentary crews do not require a permit if they are not using a tripod and no actors/on camera talent are involved.

Coverage

It is the responsibility of the director to get adequate coverage of the subject so that it can be edited into the film. This includes shots that can be edited together in a seamless fashion and other shots that may be used to create reaction or show what the interviewee is talking about. Other coverage in the form of inserts and cut-a-ways

Coverage -- Shots necessary to enable the editor to edit the scene with continuity.

is also necessary. Planning is a good way to insure that adequate coverage is obtained.

Shot Composition

It is the directors responsibility to call for the type of shot he needs and to work with the director of photography and/or camera operator to compose each shot.

Composing shots for a documentary film is important from many standpoints. Most of the same rules that are followed for theatrical films are also used for documentaries.

Lenses

There are two types of lenses used in film and digital video production. Multi-focal length lenses (zoom lenses) and fixed focal length lenses (prime lenses). Documentary productions use mostly zoom lenses because they are convenient and because most camcorders do not allow lenses to changed and come with zoom lenses.

Depth-of-field is an area where everything is in focus, in front of (near) and in back of (far) the point where the lens is focused.

Wide Angle lenses show a wider field of view than a normal lens and has more depth-of-field than a normal or a telephoto lenses.

Normal is relative to the format being used. For 35mm, normal is a 50mm lens, for 16mm a 25mm lens. Most professional camcorders use compensated 35mm equivalents. A normal lens approximates what the human eye sees at any given distance from the camera.

Telephoto lenses (long lenses) make distant images appear close by magnification. A telephoto lens has the least amount of depth-of-field and compresses the image vertically stacking up and flattening the image. Zooming in is moving to the telephoto end of the lens. Zooming out is moving to the wide angle end of the lens. A zoom-in to an object is much different than a dolly into the same subject. A zoom-in changes the focal length of the lens from wide to telephoto thereby changing the size of the shot and compressing the image vertically. Depth-of-field also changes and becomes shallow.

A dolly-in or any other way of moving the camera closer to the subject, maintains the same size lens focal length moving to the subject physically instead of optically. Depth-of-field changes are more subtle.

The two moves have different feels and say something different. The director chooses a lens that best conveys the image in context with the story, scene and emotion desired.

Shot Sizes

In Fig. 1 We move from CU, to Tight CU, to Extreme CU (ECU). There is some latitude in framing a CU on a person, but generally it's starting at the armpits and up.

Use a CU to let the viewer know where to look in the frame. A CU says look at this.

Standard Abreviations for Shots

Extreme Close-up -- ECU

Close-up -- CU

Medium Close-Up -- MCU

Medium Shot -- MS

Medium Long Shot -- MLS

Long Shot -- LS

Over-the-Shoulder -- OTS

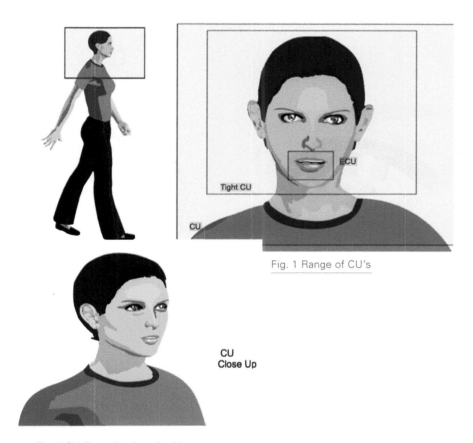

Fig. 1 Range of CU's

CU
Close Up

Fig. 2 CU From the Armpits Up.

The tighter the CU the more emphasis on the subject. There is less information being offered to the viewer. A CU of some one's hand shows entire hand. CU's are relative to the size of the object. For example a CU of truck is the whole truck filling the frame.

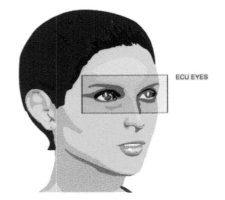

Care should be taken to frame a subjects face leaving some room around it and not cutting off part of the chin or head.

Fig. 3 Tight CU Face

Fig. 4 Extreme CU (ECU) Eyes

Medium Shot (MS)

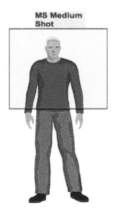

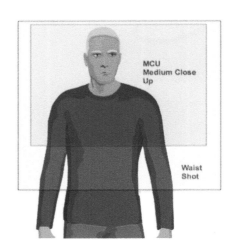

Fig. 5 MS Range

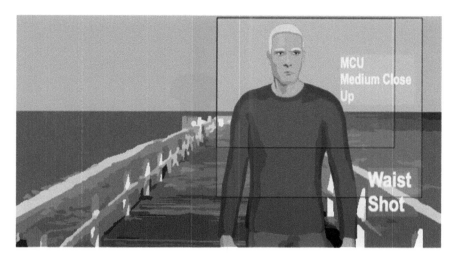

Fig. 6 MCU & Waist Shots

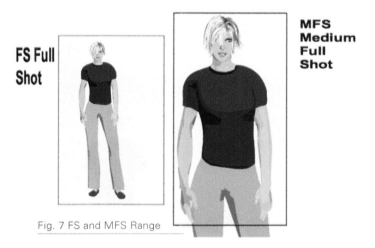

Fig. 7 FS and MFS Range

This MLS cuts off the characters at the knee which still feels a little awkward and would not be used as a static frame if a conversation were to occur. At that point there might be a push-in for a MS as the characters approached each other.

Fig. 8 FS Woman walking on highway - LS
of scene

Fig. 8 Knee shot or MLS of both
characters - not an attractive place
to frame a shot - push in as man
approaches.

A scene may have more than one perspective. Fig. 8 is a Full Shot of a woman walking in a long shot (LS) of the entire scene that gives the audience an external feel for her point-of-view. It also anticipates something may be coming from behind. In Fig. 9 , a man arrives and approaches the woman. In Fig. 10 the woman runs away up the road. This last shot is from both the audiences POV and the man who arrived and is now watching the woman run away.

Fig. 10 LS of Entire Scene and Woman

In Fig. 10, a long shot (LS), the viewer can decide to look at the whole scene, the woman running, the road, the airplane in the upper right or the dessert. Each size shot has a psychological context and should be used with that notion in mind.

Shot Angles

When setting up a shot the director considers the angle and where the camera is placed. Since the interviewee is looking at the director or person doing the interviewing the camera captures that relationship. Is the interviewer standing and the interviewee sitting? Does this require the interviewee to look up at the interviewer? Framing and camera angle create a point-of-view and send a message to the audience.

In this shot the camera is level with the interviewee but the Director is standing up next to the camera. The audience is confused and has a condescending view of the interviewee.

Fig. 11 Woman looking up at interviewer

In an interview situation a camera angle that looks down on a sitting subject conveys a condescending point-of-view. A low angle looking up at the interviewee may give a distorted or overbearing feel to the point-of-view.

If both the interviewer and interviewee are sitting or standing a neutral point-of-view would be to have the camera level with interviewee and interviewer.

If possible, avoid situations where the interviewer conducts the interview standing while the interviewee is sitting. Either have the interviewee stand or the interviewer sit down and bring the camera level with both parties.

Eye Lines

There are two choices when it comes to interviewing a subject as to where the interviewee's eye line may be directed. In most

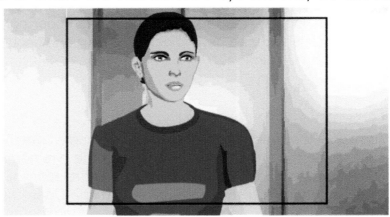

Fig. 12 Camera and Interviewer level with interviewee. TV Safe area shown on HD 16:9 frame.

documentary situations the interviewee should look at the interviewer not at the camera.

Even though the interviewer and the questions will be cut out in editing, an interviewee who looks directly at the camera is speaking directly to the audience "out there" somewhere. When the interviewee speaks to the interviewer, it is more intimate and the viewer feels as if they are in the interviewer; that they are there at the location.

Television newscasters speak directly to the camera to establish a connection with the viewer. They are reporting the news directly to the audience so this simulated form of eye contact is necessary.

This changes when there is an on camera interview in the newscast. Eye lines are directed at the other person not the viewer usually to create a conversational atmosphere.

In some cases, where expert opinion or advice for the television audience is required, the interviewee may turn from the newscaster, talk to the camera addressing the viewer directly.

Composition

Documentaries and other nonfiction visual presentations adhere to the same compositional requirements as other visual mediums. Film begins with a photographic frame and adds movement to the frame. In theatrical film as well as television these days there are frames with a number of different aspect ratios.

Aspect Ratio of Frames

Aspect ratio is the relationship between the height and width of the frame, which is the actual shape of the frame.

Television Aspect Ratios

Standard Definition Television has an aspect ratio of 4:3. Four units wide by three units high. Shots must be composed to fit into this shape, however, not everything in the frame will be seen on various monitors. Action and graphics are composed action to take place in an area called TV Safe. This is an area that will be seen on most any TV.

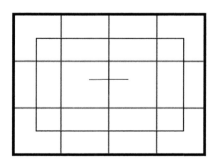

**4:3 Aspect Ratio
with TV Safe area**

Fig. 13 Aspect Ratio

High Definition (HD) Television has an aspect ratio of 16:9. Sixteen units wide by nine units high.

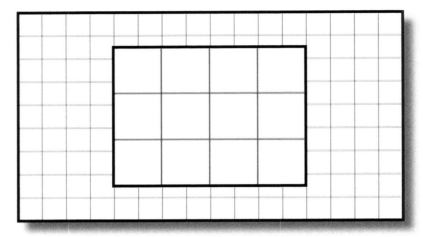

Fig. 14 HD 16:9 Aspect Ration with SD 4:3 overlay

Video shot for HD needs to be reformatted to fit into an SD format. To avoid formatting issues it is best to use only one aspect ratio for all shooting.

Film Production - Motion Picture Aspect Ratios

Standard 35mm Film and TV SD Aspect ratios

The Standard 1:33 aspect ratio equals TV 4:3 ratio.

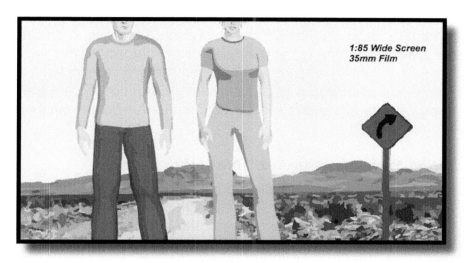

1:85 35mm Wide Screen Theatrical Format above

*Super 16mm 1:65 can be blown up with some loss of image to 35mm 1:85
and also with less loss when digitized and formatted to 16 x 9 HD TV*

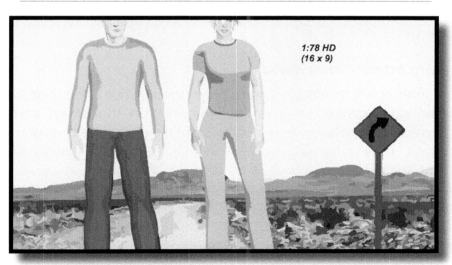

Lighting - Basic information for documentary directors.

Lighting Choices Help Tell the Story

Documentary production is almost always on the move, on location where available lighting is the main source of light. Reflectors known as Flex Fills, a light kit with several portable lights, a camera light, and LED lights are usually part of a documentary production package. In addition, camera filters and various gels and diffusion are necessary tools.

Shooting Exteriors With Available Light

Exterior shooting is less problematic on an overcast day because the light is diffused and has less contrast. When shooting video, white balancing is important, as you may find the color temperature higher than expected. Be careful of a bright color background if the auto iris function on the camera is used, as it may expose for the background not the subject. Use a flex fill to bounce some light on to the subject, even though it may be subtle. On a heavily overcast day, bounce some light off the flex fill with a portable light instead of pointing the light directly at the subject for a softer look.

In bright sunlight try putting the subject in a shadow area and always shoot with the sun behind you. A flex fill may be used in this instance as well. If you must shoot against the sun use the flex fill to bounce as much light in as possible.

To shoot exterior interviews at night try to find pools of light created by streetlights, windows and other sources. Portable lights can be mounted on the camera or held by an assistant to light the subject. For a softer feel bounce the portable light off a flex fill or other reflector to get a softer feel rather than the harsh TV news look. Always white balance for the available light. A flex fill can be used to bounce the light coming from a well-lit window to fill in the opposite side of the person being interviewed.

Lighting Interior Interviews

Many interviews for documentary projects are shot under not ideal conditions, in offices, at events, factories, on the street and in dangerous or hostile environments. Lighting is essential in getting a picture. Indoor lighting may vary in a number of ways, from daylight and tungsten in homes, to daylight and fluorescent in office situations. There may be mixed lighting sources with varying color temperatures in the same room. A light kit with a few lights will help with supplemental lighting but often it's more about working with available light.

Many offices have a window and a person's desk in front of it. There are a number of possible lighting choices. If there are blinds or drapes on the windows, see if they can be drawn and use a simple key, fill and backlight.

What if there is no way to block the light from the window? Consider shooting the interview using available light. Use the light coming from the window as a key light. For example it might be possible to shoot the interview from an angle or from the side of the desk where the light coming from the window is the key light and a reflector is used to bounce in fill light. The subject is facing the camera and both are parallel to the window. Remember to white balance for daylight.

Whenever possible think about lighting a subject with a key, fill and backlight whether it's available light, lighting instruments, reflectors or a combination of sources. A key to fill ratio of between two to one and four to one, is ideal for most video interviews and other documentary situations. When appropriate, subjective lighting may be used to obtain a certain look or feel for an interview, however, most of the time, in documentary situations, the goal is to capture the flavor of the environment; therefore try to reinforce the existing lighting so that a good exposure is obtained without adding another layer of interpretation.

In this situation (at right) a number of options of where to shoot were available, including an office, conference room, and meeting room area. An area with a neutral background that provided some minimal contrast with a lighting ratio of approximately 2.5 to 1 was selected.

If possible suggest to your interviewees that they not wear striped or blue shirts.

Barbara Koenig and David Pace - New Broad Street Development in The Baldwin Park Story Documenary Film.

Key Light on subject and back light on wall behind subject. Fill opposite and in front.

Scenes from The Baldwin Park Story

Working with Fluorescent Lights

The biggest problem with fluorescent lights is that they have a high color temperature and may have a visible flicker. If possible, turn them off and light the area. In countries with 50 cycle electrical current like Great Britain there is a flicker that might be seen in sync, if you are shooting PAL at 25 fps or film at 24 fps. In the US with 60 cycle current, the problem may occur shooting NTSC video at 30 FPS.

Turning off the lights may be impractical in many instances, so it is necessary to work with what's there. Camera filters can be used to change the color temperature. If using film, sometimes a daylight balanced film stock works better than a tungsten balanced stock since fluorescent color temperature is closer to daylight than tungsten.

Working in large spaces

In situations where it is not possible to light the entire space the best solution is to bounce light off the ceiling or walls to raise the overall levels. In a room that is lit with fluorescent light you can turn off the lights and/or try some daylight balancing gels on your lights.

Lighting, and the Director

The director has the responsibility to determine the look and feel of the film. Lighting is a big part of this vision that is done in collaboration the with director of photography. There is an obvious connection between lighting and the emotional impact of each scene similar to that of the light artists paints in to their work. There is a connection between fine art and film.

There are many elements to a painting including, composition, color, lighting, texture, style, vision, degree of abstraction and other elements that help the artist tell the story. These same elements exist in film and video. The first step in creating the look and feel is understanding the medium that is being used.

Aesthetically there is a big difference between film and video. As a medium film is considered "hot" and video and other electronic media as "cold" In his now classic book *Understanding Media,* Marshall McLuhan defines media in terms of how they engage participation.

"Hot" and "Cool" Media

In *Understanding Media*, McLuhan states that different media require different degrees of participation on the part of the person who engages it.

*In **Understanding Media**, Marshal McLuhan explains how "cool" media like television are less engaging, than film or the radio because they are low definition and require more effort on the part of the viewer to complete -- more conscious participation.*

McLuhan believed that certain media like film engage one of the senses so completely that there isn't the need to exert much effort to understand it. In 1965 audio for movies was not anywhere near the quality it is today, meaning that movies today are even hotter, engaging two senses. Movies engage vision and hearing, so completely that the viewer is engaged without having to think about it. The level of overt participation is low. McLuhan classifies movies as a hot medium based on a single sense which is vision.

McLuhan contrasts film with television, which he claimed requires more effort on the part of viewer to determine meaning, and comics, which due to their minimal presentation of visual detail require a high degree of effort to fill in details that the cartoonist may have intended to portray. "Participation" or thinking about what is being seen needs to be higher.

McLuhan considered movies to be "hot", intensifying one single sense "high definition", demanding a viewer's attention, and Television to be "cool" and "low definition", requiring much more conscious participation by the viewer to extract information.

"Any hot medium allows less participation than a cool one, as a lecture makes for less participation than a seminar, and a book for less than a dialogue." --McLuhan

Hot media usually, but not always, provides complete involvement without considerable stimulus. For example, print occupies visual space, uses visual senses, and immerse the reader.

Hot media favor analytical precision, quantitative analysis and sequential ordering, as they are usually sequential, linear and logical. They emphasize one sense (for example, of sight or sound) over the others. For this reason, hot media also include radio, as well as film, the lecture and photography.

Cool media, provide less direct stimulus. They require more active participation on the part of the user, including the perception of abstract patterning and simultaneous comprehension of all parts. McLuhan describes the term "cool media" as emerging from jazz and popular music and, in this context, is used to mean "detached."

There are a number of media that were not around when McLuhan wrote *Understanding Media*. How do digital media fit into this "hot" -- "cool" idea? Digital video is electronic because it uses video technology. High definition television and video have moved away from the interlaced image technology into progressive scan, high resolution presentation. Perhaps on day television and video will have the same feel as film. But at the moment these electronic sources fall into the "cool media" category.

What kind of medium is the mobile phone, iPhone, or the internet? The mobile phone equates with the telephone which is classified as cool. The idea that the mobile phone (cell phone) is a cool medium (not much detail and demands more attention or participation) might be supported by the number of people using mobile phones who are involved in accidents.

It's important for the director and writer to know what medium they are using and to understand the characteristics of that medium. In documentary filmmaking lighting helps to create the texture, the colors and how the audience will react to each shot and scene in the film. Video may be less engaging than film in which case the director might choose lighting that helps increase the color saturation,the mood of the scene or interview. This is a delicate process since subjective lighting may alter the reality of what is being shot.

Design and Vision

A film director and a conductor of an orchestra have a lot in common. The director has a script instead of a score. The conductor has a vision for how the score should sound. A director must turn words into images and sounds. The conductor leads the orchestra and is dependent on the ability and participation of each musician in the orchestra. If the third violinist doesn't play the right note at the proper time the conductor's vision will be flawed. A film director leads the talent and the film crew, who each bring a special talent and skill to the project. If a grip tracks the dolly too fast in an otherwise perfectly acted scene, the directors vision is damaged.

"If you don't know where you're going any road will do."

Both the conductor and the director are creating something larger than the sum of its parts. One of the main functions of a film director is not only to have a vision for the film but to also be able to bring out the talent of all creative participants involved, in a synergistic fashion.

To be able to concentrate on all aspects of production the director hears and pre-visualizes the story in cinematic terms. Each shot connects to another shot to build a scene. Scenes build into sequences and sequences into stories.

In a documentary context the director begins building a vision in pre-production. Since documentaries are an exploration of some reality, research leads to a notion of where the story might go . The director pre-visualizes the many paths the story might take, and brings those realities back to the editing room in the form of coverage. The coverage must be such that events, actions and interviews can be woven into a story.

Covering Events, Meetings, Parades, Rallies and Other Situations

There are many times when a director has the assignment to cover various events that will be used in the documentary as "B" roll or supplemental action. The actual shots will not be scripted. This type of assignment might be given to a second unit director while the primary director is doing interviews or at another location.

CU of sign establishes context for scene

With such an assignment, one of the first things to do, is shoot establishing shots of the venue along with any

Establishing LS of Hall, cut or pull out from sign.

signs or banners that identify the event or venue. Shots of people arriving and or getting seated are also good to obtain. If there is a main speaker or a speakers platform it is important to find an unobstructed camera position. Discuss options for getting the audio of the speakers audio department.

Shots of notable attendees and speakers.

It is not necessary to get talent releases from persons attending a public event. If individual interviews are conducted it is good practice to have each person interviewed sign a release.

Events are not static situations, they have a beginning, middle and end. Is this event central to the story or is just one on many similar events that might be included for a few seconds? Unless the assignment is to shoot the entire event, the director must determine what parts of the event to cover so that an editor can cut a scene that in a minute or less gives the viewer a feel for that particular event.

It is conceivable that a two hour political rally could be shot in its entirety even though it's one of many that will be part of a montage in a feature length film. Shooting two hours of coverage for what ends up in the film as a ten second

Seated audience member.

clip, is a very high shooting ratio (720 to 1). The director is looking for some basic coverage and to make choices on what parts of the rally to shoot. A member of the crew or the director should talk to the rally organizers about the program and get a copy of the agenda, press release and list of speakers if available. After getting some opening remarks the crew should standby to get

Attendee jacket helps establish venue.

some additional footage of the main parts of the speech or the "best sound bites." In all likelihood whatever is shot will be used as needed. For example, a shot of someone holding a sign might used open the scene, somewhere in the middle or at the end of scene. Shots like this are part of getting

Organizer of event.

Wide Shot audience and hall

"B" roll footage.

The main speaker for this event arrived through the main door to the hall with his entourage of security and campaign workers. The camera crew was set up on a small platform to cover the stage. Instead of coming down the camera zoomed in on that end of the room to get a high angle of the entrance.

Record ambient sounds with each shot and any source music.

Speaker enters hall and makes his way to the front and the stage where he will speak.

It's good practice to get footage of a speaker being introduced. To be able to pick and choose subsequent clips is a skill the director develops from experience, but it's based on listening and getting a sense of where the speaker is going with their speech. Get the camera rolling as these moments approach.

When the audience applauds, the camera can swing around and grab some applause shots and then turn back as the speaker continues. Good coverage of this type of event includes several audience reaction shots. These shots will allow the editor to flexibility in where to cut.

Reverse angle of speaker headed to stage

CU of speaker as he approaches stage.

Usually a speaker will begin with an introduction and end the talk with some sort of conclusion. In those times when not getting shots of the speaker get "B"roll and cut-a-ways of the audience. Get close-ups of people listening,

Cut away shot of organizer on stage applauding before introducing the speaker.

not listening, laughing, signs, others on the stage, other camera crews and long shots of the entire audience. Shots that will help tell the story are important.

It is difficult with one camera film or video to get every word of a speech and it usually isn't necessary. Start out with a fresh magazine, or other media. Time changes of magazines, tape or flash card media, so that there is never less than a minute or two still to fill on the media. The first assistant camera person should keep track of how much time is left and look for a good time to change to fresh media. Most of these changes can be made during applause or a break in the action.

MS speaker begins talking on stage.

clip: final edit scene for Wrapped In Steel documentary.

In any situation the director works closely with the DP and/or camera operator to insure the coverage will cut together and have continuity. For example, there's a break in the action or speech and media storage cards are switched; a new empty card is in the camera. The first shot after the break should be able to be cut to what happened before. If there was a MS of the speaker when the break came, it would be good to get an audience cut away and come back with a tight shot of the speaker.

Camera Movement

The motion picture medium is built on two basic ideas. The first is that what is seen on the screen is moving and that the camera recording the movement can also be moved. In the early days of cinema filmmakers didn't move the camera, they set up what is known as the "proscenium" shot. In this position the camera is set up as if it had the best seat in the house for viewing a stage play. It took awhile before it was realized that the camera could be moved thereby picking and choosing various points-of-view that would bring the audience into the story.

Today documentary filmmakers use the lightness and portability of modern film and digital video cameras to take the audience where "no one has gone before." Camera moves as simple as a pan from the speaker to audience or the audience to the speaker can facilitate a transition between two shots. Moving the camera from A to B, or changing the size of a shot makes a statement. A move from a speaker to someone listening is action and reaction. Before starting a pan or tracking shot think about where it will end. A tracking shot of someone walking leads the walker and either stops moving with the walker or stops and the walker, walks out the shot.

FEATURE LENGTH DOCUMENTARY FILM

Wrapped in Steel is a feature length documentary film produced and directed by James R. (Jim) Martin, who was also the Project Director of the Southeast Chicago Historical Project, sponsored by Columbia College Chicago, Illinois Humanities Council and The National Endownment for the Humanites.

"Wrapped In Steel is a journey to the Southeast side of Chicago where steel is boss. Where steel has dominated the lives of the people for one hundred years."

Mike Alexandroff

CHAPTER 11

CASE STUDY
FEATURE LENGTH DOCUMENTARY
FOR PUBLIC TELEVISION

*Independently produced, and aired nationally on PBS,
Wrapped In Steel was one of the many outcomes
of a four year community history project initiated by
Columbia College in Chicago and ultimately funded by
Columbia College, the Illinois Humanities Council, and
The National Endowment for the Humanities.*

Chapter Highlights

*How the project came about
and was developed*

Various phases of production

*Dynamics of producing and
directing a documentary that
takes several years to make*

*How film crew dynamics work
over a long period of time*

*Funding documentaries though
grants by local and national
humanities councils.*

CHAPTER ELEVEN

CHAPTER 11

WRAPPED IN STEEL

BLAST FURNACE US STEEL SOUTH CHICAGO

Background

Over four years in the making, Wrapped In Steel is a product of the Southeast Chicago Historical Project (SECHP). The Project was funded in part by the National Endowment for the Humanities (NEH), The Illinois Humanities Council (IHC) and Columbia College Chicago. SECHP facilitated a community history project in which residents used various media to examine their past and present condition. Over a period of four years the SECHP activities touched the majority of the areas 100,000 residents in some way.

The documentary film *Wrapped In Steel* is one of many tangible reminders of the history and culture of Southeast Chicago that remains since the project ended. Other results included a book, two years worth of articles published in a local daily newspaper, additional publications and a series of exhibits including a highly successful multimedia exhibit at Chicago's Museum of Science and Industry. In addition, hundreds of area residents compiled their family's history to pass on to future generations. The SECHP gave new life to a local Historical Society that now includes the entire area.

The first case study examined *Studio A - Profile of a Disc Jockey*, a documentary that took three, four-hour sessions to shoot, and ended up as a 30 minute film. *Wrapped In Steel* took about four years to make with 50 hours of film shot over a three year period. The first version was two hours long. A 90 minute feature length version was edited for national public television. In addition the same people that worked on the documentary were instrumental in facilitating other documentary and nonfiction productions in the community.

How The Project Came About

Mirron (Mike) Alexandroff (1923 - 2001), President of Columbia College, Chicago suggested that the Southeast side of Chicago would be a good subject for a documentary film. It was the Steel Mill District of Chicago and the neighborhoods were facing a crisis in that many of the mills were shutting down and laying off workers who lived in the neighborhood. Mike decided to pursue the notion and he set up a meeting that included people from the neighborhood, Steelworkers Union, business people, humanities and social science scholars including anthropologists, sociologists, historians, teachers, a representative from the Illinois Humanities Council and the author of this book, a filmmaker and professor at Columbia College. The meeting of such a diverse group of individuals produced something larger than the notion of making a documentary film.

Much was learned in this meeting about the neighborhoods and the working people who lived there. There were four neighborhoods comprised of every ethnic and racial group that had come to America since the 19th Century. Many scholars over the years have disputed the idea that America was a "melting pot," but according to Dr. William Kornblum, author of *Blue Collar Community*, if that theory was true, this community was the exception to that rule, South East Chicago was truly a "melting pot," and paradoxically was fueled in its growth over the years, by another type of "melting pot," the one used to make steel.

Sol Tax, a well known Anthropologist from the University of Chicago, talked about the rich ethnic diversity of these urban neighborhoods and how the people had come to live together because of shared religions and cultural similarities.

Ed Sadlowski

Edward Sadlowski, a second generation Polish American and United Steel Workers Organizer talked about his experience as a steel worker, the role of unions in the neighborhood and the role of Polish immigrants in the building of churches in the area.

Other neighborhood representatives spoke of the early friction between ethic groups like the Mexicans and Poles, Serbians and Croatians, and Swedes and Irish, and many other groups.

Rationale

The Story Needs To Be Told!

Mike Alexandrof , President Columbia College, Chicago 1961 - 1992

Most documentary films seek as wide an audience as possible and this seemed like something that had national appeal, however, this story needed to be told not only nationally but to the 100,000 people who lived in these neighborhoods. They were facing a critical time in their history and perhaps understanding how they got to this point would help them face their future. How they dealt with the current situation of unemployment and a changing economy might help other urban neighborhoods in the future as well.

Approach

The evolution of an idea for a documentary develops in an organic and natural fashion when the documentarians have an open mind about what the story might turn out to be.

Mike Alexandroff proposed that a Community History Project that would allow the people of Southeast Chicago an opportunity to look at their history, culture and lives through the use of media and the arts be planned. We would make a documentary, but also help people look at their personal family history through putting together oral histories based on family photo albums and family videos. We would create exhibits and other events to discuss various aspects of neighborhood history and support a local historical society.

The Illinois Humanities Council (IHC) said they would be willing to participate by funding a planning grant to plan a project that would ultimately be submitted to the National Endowment for the Humanities (NEH). It was important to have the support of the local Humanities Council to be able to go to the NEH. Columbia College would sponsor the project and participate in the funding.

Proposal for a Grant to Plan the Project

Working with the College Development Department a proposal was developed. The idea had grown beyond making a documentary film into a community history project that would utilize a number of media. Working along with consultants and others including Jack Wolfsohn, and Victor Margolis from the college's Public Relations department, a proposal for a planning grant was written. Planning a project like this is not as simple as just saying what it is that would like to done. Scholars, consultants and people from the community must come aboard and show support for the project. A budget and plan for the implementing the project must be completed.

Financing

The Illinois Humanities Council funded the planning grant with matching funds (in-kind or cash) from the college. Now there was a grant to plan the project, which was called the Southeast Chicago Historical Project (SECHP). Planning the project lasted for about six months. This included many meetings with academic consultants, neighborhood community groups, business groups, politicians, union leaders, religious groups and others who might be interested in what we wanted to do.

A planning grant is a grant to plan and write a proposal for a project that will be submitted for funding.

During the planning phase, a proposal to receive a grant from the National Endowment for the Humanities (NEH) was written. It was 125 pages long and included not only what was to be done but also who, how, why, what, where, how much, who was putting up matching funds, who the academic scholars consultants were and what credentials they had. In addition support letters from community groups and other connected with the project were included. There were two project directors. A historian to handle the humanities and social science issues and the author of this book to direct the documentary and multimedia efforts to be used to facilitate the community history being accomplished.

The proposal for the Southeast Chicago Historical Project (SECHP) was submitted to NEH and ultimately funded! About a year or so after the original idea was realized the project was funded and could begin. However one problem surfaced. The historian project director decided to take a job in the business sector and so that position needed to be filled. After a couple of failed attempts to find a replacement Mike Alexandroff emphatically suggested that the director of the documentary effort, become the sole project director. The SECHP had a board composed of expert humanities consultants who would advise him. At first he was reluctant to accept this responsibility, he was a filmmakers not a historian or sociologist. Mike insisted, he suggested "producing" the project as if it were a documentary film. He had one stipulation; direct the project for one year before starting to film the documentary. After that, begin the documentary and if additional funding for the film was needed he would make sure it was found. Proposition accepted! Sometime thereafter a qualified historian was hired who became the Associate Project Director.

A year later the shooting began for the documentary film. In retrospect, that year of working with the community, scholars in the humanities and social sciences and others gave the filmmaker enough reach to ask the questions that were necessary for the documentary film and for other aspects of the project. It also acquainted everyone with the unique dynamics of this working class neighborhood. During the first year, while "producing" the project and doing research for the documentary film we began writing a weekly article about the area for The Daily Calumet, a regional newspaper.

Director, DP and Sound recordist prepare to film at US Steel's Southworks Blast Furnace facility

As the project got underway staff members were hired, including some Columbia College students from the neighborhood. An office and a gallery to run exhibits about the community was established on a main street in the neighborhood. The exhibits were documentary in nature, featuring photographs, artifacts, videos, local memorabilia and local artists who's work depicted the area in someway. These exhibits led to a multimedia exhibit at The Chicago Museum of Science and Industry that was documentary in all respects, incorporating all forms of actual documentation of the four neighborhoods in an interactive multimedia format.

Making the Documentary

Based on over two years of research and study, work began on the documentary film. A second grant was obtained from NEH Special

Four Generations South Chicago Family

Projects to additionally fund the film and a book on the neighborhood by the staff and Dr. Dominic Pacyga, associate project director. Dr. Pacyga's approach for the book aided in the development of the documentary film treatment. The concept for the film was to adapt a point-of-view that would be from the inside looking out. The people of Southeast Chicago would tell their own story.

Shooting Script

In this multi-year documentary project the shooting script is more of a schedule or list of people to interview, events, institutions and cultural traditions in to cover in each neighborhood. There are four distinct neighborhoods in Southeast Chicago; South Chicago, South Deering, the East Side and Hegewich. Each of these neighborhoods had a predominance of certain ethnic groups living in them. It is important to make contact with all the ethnic groups.

There are also the steel mills and other businesses that are important to the neighborhoods. Politics is another aspect of the community that plays a large part in what people do and think.

A number of parallel themes were identified that would allow the exploration of history, culture and life in Southeast Chicago. These themes were essentially the main guide for what was documented.

The parallel themes were based on the workplace, family, ethnicity, religion, politics, history and community. Development of parallel themes throughout the film allowed the exploration of the history, and issues facing the community from the inside looking out; as observers, but also holding up a mirror for the community to see itself.

Edward R. Vrydoliac Alderman, 10th ward Southeast Chicago

Wrapped In Steel was made for the people of Southeast Chicago. As it turned out their story was universal and appealed to a wide range of people nationally in other urban areas.

Certain things in the neighborhoods remained constant like the steel mills, the churches, ethnic diversity and rivalry, family life, and the harshness of working steel. The shooting script evolved around these ideas, interviews with residents and ongoing documentation of the neighborhood. Hundreds of historic photographs mainly from the residents of the area and from businesses including US Steel were collected and archived. These historic photographs provided a chance to look at the past as well as the present. As shooting continued a number of themes, characters, conflicts and drama became evident.

Family life and unemployment discussed with the Mulac family

Pastor of a local church discusses the role of the Church for its "Black" members in the community

Chicago is known for its parades and the SE side of Chicago is no exception. Visually appealing, the parades revealed much about how the community feels about itself.

Mexican Independence Day Parade in South Chicago celebrated by Mexican Americans and the community.

Polish immigrants built a number of churches in Southeast Chicago. St. Michaels (right) has services in Polish, English and Spanish at this Christmas Midnight Mass.

Orthodox Jews celebrate Passover in South Chicago.

Every effort was made during the shooting of *Wrapped in Steel* to document daily community life. This included interviews with residents from South Chicago, East Side, South Deering and Hegewich; then moving to even smaller enclaves in each of neighborhoods.

To help understand this working class, multi-ethnic, multi-racial community it was decided to document activities and traditions from all groups. This included going to churches, parades, weddings, funerals, social and political events.

Easter Service at Serbian Orthodox Church on the East Side

Initially contact was made with people in the community, arranging interviews and asking to attend events. Within a short time most everyone stared calling the project, wanting to be part of the documentary film and the community project. Every effort was made to cover as much as possible without repeating coverage of similar events.

Author Studs Terkel speaks at local political rally.

In some instances there were competing spokespersons for ethnic groups, local organizations, events and other situations. Residents wanted their point-of-view known. In this situation it seemed important to document whatever possible within scope of the project.

Mayoral Candidate Harold Washington visits the East Side on St. Patrick's Day.

Budget Notes Wrapped In Steel

There was an adequate budget to cover shooting the documentary over a three year period. This included all aspects of pre-production, production, post-production and shooting on 16mm color negative film stock with enough stock to ultimately shoot about 50 hours of film. All film shot was work printed and synced with sound, transferred from 1/4" reel-to-reel audiotape, to 16mm magnetic film stock. Editing began with syncing of dailies and logging of all footage. All interviews were budgeted to be transcribed by a typist which was accomplished at our field offices in South Chicago.

Today this documentary could be shot on super 16mm film or on a digital HD format. In all likelihood whatever the recording medium it would be edited digitally. If shot digitally, there would be a large amount of storage space required to store all the footage. Since no negative or tape would exist, triple redundancy backup of all elements would be required with two of the backups stored at different locations. Logging of all footage would be critical to finding individual shooting days.

All or part of this documentary, if shot now, could also be shot "double system" using DSLR cameras like the Canon 5d Mk II with separate audio recording using a suitable digital audio recorder. Picture and sound are synced in postproduction .

Budget Considerations for Wrapped In Steel

Above the Line Costs

Include Producer, Director, Consultants and a Narrator (if one is used).

Production Crew

(Below the Line usually but since this was an long term project certain key personnel were salaried.)

Director of Photography/cameraman was involved in the project for the entire three years of production. On occasion, if he were not available a freelance person would be hired. He had a regular 1st assistant and loader who he liked to work with, but if she was not available there were other people.

The usual crew consisted of:

Director who also did the interviewing (full-time with other responsibilities.)

Assistant Director/Script/Coordinator (full-time with other responsibilities)

Below the Line Costs
First Assistant Camera and Loader
Sound Recordist
Production Manager (full-time with other responsibilities [Sound Recordist]

Production Photographer and Archival Photographer (copied and archived photographs from the community, full-time)

Additional Crew (as required for special events)
As seen above most everyone did more than one job, which included working on the SECHP staff and the documentary effort.

Director of Photography Mike Goi (top) crew setting up on the street (center) . Camera Assistant/loader changing film in magazine black bag (bottom).

Crew Dynamics on a long-term documentary project are an important part of how successful the production will be. Film crews of any type foster a familiarity and synergy that is unique for short term or temporary work groups. Unlike typical office situations where people take years to get to know each other, film crews quickly share enough personal information to allow themselves to work closely and under sometimes stressful situations. It is for this reason that film crews become groups of people who like to work together and enjoy each other's company. This works well in most cases where production lasts for up to several months. But what happens when the production continues for several years and some crew members leave and are replaced by other people?

The new people must integrate into the existing group that has taken on an extended family kind of feel. Newcomers must conform to the existing culture or they will not be accepted.

Most film crews expect everyone to pull their own weight and pitch in to help each other in all situations. Anyone who is perceived as not working as hard as everyone else will be shunned and ultimately be released or leave on their own.

Key personnel including the producer/director,   director of photography, production manager/audio engineer, and first assistant director were hired full time for *Wrapped In Steel*. All full time crew had other duties in addition to their specialty. The director and DP edited the film based on an editing script written by the director. Budgetwise it made sense to hire most everyone else on a freelance basis. The same free lancers were usually hired because someone liked working with them and because they were very good at what they did.

Shooting the Labor Day Parade on the East Side. Documentary crews are usually small.

(Above) Documentaries are shot on location, the crew needs to adapt quickly.

(Right) DP And audio mixer set up a shot and shoot.

It is important for the documentary Producer and/or Director to set the tone of the production. Their enthusiasm and leadership ability greatly determines the morale and dedication of the crew. Of course like any family there will be occasional problems, but most of the time they can be worked out.

Equipment Used for Wrapped In Steel

Equipment in the original budget

16mm film camera package, including lenses, four additional magazines.

Tripod and other camera supports

Camera accessories and supplies

Sound package including recorder, microphones, (shotgun and lavalieres) boom poll)

Lighting package. Colortran light kit with four 3200K lights

Grip equipment

Still cameras and lenses, Polaroid camera

Example of Equipment Required if Shooting In Digital Format.

Panasonic HVX 200 HD Camcorder (or similar HD Camera like Canon XL HD with interchangeable lens capability)

6 32 gig P2 Storage Cards or DV recording tape

Hard Drives/fire-store and laptop computer
Sound package – wireless lavs, mixer, boom, shotgun mics

Light Kits -- total of 8 lights, stands additional specialized lighting elements

Grip Equipment

Digital SLR camera and lenses

Stand-alone photo printer

Postproduction

With 50 hours of film how does editing begin? While there was an initial concept, treatment and a shooting script; which footage should be selected to make the documentary? The process includes reviewing all the logged footage, reading interview transcripts and then writing an editing script. Writing the editing script begins with a review of all the interviews and footage. Edited portions of the interviews are used to create a narrative for the film.

Reading the transcripts of the interviews helps find the feelings and emotions voiced by the people of the neighborhoods. Things that are important to them are brought into focus; their ethnic heritage, religion, family, work, relationships, community groups, politics and pride in their neighborhoods emerge as themes that can be explored in the creation of a narrative for the documentary.

A story needs a beginning, a middle and an end. All the usual dramatic elements of story telling like conflict and plot are important to the documentary. Many filmmakers believe that a story should, "begin with your second strongest scene and end with your strongest." The thinking is that starting with the strongest scene leaves no place to go but down. In this case there were many strong scenes and other dramatic elements that could be used but something that would engage the audience for the entire film was needed.

The notion to use parallel themes based on the workplace, family, ethnicity, religion, politics, history and community were discussed with academic consultants and others to determine if what was being portrayed was accurate and factual.

Labor consultant and local steelworker, Ed Sadlowski pointed out that there was newsreel footage from 1937 that was an important part of the history of the area. This dramatic footage known as the Memorial Day Massacre was obtained, the footage reviewed and scripted for use in the documentary.

The editing script evolved and a rough cut of the documentary begun as footage was obtained. In addition to film there were many hundreds of historic photographs that could be used in the documentary. These were cataloged, reviewed and made available.

The editing script provided a pre-visualized story line for the documentary based on available information, footage and most importantly, narrative built on interviews and dialogue in the form of action on the part of the subjects. Also speeches and situations where the people and groups in the story interact. However, since shooting was still going on many revisions and changes happened in the editing process. This is to be expected as new facts emerge.

Editing Equipment for Analog Film Editing

Steenbeck six or eight plate flatbed editing machine*
Table, rewinds, viewer/synchronizer (Acme Pic Sync)
Editing supplies
Split reels
Splicers
Trim bins

Editing Digitally

NLE system (Avid or Final Cut Studio) for duration of post-production
Two or more terabytes of server storage capacity for captured footage
Software including After Effects , Photoshop etc for special effects and photographic sweetening.

*Even if a documentary is shot using film instead of digital media today, it is usually edited on a NLE system with software like Avid or Final Cut Studio.

Postproduction Budget Items

Narration recording and talent
Music recording and composer
Assistant editor
Syncing dailies
Logging
Effects editing
Sound mixing
Film finishing including answer print (if film)
DVD design
Release prints or DVD's
Local travel, transportation and crew meals.

Be realistic about the expenses of moving a crew around and feeding them. When traveling out of town a per diem stipend is paid to each crew member. All of the shooting for Wrapped In Steel was on the Southeast side, but meals were provided depending on the length and time of the shoot. A vehicle for transporting the crew should be in the budget.

Raw Stock, Work Print, Transfers, Audio Tape and Other Recording Materials and Supplies

Wrapped In Steel was shot entirely using 16mm Kodak Color Negative Film Stock. Regular 16mm film and super 16mm film comes in 400' rolls, that when shot at 24 fps last for approximately 10 minutes. After exposure each roll of film is sent to a film processing lab, where it is developed, timed and printed on to positive stock for editing. This print is called a work print, because it is the print that will be edited. Sound is recorded separately, in this instance, on a 1/4" tape, reel-to-reel Nagra sound recorder. *Wrapped In Steel* was shot "double system" – picture and sound (in sync) on separate media. Newer audio recorders record to a hard drive and are digital.

Wrapped In Steel was edited traditionally using a work print and the sound was transferred to 16mm magnetic film stock. The budget provided for all of these steps.

Today if this project used film it could be shot on super 16mm negative stock (transfers well to HD and can be blown up to 35mm film). A work print would not be needed because the negative would be digitized and transferred, for editing, to a NLE system. Audio would also be transferred to the NLE system and synced to the picture. If shooting using a digital format such as DVC Pro Hd, or DV the budget would need to include all of the tape stock needed unless a tape-less camcorder system is being used. In this case media to store footage on is required.

Distribution

Distribution for a feature length documentary film today can run the gamut from theatrical release, cable, public television, education to independent distribution on DVD. The following is an account of dealing with public television as an independent producer. Because the film was funded by NEH, PBS had the right of first refusal to air the film. The "Directors Cut," a two-hour version was screened for PBS and they said they wanted to air it, but asked that it be cut down to 90 minutes. A letter of agreement was written by PBS with a national air date in three months on labor day. The PBS contact was enthusiastic and supportive.

About the time the re-edit was finished a letter from was received from the contact at PBS. She wrote that she was taking a position at PBS affiliate in Los Angeles, and that a new contact at PBS had been assigned to the documentary. The new contact was phoned and informed that the 90 minute version was finished and a copy would be sent to her to review. She stated that she would need to see the original version and see what she thought was needed to be done with the film. She was told there was an agreement and that the film had already been re-edited as requested. After some discussion she agreed to view the re-edit and to a meeting at the PBS offices in the Washington DC area to speak with her.

The meeting was held in her cubicle, in a sea of cubicles at PBS. It was noticed that the review copy that had been sent her was sitting on her desk, it appeared that it had been viewed for a few minutes. She said she had viewed the film and decided that it need to be narrated. It was explained to her that the documentary had an opening narrator who introduced the film and that the people of Southeast Chicago did the rest of the narration. She said, "the 'merican' public won't understand what's going on, there needs to be third party narration to explain everything to them." The reply, "The American people narrate this film; don't you think they can understand what they're saying? This film was screened for the people of Southeast Chicago and others and apparently no one had problems understanding the culture, history, hopes and fears of working class people." She insisted that it would have to be narrated and she would have to supervise the re-editing. It became obvious that this person had an agenda of her own and no intention of honoring the letter of agreement.

A few days later back in Chicago Dick Bowman, at that time, the Vice President of Programming at Channel 11, a PBS station in Chicago, suggested meeting with him at his office to discuss the situation.

Dick proposed that Channel 11 offer the documentary to all the other PBS affiliates via satellite as all PBS affiliates may originate programming for the use of other PBS stations. Channel 11 had originated many national programs including the original *Sneak Previews* with Siskel and Ebert and *The Frugal Gourmet* (Dick mentioned that this same person at PBS had tried to cancel *The Frugal Gourmet* and that it appeared she just hated Chicago) and many other programs.

Dick Bowman's offer was accepted. About 305 PBS affiliates including Guam, 98% of the PBS affiliates, ran *Wrapped In Steel* on Labor Day and on subsequent days over the next two years or so and received high ratings.

Wrapped In Steel was subsequently nominated for an Emmy. It won a golden plaque for best national network documentary at the Chicago Film festival and other awards around the country. It was distributed by Columbia College, J R Martin Media, Inc and Illinois Humanities Council who helped fund the film and the SECHP project.

The experience with PBS by an independent documentary filmmaker, is reported here because it served as a lesson in that, you can never expect things to go according to plan in this profession; that there may be someone out there who just doesn't like you, where you're from or the cut of your clothing, and that will be enough for them to try to destroy your work. You must look at the facts and if they support your position move ahead, no matter what obstacles you encounter. Never take anything for granted. Faith and determination in what you want to do is important and necessary.

This experience also shows that there are a lot of good people in the media world who care about getting the story made and out to the public.

ADVOCACY

John Grierson -- Photograph by Virginia Leirens

"Art is a Hammer not a Mirror" -John Grierson

"I look at Film as a Pulpit" -- John Grierson

Bertha Gilkey leads training session

CHAPTER 12

CASE STUDY
THE MAKING OF FIRED UP:
PUBLIC HOUSING IS MY HOME

EMMY AWARD WINING
SOCIAL ADVOCACY
DOCUMENTARY

CHAPTER TWELVE

CASE STUDY
THE MAKING OF FIRED UP: PUBLIC HOUSING IS MY HOME

Working with a Foundation

Background

According to their web site, the Metropolitan Planning Council (MPC) "was founded in 1934, is a nonprofit, nonpartisan group of business and civic leaders committed to serving the public interest through the promotion and implementation of sensible planning and development policies necessary for an economically competitive Chicago region." MPC researches and develops policy recommendations and conducts outreach and advocacy in partnership with public officials and community leaders to enhance equity of opportunity and quality of life throughout metropolitan Chicago.

One of their primary areas of interest is housing. Their mission is "to increase supply and access to high quality affordable housing in divested and high job growth areas and leverage private sector leadership and investment through employer-assisted housing and other financial incentives and expand public housing resources in quality homes and neighborhoods."

How The Project Came About

Mary Decker. The President of the Metropolitan Planning Council was interested in the possibility of making a documentary film about an initiative they were planning that involved public housing in Chicago. They wanted to make a documentary about their plan to introduce the concept of tenant management to Chicago public housing residents and the process of training residents to implement tenant management in high rise developments. This project was to last for one year.

Mary Decker President MPC

Approach

Tenant Management

Tenant management had been done successfully in St. Louis, at Cochran Gardens. The effort, led by Bertha Gilkey, a Cochran Garden resident, had produced amazing results and Bertha would be involved in a major way in the Chicago project.

Rationale

National Distribution

MPC wanted this concept to be considered as a national solution to the overall problem public housing had become in most cities around the country. It was also explained that if the MPC wanted a documentary that might be seen nationally on public television or some other venue, the filmmaker would need to have creative control of the film and own the copyright..

Background

Creative Control and Copyright

If MPC, a foundation with a mission, had creative control and owned the copyright, the documentary would be considered propaganda and not eligible for public television distribution. This has been the case since 1937 after a government-sponsored film was shown in theaters. The film, *The Plow That Broke the Plains*, made by Pare Lorenz was commissioned by the Department of Agriculture. Franklin D. Roosevelt was President, and the "New Deal, was trying to show what had happened to the "Breadbasket," of the United States and how that had led to drought and the "Dust Bowl." All leading up to the

"Depression Era, that preceded FDR's election as President.

The Republicans and others argued that government-sponsored films could not be shown to the public, since by definition they were propaganda.

Cabrini Green Children return from school

Even though their motivation was political they were correct. A law was subsequently enacted that prohibited films made by government agencies from being distributed to the public. This idea carried over to those films sponsored by institutions, foundations and others with social or political agendas. Public television was sensitive to these concerns.

If an independent documentary filmmaker made the film, with creative control, a point-of-view that was removed from the organization could be established. It apparent this was an interesting and unique approach that might help people in public housing and that examining the current state of public housing in Chicago was an important issue to explore.

Resident unlocks her front door

If there had been any misgivings about the project the commission would have been turned down.

Financing

A contract was drawn up which detailed the relationship. MPC would

Financing and Budget

raise the money needed to make the documentary. A concept and treatment was written along with a preliminary budget. MPC wanted to shoot the documentary on film so the budget was based on a one hour documentary shot over the period of one year on 16mm film. The budget also detailed a certain number of days per month for shooting, events, interviews, and other aspects of creating the film. Equipment, staff, film stock, processing and work print were all based on the amount of coverage needed. It is possible to come up with a fairly accurate budget if enough is known about what is required. Also included was a contingency fund based on about 10% of the below the line costs, to cover any unforeseen expenses.

Preproduction

MPC agreed on the general terms and work began making the documentary. After consultation with MPC staff and others a concept and treatment was developed. This is an important phase of pre-production. MPC was a client in that they were putting up the money to make a documentary film about something they believed was important. It was necessary to understand the rationale for the project, to teach tenants of public housing about tenant management and to learn something about the mission of the foundation – what their objectives and goals were for their foundation and this project.

In this situation the filmmaker should be able to connect with the sponsor's goals and objectives from a moral, ethical, social or political standpoint. If this is not possible, the project should not be accepted. For example a humanist would not work on a documentary project that demeaned a racial, ethnic, or gender group in anyway. This would be against their humanistic values and therefore not acceptable at any price.

Concept, Treatment, Shooting Script

The basic concept was to interview various people associated with MPC, Chicago Public Housing (CHA), the trainers, led by Bertha Gilkey, and residents of public housing involved in the MPC tenant management training program.

Bertha Gilkey, President
Cochran Tenant Management Corp.
St. Louis, MO

In addition the training classes, seminars and other aspects of the program were to be covered. A trip to St. Louis to visit Cochran Gardens was also planned. Cochran Gardens was where Bertha Gilkey and others created and implemented their version of tenant management successfully.

Archival Photographs were used in Film.

Children in Chicago Public Housing Circa 1946

Budget

The Metropolitan Planning Council (MPC) accepted a budget of $70,000 to make the film. The budget included local travel and travel to other locations including St. Louis. Post-production included the writing of a shooting and editing script by the Director.

Motion Picture Equipment

16mm or 35mm is much more expensive than the digital counterpart. So this equipment is usually rented or leased. Cranes, dollies, jibs and other camera supports often may only be available for lease. It also makes sense to rent equipment that will only be used occasionally.

Equipment For Fired-Up

Film camera package, Éclair NPR – 12 to 120 zoom lens including lens and additional 400' magazines.
Tripod
Camera supplies
Sound package including Nagra recorder, microphones, (shotgun and lavalieres) boom poll).
Lighting package. Colortran light kit with four lights and stands.
Grip Equipment
Still Cameras and lenses
Polaroid Camera

Editing Equipment

Steenbeck six or eight plate flatbed editing machine.*
Table, rewinds, viewer/synchronizer (Acme Pic Sync)
Editing supplies
Split reels

Splicers

*Even if a documentary is shot using film instead of digital media today, it is usually edited on a NLE system with software like Avid or Final Cut.

Production Crew

Our team included a producer/director/writer, director of photography/camera operator, first assistant camera, loader, grip/gaffer, sound recordist, script supervisor, production assistant and interns. Everyone was hired for the project on a freelance basis. The director and director of photography coedited the documentary.

Production

Production of Fired-UP

In the first few months of production a number of people involved in the effort to train residents of Cabrini Green and other Chicago Public Housing (CHA) developments were interviewed. Initial meetings and contacts with the residents were also shot.

Cabrini Green was a notorious public housing development with about 10,000 residents. Violent incidents involving residents happened Daily. "Gang Bangers," ruled many areas and regularly fired guns at each other and "sniped," at rival gang members who crossed open areas. Non-residents of the development did not go there very often. The crimes and violence that occurred at public housing developments were perpetrated by residents on each other not usually on non-residents. In addition there were two main areas, the red brick buildings and the white brick buildings. The white brick buildings, were safer because there were families housed there and the female head of households in the white brick buildings were more in control of their environment and kept clear of the "gang bangers." In addition the press or television crews, were not usually harassed. Day time visits to this development were relatively safe under these circumstances.

On the day before the first day of shooting on location at Cabrini Green one of the interns became apprehensive. He was serious when he inquired if the crew going to wear bulletproof vests! When he was told they were not available, he declined working on the shoot. The next day when the crew arrived at the back of the building on Burly Ave. in Cabrini Green, to film a tenant meeting, there was a moment before opening the door of the van that seemed a little long, but once out of the van a number of children appeared who inquired if the crew was there to see Ms Wilson (a resident). The children led the way into the building. The crew experienced no problems visiting public housing developments; no one was ever threatened in any way.

Over the next year the progress of the tenants in their efforts to learn and hopefully one-day implement tenant management was covered. We budgeted this documentary for one year. It became apparent late in that first year that this process was going to last longer. As it turned out shooting continued for an additional year. Additional funds needed to be raised by the Metropolitan Panning Council to fund the second year and the post-production of the film. They were slow in doing this and some tension developed, straining relations

Resident Training Session

In a 9 Week Period in 1981
10 Cabrini Residents Murdered
35 Wounded

but these issues were resolved.

Establish a payment schedule with a client and avoid letting the production continue without the payment schedule being followed. There are a number of methods to schedule payments. One way is to have the client put up 25% of the budget to start, 50% when shooting begins and the final 25% on delivery of the finished film.

But what if the film goes over budget because the client extends the parameters of the project or it takes longer to shoot than was originally planned? The filmmaker has stayed within the original

Al Raby, Director
Chicago Commission on
Human Relations

parameters of the agreement and budget. If the client extends or adds goals that were not included in the original agreement and budget the relationship between the client and the producer should be amended or renegotiated. These contingencies should be explained to the client up front so that they understand the potential consequences.

Contracts or agreements include the number of revisions a client can make to the film once it is initially approved. If for some unforeseen reason, the client wants changes or additional scenes, they must find additional funds. Ensuring everyone is on the same page to start helps resolve issues down the line. You should not fund a clients project if they go over budget while you wait for them to find money.

In the case of Fired-up the client did not have approval of the final cut, since creative control was in the hands of the filmmaker/producer. They were invited to screen the fine cut to help with any errors or omissions.

The Story

The focus of the story was about the residents going through the process of learning about tenant management. The seminars they attend ended covered a wide range of topics including, reading a lease and understanding the

Residents Cabrini Green

relationship between landlord and tenant. There were also sessions on the responsibilities of having tenant management organizing their buildings and managing services.

One thing that was noticed early on in the training process was that

CHA Board Member

some of the residents appeared to be changing, dressing differently and taking charge of certain affairs. It was decided that the filmmakers are observers in this process; the documentary was not advocating tenant management. Rather it was reporting on how it might work in certain public housing developments in Chicago.

Exterior Walkways on High Rises

Editing Script

The editing script for *Fired-up* was written based on transcripts of all the interviews conducted. Below are excerpts from Fired-Up Interview Transcripts -- Interview with Bertha Gilkey. *Bold underlined type shows what was included in the editing script and ultimately the finished film.*

Tenant Management Training

Doris Wilson, Resident

Highlight or underline parts of the interview to be used. These sections will be pasted into the Editing Script.

Interviewer:
How much of that [money for services] gets down to the tenants?

BERTHA:
Because they've got it built in all kinds of places. For example, ***most housing authorities when you go into their offices they have lavish furniture. That's bought out of the subsidies and rent of public***

Residents at Training session

Residents must pay 30% of all family income as rent.

Graphics are used in the film to furnish factual information.

Very few Male Residents attended Training Sessions

housing tenants. In St. Louis we had an executive director that spent $15,000, $8,000 on one chair. I swear to God. He had eight chairs and you know how much money he spent. He spent... his desk cost $50,000. He bought him not a Ford, like a little Ford, he bought him one of these long cars, almost a Cadilac, out of public housing dollars. And here we have public housing developments that didn't even have screens in the windows. Babies were falling out the windows dying because there were no screens in the windows. And he was spending $50,000 for a desk. Then, you look at the public housing budget, they have deputies, and deputy's deputy. And deputy's deputy's deputy. And executive secretaries and executive assistant secretaries, and assistants to the executive secretary. That's where the money goes. Then each department head has there deputy, and their assistant, and their executive secretary. And they staff all of this. And it's staffed off of the backs of the taxpayers and the public housing tenants.

Transcript Continued

So finally when they get through furnishing their offices, hiring all of their friends and their girlfriends and their boyfriends and their lovers, and then furnishing their offices with drapes and carpeting and plush furniture and all of that. And everybody gets a car, and then an expense account, and an elaborate salary. Then you get into the leaves because they've got this benefit package.

BERTHA:

They have every kind of leave you want to name. Funeral leave, which is alright, they've got special leave; now don't ask me what special leave is, birthday leave. The man has a paternity leave. The man. If his wife is having a baby, he gets time off for the wife having the baby. I mean it's crazy, and we're paying for it. They have every vacation, I mean every holiday for every person that done died. Even people that nobody even knows about. This is the personnel manual for the group in Cleveland Ohio, I mean it is ridiculous. Then the housing authority pays them for going to school. And they don't even require that the school that they are going to has to be related to the job. And we're paying for that. Then they get health and

Bertha Gilkey

sick benefits, and annual leave, and sick leave. All of that's paid for out of our budget. ***And then finally somebody says "Oh, we got to do something for the tenants because after all this money is for public housing." Then maybe 10% of the budget is used to buy some windows, some doors, some paint, no stoves, no refrigerators, very few maintenance workers, no security. So there is nothing left to operate the development off of. Because all the money is going towards the administration. That is a fact. And I challenge any housing authority that's hearing me talking, I challenge them to say that I'm not telling the truth. Go through their budgets and let them explain their budgets to you and you will find that 85 to 90% of their budgets is fat.*** It's administrative top-heavy.

The highlighted areas are cut and pasted into an editing script on the next page.

Excerpt Editing Script Fired-Up

Clip of edited interview. Entire interview begins on page 208.

	PICTURE		AUDIO
	CU Bertha 		...Most housing authorities when you go into their offices they have lavish furniture. That's bought out of the subsidies and rent of public housing tenants. In St. Louis we had an executive director that spent $15,000, $8,000 on one chair. I swear to God. He had eight chairs and you know how much money he spent. He spent... his desk cost $50,000. He bought him not a Ford, like a little Ford, he bought him one of these long cars, almost a Cadillac, out of public housing dollars. And here we have public housing developments that didn't even have screens in the windows. Babies were falling out the windows dying because there were no screens in the windows. And he was spending $50,000 for a desk. Then, you look at the public housing budget, they have deputies, and deputy's deputy. And deputy's deputy's deputy. And executive secretaries and executive assistant secretaries, and assistants to the executive secretary. That's where the money goes.

| MS Bertha  | And then finally somebody says "Oh, we got to do something for the tenants because after all this money is for public housing."

Then maybe 10% of the budget is used to buy some windows, some doors, some paint, no stoves, no refrigerators, very few maintenance workers, no security.

So there is nothing left to operate the development off of. Because all the money is going towards the administration.

That is a fact. And I challenge any housing authority that's hearing me talking, I challenge them to say that I'm not telling the truth. Go through their budgets and let them explain their budgets to you and you will find that 85 to 90% of their budgets is fat. |

Editing Process

Editing starting early in the process of developing the story along several parallel themes like the training, daily living and current problems. It was decided to broadly focus on three or four women and see how they reacted to the training.

The interviews with Bertha Gilkey showed she was knowledgeable about public housing and the training process. Her prior experience working with tenant management concepts, success in St. Louis and ability to communicate made her perfect person to articulate these ideas in the film.

The interviews were used to create a narrative for the story. This was done by reviewing transcripts of all the interviews and piecing together the beginning, middle and end of the film. It seems that once there is theme and a feeling about telling the story a lot of things fall into place as editing proceeds.

Based on what had been edited and gradually refining the rough cut it appeared the length of the documentary would be an hour. No particular length was envisioned at the start. What is best is to work to tell the story as succinctly as possible, and then see where the length might be headed.

The final scenes in the film were shot just before editing was finished. They were scenes of the tenants getting their diplomas for completing the program. This seemed like a fitting ending for the highlighting training and the hopes of the women involved. Another documentary might be to look at the attempt to implement tenant management.

At various stages in the editing process the rough cut was screened for consultants, ranging from other filmmakers to individual with insights about public housing. They provided their reactions or questions to the film from their own POV. One outcome of these screenings was the addition of factual information shown as subtitles on the "lower third" of the screen. Once editing was completed the fine cut was screened for MPC. Their comments were considered and the fine cut finished.

Postproduction

Narration – no 3rd party narration used.
Music recording – source music only.
Assistant editor
Syncing dailies
Logging
Effects editing
Sound mixing – Sound mixing for film productions is done in a dub theater where multiple tracks of Dialog, Effects and Music are mixed. Even if the sound is edited on a NLE system it may benefit from being mixed in a dub theater by engineers experienced in mixing sound and enhancing the audio.
Film finishing including the answer print (if film)
DVD Design

NLE also requires the Audio tracks to be balanced and mixed in three main areas, dialog, effects and music.

Distribution

Chicago public television station, channel 11, put the film up on satellite and offered it to be aired nationally in much the same way *Wrapped In Steel* had been handled previously. In each case there was no payment, to anyone, for the national airing.

The film was seen nationally on most PBS affiliate stations and requests for copies were received from the White House and the Secretary of the Department of Housing. Viewer ratings were high for the time slots the documentary aired in various cities around the country more than once over a two year period. A number of university sociology and urban studies programs requested copies for their curriculum.

Metropolitan Planning Council distributed copies of the documentary to other housing authorities around the country who were interested in Public Housing and tenant management. Distribution rights were also given to the University of Illinois Film Library. They listed it in their catalog. There was a contract to receive a small royalty on the films. Distribution was on VHS at that time. The film is now available on DVD.

Residents visit Cochran Gardens in St. Louis, Missouri.

Young Residents Cochran Gardens

Fired-up was successful as a documentary in a number of ways; it offered a solution to a problem that existed at the time. It explored a topical issue. It showed that while tenant management can be a solution to problems existing in high rise developments it requires strong leadership by residents.

Fired-up was entered in a number of film festivals and received awards from the Chicago Film Festival and other festivals. The film was nominated for an Emmy Award and went on to win an Emmy for Best Independently Produced Network Documentary. Winning awards is an honor and shows recognition from others associated with the industry. It can help you get other work in the future.

Fired-up, produced today would consider broadcast quality HD or another digital format as an alternative to 16mm film (or super 16mm). This would be for the fact that the documentary would be seen exclusively on television or on DVD.

Update

The concept of tenant management that was documented in Fired-Up offered a possible solution to some of the problems facing public housing in many urban areas in the United States. Apparently it did not succeed at Cabrini Green and much of the development has been torn down and the residents dispersed into other types of public housing including low rise dispersed housing. It appears the future of Public Housing while, "up in the air" will not be in high rise buildings.

Fired-up! Public Housing is My Home won an Emmy Award for best Independently Produced Network Documentary.

Documentary storytelling techniques are used for all sorts of nonfiction films, videos and multimedia projects. These productions can be a corporate year-end report, image piece, or public relations video; an industrial, training or educational film; an informational video or public service announcement (PSA).

CHAPTER 13

CORPORATE, INSTITUTIONAL, SPONSORED, MADE FOR HIRE, NONFICTION AND DOCUMENTARY FILMS

CHAPTER THIRTEEN

CHAPTER 13

Corporate, Institutional, Sponsored and other made for hire nonfiction and documentary films.

The Maysles Brothers, Albert and David, made some important documentaries over the years, like the *Salesman* in 1969, and *Gimmie Shelter* in 1970 and previously *Showman,* 1962, *The Beatles* in the USA, 1964, and *Meet Marlon Brando* 1965. They also made many corporate and industrial films for various clients.

Documentary story telling techniques continue to be used for all sorts of nonfiction films, videos and multimedia projects. These can be anything from a corporate year-end report or image piece, public relations video, an industrial film, a training or educational production, informational video or Public Service Announcement (PSA).

Training, Educational and Informational Films

One of the biggest clients for training films is the US Government and the US Armed Forces. There are also State and local governments and other entities who regularly produce various types of videos and multimedia presentations.

Working With Clients

Working with a client is a different experience than making a documentary film and having total creative control of the film. Clients have priorities and needs that the filmmaker must adapt to and understand to tell the story that the client wants to tell.

A client may contact a number of production companies that make nonfiction films, videos and multimedia presentations and ask for a bid on a project they are considering. The actual client may be working through a third party like their advertising agency or public relations firm.

Many clients are not aware of just how expensive it can be to make a film or video. In many cases they are trying to decide between a power point presentation and a film. Of course there's no comparison. In reality all they might need is a power point show. When confronted with the cost of making a five or ten minute film it's apparent their budget won't accommodate the price. By discussing the project with the client it can be determined what will best meet their needs. When approached directly or by an agency about a project ask for a meeting with client so that you can access what their needs are, the story they want to tell and what kind of budget they have to work with. There is no way to come up with a budget that makes any real sense if you don't know what's required. It is possible that the agency will have already gotten this information from the client, in this case the meeting will be with the client's representative.

Many times the client will have a rough idea of what they want to do and an experienced producer may be able to come up with a "ball park," estimate a very approximate cost – like the ball will land somewhere in the ball park -- this is dangerous to do even for an experienced producer, but it can be used much like the cost per square foot used to calculate how much it might cost to build a house. A lot depends on how many bedrooms, kitchen equipment etc and the quality required.

When asked for "ball park" estimates try to first get a handle on what type of film they want to make and how much they have in mind to spend. Film and video projects, like cars, come in all shapes and sizes. Before shopping for a car it's a good idea to know what price range you can afford.

Determining What The Client Wants

First ask questions like: What is the story you want to tell? Who is the audience? How do you intend to distribute this film or is it strictly for "in-house" use. Is it for the Web and/or DVD?

With answers to these and other questions try to determine if the client really needs a film. Is the subject cinematic, is it all static subjects and/or talking heads and charts or is there some action involved?

If there's no action, perhaps still photographs with a voice over and music is something that would tell their story at a lower cost. Is a narrator or spokesperson in the film? Where will the shooting take place?

Sponsored Documentary or Nonfiction Projects

Suppose a client who manufactures baby carriages and car seats wants to make or is sponsoring a documentary about the first five years of a child's development. The script for the film is aimed a new parents and is educational. It uses child development experts and others to present the information. The manufacturer wants product placement in the film. Does this present an ethical or conflict of interest problem? A lot depends on how the product is placed.

If the product placement is incidental, for example, the manufacturer's car seat is seen in the back of the car, there might not be a problem. Consider if the manufacturer also wants to change the content of the documentary to somehow endorse its products or falsify facts about its products. Public television has sponsors that are announced at the beginning and end of programs and help to fund the program. They do not get any mention in the program but gain the association with the program.

Product placement has become a huge part of theatrical and television venues. Documentaries do not employ product placement. Sponsored nonfiction films may do so.

Corporate and Industrial Documentary Case Studies

The following case studies look at a few projects covering a range of nonfiction projects that use a documentary format. The projects range in budget and purpose. Each project had different priorities, for different clients. With one exception they were done as work-for-hire. A work for hire means that the client is paying someone to do the work required to do the project. Therefore the ownership of the project and all related elements belong to the client.

Usually, even if the client terminates the relationship, as long as they have paid for all services required up to that point, they retain all rights. The client only has rights to what they have employed and paid the contractor to do for them. The issue of non payment does not necessarily mean that the contractor owns the rights to the work. It may only mean that the work does not need to be delivered until payment is received. *Legal council should be consulted for specific guidelines.*

A contract or letter of agreement helps to define the relationship and the services required. For example, unless otherwise specified the raw footage shot for a contracted project would be owned by the company or person paying for it to be shot. The filmmaker shooting the footage does not own it and could not use that footage for another project unless they had permission from the client or it was agreed on in the original contract, perhaps as payment in kind.

Corporate Institutional or Religious

On Campus is a short public relations documentary made for the Chicago Episcopalian Arch Diocese Campus Ministries.

The Producer was contacted by a representative of the Diocese about the prospect of making a short documentary about what they believed was a successful approach their campus ministry on the Circle Campus of the University of Illinois, Chicago. The video would be distributed to other campus ministries in other Episcopalian Dioceses.

Background

Concept, Treatment, Script and Budget

After meeting with the client and discussing what they wanted a concept, treatment and preliminary budget were written and submitted to the client. Once the concept, treatment and budget were approved a shooting script and final budget, was submitted and also approved by the client. The script included interviews with the pastor of a church adjacent to the campus ant others clergy and laypersons involved. Shooting days were also planned to shoot on campus to acquire footage of the campus as "B" roll for the interviews.

How the project came about

Students gathered in central area on campus

Contract or Letter of Agreement

A letter of agreement is a simple form of contract between a client and a service provider. It states the terms of the relationship, i.e., who will do what, when, and how. It also details payment considerations. In this case the agreement stipulated that after acceptance of the concept, treatment and budget, the production company would receive 25% of the budget. After acceptance of the shooting script another 25%; after shooting and a rough cut screening another 25%; and the final

Rationale and Approach

Financing and Budget

Students who commute to classes daily don't have as much opportunity to socialize with other students.

payment on delivery of a finished video.

Other payment schedules are possible, for example a variation might be, 50% to begin, 25% after principal shooting is finished and 25% on delivery.

The idea behind having a formal contract or agreement is so that each party knows what to expect in the relationship. Details in the agreement include the amount of time to spend on shooting, client approval of shooting script, and the number of revisions of the final edit are

Campus located in heart of Chicago

allowed. The client signs off on various stages by written approval and payment.

Production

To convey the University of Illinois Circle campus life, it was important to get as much activity and shots of the students as possible. As an urban campus there was a diverse mix of students attending. In addition Circle Campus was a "commuter campus" in that not many students actually lived there. So there was not much activity at night.

Agape Episcopalian Church, Circle Campus Chicago

The documentary was shot on professional format video tape since distribution would be on VHS tape. Currently the documentary would be distributed on DVD and shot on broadcast quality equipment.

Postproduction

Editing was done entirely off-line with what was called A/B roll editing machines. This was an economical way of doing a low budget documentary at the time. 16mm would have been expensive and over kill for this type of project.

Interview with Clergy Agape Campus Church

Off-line is a term used for editing with basic equipment that sometimes used two playback tape recorders (decks) and a record deck or just one playback and one record deck to edit professional Beta, 3/4", SVHS and VHS video tape.

All linear editing resources that do not utilize major switchers and consoles for video editing and do not send the program out over the air (on-line) are usually said to be off-line. An on-line resource may also be utilized, off-line for editing to tape. Some of these resources may still be found in small TV stations or high schools but most have been replaced with NLE systems.

Crew

The crew was composed of a director, DP/camera operator, camera assistant, sound and boom operator, and production assistant who did logging, script supervising, and a first assistant director who worked on the schedule of shooting, crew management and arranged for meals and transportation. Post-production included the director and an editor.

Distribution

A rough cut was finished in a few weeks and screened for the client. After the rough cut was reviewed and approved, a fine cut was edited and screened. At the end of the project the master tapes and dubs were to given to the Diocese. In most projects of this type all original elements are the property of the client, who may want them or ask the production company to store them. The client handled their own distribution by taking the master tape to a video tape dubbing facility and ordered dubs as required.

Many producers bid on making DVD's or CD's for their clients. If large numbers are required a profit can be made on producing the DVD and at the same time save the client time and money. This aspect may be included in the original bid and budget. If more copies are needed in the future the producer furnishes them also.

Not For Profit/Pro Bono Projects

Pro Bono - A term used in the legal profession which means services are donated or done without pay.

On occasion a Not-For-Profit charity may wish to make a documentary about their activities or special events. They may not have the resources to pay for a large production budget and ask the filmmaker to work "pro bono" (with out pay) and to donate their services to make the documentary. Depending on the scope of the project it may be possible to help the organization. While personal time donated is not tax deductible, certain other hard expenses may be.

Make-A-Wish Documentary

On the occasion of making its three thousandth wish, the Central and Northern Florida Chapter of the Make-A-Wish Foundation wanted to make a documentary both to document the event and for possible use in fund raising and other purposes. The documentary was envisioned to be six or seven minutes in length and distributed on DVD.

The recipient of the 3000th wish was to visit the Orlando Magic basketball team and meet some of his favorite players. The major potion of the event would happen in one day with an early visit to the airport by the recipient and his family to tour the private jet used by the team and the facility where it is housed. The rest of the day was planned to be at the arena where the Magic were playing that evening. A number of events including meeting players, being a ball boy, and having dinner with one of the players would be happening at the stadium before and during the game. A second day was also planned for the recipient and family to visit Universal Studio Theme Park in Orlando for the day.

The filmmakers met with

Family visits Airport tours Jet

the Make-A-Wish staff involved, to discuss their priorities and decide on how to approach the project. It was decided that a traditional documentary approach would be used and that the short seven minute documentary would be based on first person interviews with all the participants and documentary coverage of the events on one day. "B" roll was also planned to be shot on a second day as the wish recipient and family visited Universal Studio Theme Park.

Preproduction

Before shooting it is a good idea to think about what the story is and how it can best be told. Writing a concept and treatment for a documentary project helps focus on what the beginning, middle and end of the story might be. With this notion of where the story will go, the style and type of coverage required can be finalized and a shooting script or shot lists can be made for each event.

The crew was composed of two camera operators, one audio recordist, assistant camera, production assistant, line producer and producer/director/editor. A still photographer, the production assistant and the director took photographs of all aspects of the action and also production stills. Two cameras were included so that coverage of the basket ball activities could be shot from different angles. While the director did interviews and covered the main action the line producer would work with the second unit camera operator to gather "B" Roll footage or get additional coverage of the main action.

Preproduction included some basic research on the subject's condition, the Make-A-Wish Foundation, questions to ask participants and how and what to cover during shooting.

Since this project was done on a "pro-bono" basis (at no charge to the Make-A-Wish Foundation) no budget was submitted to the client; however there were some expenses for transportation, equipment and crew meals that were budgeted for in-house purposes.

On low budget or no budget shoots a production assistant (PA) may assist the director as a script supervisor and/or first assistant director, keeping communications going between the director and both cameras, setting up interviews and checking on upcoming events. Whatever the budget many documentary and nonfiction productions keep the crew small for logistical purposes.

Using two cameras on a shoot where it is important to cover action from more than one angle simultaneously is a good idea. But there must be coordination between both cameras and communication regarding what the second camera should shoot. The director should sit down with both the first camera and second camera operators to define what they are looking for as far as coverage and type of shot. A second camera wandering around doing pick-ups without direction may a waste of time as the shots will not cut with the first camera and might not make sense as "B" Roll. In certain situations wireless communication between the director and both cameras might be worthwhile. Depending on the scope and amount of coverage needed from the second camera unit a second unit director may be required.

Digital Equipment

This shoot utilized Panasonic HVX 200 cameras and recorded on P2 media. A P2 card is similar in size to a PCMCIA card and is a solid state recording medium. At this time, cards are available that can hold up to 32 gigs of data. HD shot at 720p uses about 8 gigs to record 20 minutes of footage. Shooting with P2 media creates a somewhat different work flow than shooting with tape or film. The HVX 200 holds two P2 cards and will shoot continuously automatically switching from the first card to the second. With two 32 gig cards shooting at 1080p you could shoot for 40 minutes and replace the cards with two fresh cards while you downloaded the footage from the first pair. However, it may be best to use only one card at a time since the camera can

SAMPLE DOCUMENTARY FILMMAKING PACKAGE

HVX-200 W/ BATTERIES, AC ADAPTER, AND CABLING
P2 STORE 60 GB DUMP DRIVE AND TWO 16GB P2 CARDS
BOGEN 503 TRIPOD KIT AND COLLAPSABLE REFLECTOR
SHORT SHOTGUN MIC AND DEDICATED AUDIO PACKAGE....

create "spanned" files when there are two cards that create files that may be difficult to bring into some editing programs.

There are a couple of ways to download the footage. Early on Panasonic had a small hard drive device on which you could download up to 60 gigs of data. You can bring the footage through Final Cut and onto an external hard drive. On location, the most practical system is to download the cards to a large external hard drive via the data card slot on a PC laptop or with the latest Panasonic P2 transfer device if using a Mac.

The Make-A-Wish staff supplied the filmmakers with an itinerary of the events for each day. The director worked on a shot list for each event and questions for the interviews. The wish grantee and family, as well as the staff of Make-A-Wish and the Orlando Magic, were all scheduled to be interviewed. All the events and interaction between the wish recipient and the Orlando Magic players were also to be covered. Several key players of the team volunteered to work with the wish recipient.

Production

Shooting was scheduled for one day of coverage of the wish recipient and his family starting at 9:00 AM at their hotel, going with them to the airport to visit the Orlando Magic's corporate, team jet and then to the arena where the Orlando Magic were playing that evening and where the family would have a lunch with team members.

Dwight Howard Orlando Magic with Wish Recipient JP

Shooting

The day began with an interview with the wish recipient and his family while they were being transported in a stretch limo to the airport to see the team jet. The director and the camera operator sat on the back seat. The director hand held a shotgun mic. The interview started while parked at the hotel and was going well until the limo started to move. The noise levels were too high to do the interview so the driver pulled over and the interview was finished. The interview in the limo was a good idea but not practical while the vehicle was moving. Individual lavalieres could have been set up with a mixer, preferably wired, since wireless lavs might pick-up radio frequency (RF) noise, especially since the vehicle was moving. There were sounds coming from outside the vehicle, road noise and the interior of the limo had a bar with glass objects moving and making clinking sounds.

Family interviewed in Limo

It was important to see the limo arrive at the airport. The second camera was used to show the vehicle arriving. If only one camera had been available it would have been necessary for the director and camera operator to either get there ahead of the limo or get out of the limo before it got to the entrance, run ahead and have the limo drive up.

Arrival at Magic Jet Hanger

Inside the airport terminal and hangar there was much to cover. JP, the wish recipient, was greeted at the door by Orlando Magic staff where everyone was introduced.

Shooting events as they happen doesn't usually allow for setting up lights. Most of the time shooting is done with available light and small portable lights often attached to the camera. Available light ranges from daylight at all times of the day either as an exterior source or filtered in through windows on interior scenes. This may give rise to situations with mixed daylight, tungsten and/or florescent lighting. When shooting any form of video, attention to white balancing in each environment is crucial.

Family views Magic Team Jet

Airport Hanger with mixed daylight and other lighting

White Balance for each shot in mixed lighting situations

Interior arena with mercury vapor lighting

Wish recipient tours jet and meets Orlando Magic team players Dwight Howard and (right) Carlos Arroyo.

Interior jet cockpit using brick LED camera light and available light.

Interior arena with mercury vapor lighting

Exterior - cloudy near dusk available light usually requires fill light

Postproduction

All footage was downloaded or transferred from the P2 cards to an External Hard Drive using Final Cut Pro where it was logged. The footage was reviewed and a draft editing script written based on the original concept, treatment, shooting script and actual footage shot.

Transfer, log, review actual footage shot then write edit script.

There may be a temptation with a short documentary to skip logging, review of footage, and writing a shooting script. However, these steps are important and give the director and editor a firm insight into the story and how to use the footage that has been shot to tell the story. Typically in a documentary which asks questions and explores issues surrounding the subject, the footage may reflect new discoveries and issues that were not thought of initially.

In the Make-A-Wish project there was a basic concept to document this event and create a seven minute documentary about the recipient, the wish and how it was received. The family of the recipient was asked to furnish photographs of JP growing up that were used in the documentary. The photographs were scanned and returned.

A fairly fine cut version was finished it was shown to the client, the Make-A-Wish foundation. The foundation staff made some requests for changes which were incorporated into the final cut of the documentary. The final cut was taken into a mixing theater and a mix of all sound (dialog, effects and music) made. This could also have been done with Pro Tools software that goes beyond the capabilities of Final Cut Pro.

A preview screening was held and a number of DVD copies of the documentary given to the recipient and the Make-A-Wish® Foundation.

JP's Wish was awarded a 2008 Bronze Telly Award as a documentary.

Baldwin Park is an urban neighborhood that grew from the ashes of a naval base in the middle of Orlando, Florida in 2003.

Baldwin Park, Orlando Florida

CHAPTER 14

THE BALDWIN PARK STORY
A WORK IN PROGRESS

Chapter 14

Developing an Idea For An Independently Produced Documentary

It isn't difficult to come up with an idea for a documentary but where do you start in assessing the viability of the notion?

Background

Baldwin Park is an urban neighborhood that grew from the ashes of a naval base in the middle of Orlando, Florida in 2003. At first it appears as most "planned communities" might appear, new single family homes, apartments, condominiums and city town homes. What makes it unique enough to make a documentary about it? Is Baldwin Park part of a larger story?

Rationale

Stories are mostly about people, in this case why they have chosen to live in this new neighborhood or community. How did this community come to be born? What makes it a community? Why does it appear to be a successful modern planned urban development? What makes a neighborhood livable? What turns a development like Baldwin Park into a community where people enjoy walking to nearby shopping, schools and restaurants?

How does Baldwin Park compare to other communities new and old, to neighborhoods in Orlando and other cities. How does it fit in to new urban planning doctrine? It begins to be clear that the story is not only a look at Baldwin Park but a look at urban life past, present and future. Are there lessons learned for the future of urban renewal?

Approach

Preliminary research, including going online and consulting sources knowledgeable about urban studies, indicates a broad base of interest in not only urban affairs but in the notion of "New Urbanism" and how the financial crisis facing the country in 2009 will impact urban life. Further research in order to define the focus of the documentary, can be accomplished by contacting additional sources knowledgeable about planned communities, new urbanism and urban history and other sources for information.

The Idea Takes Shape

Once the idea shows potential and starts to take shape, it's time to write a concept and treatment for the documentary idea. This is used to give people in the community and at large an idea what we're proposing to do and to seek support.

The Baldwin Park Story

Concept

Concept

Explore the community of Baldwin Park in Orlando Florida, from its birth which is the result of the closing of the Naval Training Center in Orlando, Florida to the successful planned community it has become today.

Treatment

Treatment

The story begins with the military history, in the form of archival photographs and footage, of the Orlando Air Force Base in 1940 and its evolution into the Naval Training Center that ultimately closed in 1998. From there begins the acquisition of the land by the City of Orlando, political wrangling and finally the planning and the demolishing of the Naval Training Base to make way for the planned community of Baldwin Park.

What follows is a look at how Baldwin Park has evolved over the years; how it has evolved into the dynamic community it is today; what kinds of community groups and organizations have been established and how the community functions; why its cycling, running and walking trails along the lake are so popular and friendly.

Baldwin Park is a new neighborhood community with its own shopping and restaurants in the middle of the established urban setting of Orlando and nearby established suburbs like Winter Park. Baldwin Park is unique in that it apparently has blurred the lines between old fashioned neighborhoods, planned communities and urban renewal. How did this evolved? What does it predict about the future of urban planning and urban life?

Interviews with businesses, residents, community leaders, planners, residents association, business association and others would be used to narrate the story. Who are the residents of Baldwin Park and why have they chosen to live there? Special events and activities would also be incorporated into the story.

Areas of interest to the story are the efforts, trials and tribulations that have led to the community as it is today. What schools exist and how are they part of the community? What other institutions exist or are planned?

This story is an exploration of a modern urban community that has emerged in a unique way representing a contemporary effort to establish a new residential area in the heart of an established city. What does the future hold for this type of development and Baldwin Park?

Finding Support and Interest

Preproduction

After developing a concept and treatment, the next step is to identify individuals and organizations in the community who might be interested in the idea and in seeing the documentary get made. In the case of Baldwin Park it turned out to be the developer of Baldwin Park, but not knowing where to start we contacted the Home Owners Association and the public relations representative pointed us in the right direction. It is important to find support with individuals and institutions who are knowledgeable and might care about the documentary getting made. More than one source of support should be developed to gain more than one perspective on subjects and issues concerning the community.

As part of the pre-production and production effort, the first interview with the developers was set up an shot in July of 2009. The next step is to continue research based on tis interview and conduct additional interviews with other entities in the community and at large.

This process will be updated online as it progresses at TheBaldwinParkStory.com.

Barbara Konigh and David Pace of The New Broad Street Development Company

Crew consisted of four persons including the director interviewer.

Director Jim Martin conducts interview in New Broad Street Realty offices in Baldwin Park

The first interview with the developers was conducted at the offices of New Broad Street Realty in Baldwin Park, Orlando, Florida. There were a number of places in the office where an interview might be conducted including a conference room and a more casual setting in the lounge area. We choose an area with a neutral background and used simple key, fill and backlight three point lighting.

Future Interviews are planned with a diverse group of individuals and groups in this community as well as other planned communities nationwide. Experts including new urbanism advocates and city planners will also to be contacted.

Reaching the Community

To help reach the local community and others interested in planned communities and new urbanism a web site and blog have been established at the production company web site. As shooting continues posts on the progress will be put on the blog, including a preview of the documentary as a work in progress.

A new idea in the development in the project is the notion of following a number of new and current home buyers in Baldwin Park as to why they decided to move to this community. Interviews with various age groups and types of buyers including young couples starting out; singles, and senior citizens are planned. As all levels of housing exist in this large development, a diverse group of people are moving into the community.

Searching for Financial Support

Additional financial support needs to be obtained to make this documentary a viable undertaking for the producer who has put up the seed money to get the project off the ground.

There are a number of possible sponsors in the community and in the city that can be approached as well as foundations and other agencies interested in this subject.

The Baldwin Park Story could be registered as a not-for-profit corporation and then apply for tax exempt status so that donations to fund it would be tax deductible. However, this is a lengthy and expensive process that requires legal counsel.

Production Continues

Currently production continues to document local events and to do interviews with residents. In addition documentation of a number of new construction sites is underway.

It is expected that full production will get underway in the late summer of 2010. Updates to this process including final preproduction, fund raising, production, postproduction and distribution will be continued on thebaldwinparkstory.com and jrmartinmedia.com.

*Archival Documenta-
tion of events in the
community.*

*2010 Orlando Chili Cook Off held in Baldwin Park was well at-
tended by Baldwin Park residents and many others from the area.
Documentation including both still photography and digital video
was shot using the Canon 7D SLR. Video included interviews as
well as general archival footage.*

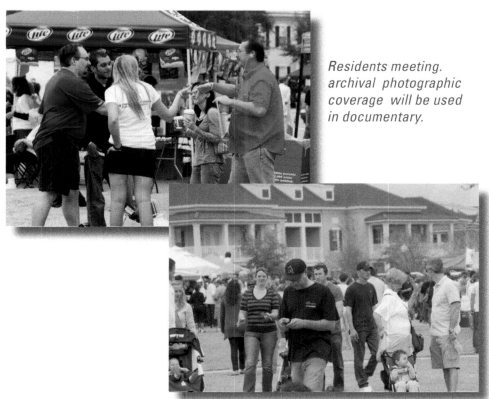

*Residents meeting.
archival photographic
coverage will be used
in documentary.*

Archival Documentary coverage of people and event.

Archival documentary coverage of people and location.

Baldwin Park Lake Front

2010 new construction underway in community

Cycling paths in Baldwin Park

New Broad Street Downtown Baldwin Park

There's a difference between making a documentary about an event and recording the event. The documentary goes beyond point and shoot. It explores the who, what, when, where, why and how of what is happening whether it's a concert or a wedding event.

Hampton Court Palace Dinner By Candlelight

CHAPTER 15

**PRIVATE EVENT
DOCUMENTARIES**

CHAPTER FIFTEEN

Private Events

Private events take many forms. They could range from a local wedding to an international event. Special events also include corporate sales rallies or similar events where thousands of people attend to hear a speaker in a stadium setting.

International Private Event

Background

Suppose you were the son of a wealthy person who was having his 65th birthday and you couldn't think of anything to give him that he didn't already have what would you do?

How about throwing him a birthday party at Hampton Court Palace in England and flying in a couple hundred of his closest friends for a fantastic celebration. Also, as a party favor to remember the event, a documentary video of the entire affair.

How the project came about

Producing and directing this event required knowledge of working in England and dealing with the logistics of covering multiple events over the course of one afternoon and evening.

Concept and Treatment

Essentially the goal was to cover the event from start to finish. This would include a reception in the afternoon, a train ride on the Orient Express from London to Hampton Court Palace, dinner, after dinner events with the Royal Marine Marching Band, fireworks and a train ride back to London Victoria Station.

Rationale and Approach

Pre-Production

This would need to be a multi-camera shoot since multiple events needed to be covered at the same time. Also logistically required to cover large gatherings where a great deal of coverage was required.

Reception

In a documentary of this nature it is important to get lots of close-ups of the attendees and as many interviews as possible. For example there is one camera covering everyone arriving at the reception, another camera roaming the

Orient Express leaves Victoria Station for Hampton Court Palace

reception, a third camera waiting at the train station for people to arrive. One camera will go aboard the train with the attendees while another camera will go with some guests leaving for the station, from the reception. One camera shoots the train leaving Victoria Station. Assignments for each camera assures adequate coverage.

Multi Camera Shoot

Two cameras and the rest of the crew headed for Hampton Court Palace where a crew was sent in advance to set up lights in the banquet hall. Of course there would need to be a camera to shoot people debarking the train and walking or being transported to the palace.

Guests Arriving Hampton Court Palace

Coverage

Dinner is by Candlelight

This project was solely intended for video distribution and it was shot on video. The client wanted to release the film in PAL which is used in Great Britain, Europe and Australia where most of the attendees lived. But the production was to be edited in the US, which uses NTSC. The question was whether to shoot in PAL 650 lines or NTSC 450 lines. The two formats are incompatible.

PAL versus NTSC

Whatever system was used it would need to be compatible for

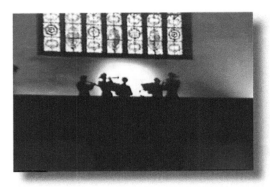

Banquet Hall Musicians play period music

shooting and editing. Had NLE systems like Avid or Final cut been available at the time shooting and editing could have been done in PAL because editing would have only been a matter of using the correct software settings. The editing resources for this project were in the US and NTSC.

One alternative was to shoot on NTSC equipment, edit and have the NTSC converted to PAL for distribution. There would be some quality loss, but it was deemed acceptable for first Generation VHS release.

Budget and Equipment

As this was a multi camera shoot, it was necessary to check out the cost of supplementing in house NTSC Beta Cam equipment with rentals and shipping it all to England. There would be less chance of equipment loss if the equipment was on the same plane on which the crew traveled. It is not unheard of for a production manager to actually supervise or observe motion picture equipment being loaded on and off the plane to insure it's safety and security.

Lights, audio and grip equipment would also be required. Everything would need to be able to use 50 cycle, 220 amp electrical power which is the standard in England. There would be paperwork to file with the British Government, which also might want the client to justify why they were using an American crew instead of a British crew to shoot. There may have been some justification for using this

The Royal Marine Marching Band provided after dinner entertainment.

particular American crew, because of financial connections between corporations, however there was another alternative.

After some research an equipment rental company was found in London that rented NTSC equipment to visiting television crews from the US, shooting in England and Europe. All the equipment needed could be rented from them. The American crew could travel with no equipment and return from England with the videotape that had been shot. Rented equipment included communications gear, mobile phones for location and walkie-talkies. This turned out to be the most practical solution.

NTSC Equipment Rental in England

Two camera operators, recommended by the rental company in London, and additional support crew were hired in England. This saved the expense of flying an entire crew from Florida to London, hotel accommodations, per diem and meals.

Local Crew Members

Of course all crew and personnel coming from the US needed passports. Everyone entered Great Britain on business. Technically anyone coming to England to work needed a work permit. The US production crew (mainly above-the-line personnel) came in under a corporate umbrella, which seems to have been accepted at the time. Possibly as "above-the-line" staff and because of the fact that additional British crew were hired and equipment was rented locally.

The US crew consisted of producer, director, DP (who also would operate and light), a second camera operator, first assistant, an assistant director, video technician, audio technician, and production manager.

US Crew Members

Shooting Isolated (Iso) Cameras and Genlock

There are a number of ways to work, using video in the field with multiple cameras. Field Cameras (Camcorders) as the name implies are able to record video in the camera. Each Camera has its own synchronous time code system that should allow it to be synced with what other cameras are recording.

In studio situations where cameras do not have built in recorders they are synced using a sync generator that produces synchronization pulses for cameras and recorders to keep the signals in synchronization. Genlock allows switching between the video signals coming from all sources. In the field it is possible to record in the camera while all the cameras are genlocked so that the signal from each camera is in sync and can be switched to for a live feed. Tape in each camera would provide backup and allow the ability to edit afterwards. In this shoot there was no need to switch between cameras as the event was not being broadcast live.

At the banquet, a control center with monitors was set up so that the director could see what each camera was shooting, talk to the camera operators and call shots. This is a typical multi camera shoot situation set up so that the director can pick which camera to put on line but in this case the event was solely being recorded to tape.

The entire crew arrived a day early so that equipment and locations could be checked. The DP and a camera operator went to the rental house, checked out the equipment and met with the local crew members that were being hired in London.

Scouting Locations

The director and others went to scout the locations. Based on the scouting trips, camera placements were picked as well as how to cover the event at each location. The director could not be at all the locations so the type of coverage required was discussed in advance, plus there was radio communication.

Hampton Court Palace is not far from London by car so the DP and a some crew were sent ahead, to set up lights in the banquet room, the morning before the event. This room was large and had priceless old tapestries hanging on the walls, from near the ceiling to near the floor. Great caution had to be taken not to shine any of the hot lights on the tapestries for fear of damage or fire!

High ceilings made it difficult to light the room. There were many tables lit with candles that actually helped the lighting. But the head table was difficult to light. Audio was another problem. Only shotguns and a table microphone used for the head table. It was not possible to tie into the PA system that was used for the head table and speaker's podium since it was not adequate for our purposes. Audio in these types of situations is always a problem.

Piper bids farewell to guests

A microphone may be placed next to the one at the speakers podium with the line run to the mixer for decent sound. Wireless lavalieres, when you get people to wear them, provide good sound, however, wireless microphones can sometimes be subject to random RF and noise. Also multiple wireless lavalieres require a receiver and a multi-channel mixer. Always bring plenty of microphone cable and microphone options when shooting at any type of large event.

One of the goals was to interview everyone in someway; either with a few questions or at the very least having each person introduce themselves. In this type of documentary everyone will look for themselves in the video. The guests were in "party" mode so interviewing went well. The interviews were spread out over various locations so that there would be a variety of backgrounds and situations.

The plan for covering the day went well. The crew was able to stay ahead of events and cover everything that was needed. When walkie-talkies or cell phones did not work runners were used. Some events like the reception in London took longer than expected and so one camera stayed behind to do pick-ups while the crew went to Hampton Court or to Victoria Station to get people boarding the train.

One area that was a surprise was the Royal Marching Band and the fireworks. One camera went up on the roof of the palace, one on the side and the other handheld on the ground with the band. This camera was able to move up and down the rows of the marching band.

Post Production

Post Production was done in Florida. A concept, treatment and basic editing script for the edit, based on what was shot, was written on the plane coming back from England. The Executive Producer and the client approved the edit script and asked the director to supervise the edit.

All editing was done at an online editing facility at Full Sail University. When a rough cut was ready, the client came to Florida and sat in on the editing as a technical advisor which included identifying people in the documentary.

The first version was about 60 minutes. A second thirty minute version was cut for the party attendees. Both versions were converted from a 1" edit master to PAL and VHS dubs made.

The quality of the color and image suffered greatly in the conversion from NTSC to PAL.

With today's NLE tools and the superior quality of the PAL system it would be best to shoot with PAL 25 FPS and work with a PAL

Grand Finale of Fireworks as Marching Band Played at Hampton Court Palace

based NLE system. By working in PAL the film would not need to be converted and the quality would be excellent for distribution to Europe and Australia. NTSC conversions would look pretty close to or better than native NTSC because of the hire resolution of PAL. Shooting in High Definition (HD) would also be a worthwhile option.

USING A DOCUMENTARY STORYTELLING APPROACH FOR NONFICTION PERSONAL EVENTS

Creative-Cinema.com is a production company that specializes in personal event documentaries including weddings. Ted Juras, owner of the company, feels strongly about telling the story in a way that will best serve the clients needs. He outlines his approach to shooting weddings.

**Ted Juras
Creative-Cinema.com**

"It's important to capture the story of the bride and groom's day. For each couple this moment is personal and unique, so the goal is to help them relive this day when they watch the documentary in the future. For example, an outside wedding with the threat of a huge thunderstorm and an anxious bride sounds like it could result in a terrible tragedy, however, the documentary can show how they overcame this threat and find happiness despite the weather, creating a positive memory for life. From a story standpoint it also adds a little real life drama!"

"When we shoot events, such as a wedding, our main purpose is to capture every tiny detail that the bride painstakingly put in place. As anyone who has been a bride or groom can attest, your big day can be a blur, so at times it's hard to recall exactly what happened. Details such as table numbers, place cards, the room number where the bride gets ready, all details that bring the couple, family and friends back to that day and help them remember each time they view the video over the years."

"Lastly, our approach is a 'direct cinema' or 'verite fly-on-the-wall' style shooting. Not directing, imposing on, or orchestrating this special occasion creates an intimate reality. Coverage includes mixing up the composition and framing of establishing shots and close ups. The job of the videographer is a piece of cake compared to the wedding photographer who does need to set up shots. The photographer is also part of the story! We simply stay on the photographer's hip and include them in some of the shots. The idea here is to help the bride and groom remember what their day was like. It's important to include both the 'Official Photograph' and the 'behind the scenes' reality of the day. The finished documentary spontaneously brings to life the event and the actuality of that day."

One of the key elements in putting together any documentary style event video is obtaining adequate coverage, starting with shots that include action; something happens that helps tell the story. In certain situations interviews with key individuals and attendees adds another facet to the storytelling. "B" roll inserts and cut-a-ways for each scene will help in editing. Emotion and drama may be found in nonfiction situations and used to help tell the story. Every story has a beginning middle and end. It is best to shoot with this in mind.

The Auto Tuner's Center is one area of the Lyndale Island Documentary Style television series proposed and currently online at Lyndale Island.

*Interview With First Mate of the Bounty
for Lyndale Island Documentary*

CHAPTER 16

MAKING DOCUMENTARIES
FOR TELEVISION AND
THEATRICAL RELEASE

CHAPTER SIXTEEN

CHAPTER 16

Television & Internet Pilot for Documentary Series

Captain Tom Martin (left) and Filmmaker Jim Martin on location in Lake Michigan boat yard in Chicago

It was a cold and wintry Chicago evening in February when I received a call from my brother Captain Tom. "You know you should make a documentary about boating," he said. "Come down to St. Pete, Florida and I can show you some of the boats we're working with."

Rationale and Approach

When you make films, friends, relatives, people you meet in a bar, all have these great ideas about a film you should make, most of the time the ideas are not viable for one reason or another. But after thinking about Tom's idea a concept materialized. Instead of This Old House, the popular PBS "How To" series, what about "This Old Boat?"

This series would be about more than fixing up your boat; it would be about the whole world of recreational boating. A brief concept and treatment was written and given to associates in public television to see what they thought of the idea. The feedback was that there should be an audience for this type of programming.

Public television stations don't finance very many independent projects. They have their own "in-house" productions and get most everything else from the PBS Network. So while they might be willing to sponsor a series the financing would have to come from somewhere else.

At the time sponsors of a public television program could only have a minute or two at the beginning and end of a program. So a sponsor basically paid for the whole production. The could be more than one sponsor but they would have to divide up the time at the beginning and end of the show, so you might end up with 5 sponsors who each got 10 seconds mention at the beginning and end of the program.

Proposal

The next step would be to write a proposal for the series, scripts for at least six of the 13 episodes comprising a season. The final seven episodes would be summarized. In addition a pilot episode or at the very least a trailer should be produced that would serve as a preview of the series. Research was conducted in Florida with Captain Tom Martin to see what topics might be included. this research was important for a number of reasons including an assessment of the viability of the project and cost of doing the proposal and pilot. Research was also done to assess how big an audience existed for a show about recreational boating.

At the time, according to the National Marine Manufacturers Association (NMMA) there were, 80 million registered boats in the United States. Florida had the most boats with Michigan second. The industry generated about 20 billion dollars a year in revenue.

There isn't much on broadcast television or cable except for fishing shows. Fishing appeared to be popular in most markets.

Demographics concerning who all the people interested in boating are and what their income and life styles might be were studied. The information helped to decide that the project had viability and that it could be a profitable venture.

Captain Tom reviews sailboat restoration

The format for the show would be documentary with two hosts. Captain Tom and someone else who would interview and cohost. Captain Tom would be the resident expert. Research including visiting boat yards, yacht clubs, marine supply stores and other recreational

Co-hosts (left) interview Sea Ray boat owner (right) for pilot

boating related places to speak to professionals and other people involved in the marine industry. These visits not only aided in the writing of scripts for the series, it sparked the idea that the show would include visits to these same sources.

The next step was to write scripts for the pilot and for the series. In addition a proposal had to be written to present to possible advertisers (sponsors) and a proposal for possible investors. All of the initial efforts were self-funded.

The proposal, concept, treatment and script for a pilot production which would be the first episode with six more ready for production were written. A major corporate sponsor interested in supporting the series on public television was found.

St Pete, Florida

The finished proposal and pilot was accepted by WTTW Channel 11, a public television channel in Chicago. They had other national shows and had been interested in the program from the beginning. Contract negotiations began with executives at the station.

After three months WTTW presented a contract. Review of the contract with legal council determined that it was unacceptable, since it stipulated that WTTW would have Creative and Financial Control of the program. They would not negotiate this aspect of the contract. This agreement was unacceptable because it would mean that the show would not belong to the producers anymore and that WTTW, with total control could actually dismiss the producers and own the program.

So everything came to a halt. Public television Channel Two, in Miami was contacted and they were not interested. A contact at an LA public television channel had the pilot and proposal reviewed there and they were interested, however a move to LA was not possible since the production company had just made a move to Florida. It was decided that public television was not the best venue for this series.

A new approach to the idea was conceived that would begin with an internet presence for the series. The following is an abbreviated version of a proposal put together for Lyndale Island Yacht Club.

The original proposal was 32 pages long including a pilot script, all aspects of the production and a business plan. What follows is a brief overview.

Concept

Lyndale Island Yacht Club explores the rich diversity of our national love affair with recreational boating and life on the water. It is accessible 24 hours a day, 7 days per week on the internet.

Treatment

The program utilizes a magazine format with documentary style segments on all aspects of recreational boating. The series is designed to inform and entertain. The world of recreational boating is exciting, interesting, and fun. The people involved are friendly good neighbors; they come from every walk of life, age, sex, and ethnic group. This series should appeal to arm chair enthusiasts as well as "dyed-in-the-wool" boaters.

The hosts for the series keep the family feel of boating alive by maintaining a friendly personal relationship with the viewer and other participants in the program. The show has a sense of humor and often keeps the chats on the lighter side as they explore various aspects of the boating world. Boating is often a family affair and host Captain Tom Martin, and Cohost Jim Martin are "boating brothers" who often have different perspectives on various subjects. Captain Tom is the knowledgeable expert and Jim represents the audience asking questions they might have about what's being discussed.

The magazine format breaks down into six regular feature segments: From The Keel Up, Life On the Water, Care and Feeding, The Boat Show, Bosun's Locker and Getting There.

Magazine Format for series.

From The Keel Up
Documents a major restoration of a motor boat and a sail boat each season.

Life On The Water
Explores the human side of boating through a series of related topics including living aboard, cruising, racing social life, families afloat, yacht clubs, marinas, travel planning and livability at various "ports-of-call."

Care And Feeding
Maintenance of equipment and the boat and preventive maintenance.

The Boat Show

Shopping for a Boat and all it entails. Boat Reviews, Boat Shows, Owner Interviews, Boat Brokers, Bargaining, and Surveys are a few of the many topics covered in this segment.

Bosun's Locker

Looks at the huge array of nautical hardware currently available.

Getting There

Help in Developing skills in navigation, piloting, marine communications, learning the rules of the road, heavy weather techniques, and safety are some of the topics covered in this segment.

Lyndale Island

Lyndale Island is currently online at www.lyndaleisland.com. The concept has been expanded to include two more areas on the island; the Auto Tuner's Center and the Aviation Center.

The Yacht Club area has dozens of articles and documentary videos in the various areas outlined here. The Auto Tuner's Center has focused on Corvette sports cars and is divided into a number of areas including a focus on aftermarket modification, restoration, life on the road, maintenance and links to sources and vendors. The Aviation area is being developed in the same fashion as the other two areas.

A unique feature of Lyndale Island is an interactive 3D version of the site where you can take a boat out for a spin around the island, drive a Corvette on island roads and enter buildings with shops and informational programming.

Documentary and Nonfiction Feature Production

There are many documentary nonfiction programs on both network and cable television today. So-called "Reality" shows that use a pseudo documentary style that pretends to be actuality are not considered documentary or nonfiction. In fact shows like Survivor, and Idol are highly scripted and manipulated realities with "talent" selected to react in predicted ways in various situations.

Nonfiction and Documentary Areas

Broadcast Television

Network news productions like CBS's *60 Minutes* carry on a tradition started by Edward R Murrow and Fred Friendly with documentaries for television like *Harvest of Shame* and the McCarthy Hearings. While today's magazine format is different than the original program, 60 Minutes has its roots in the investigative documentary style they used. Public television documentaries produced independently and by PBS Network affiliates like WGBH's Front Line are usually traditional documentaries. *The Civil War* and other documentaries by Ken Burns are excellent examples of television documentaries.

Cable - Non-Broadcast

A number of Cable Channels like HBO, Showtime, Discover and others feature nonfiction programming with emphasis on a particular subject. They either originate the programming or pick it up from independent producers and syndicators. The programming is a mixture of nonfiction subjects and documentary productions.

Theatrical Documentaries

Documentaries made with the specific goal of playing theatrically, i.e. in the theaters may cover a wide range of subjects. Every year the Motion Picture Academy awards an Oscar for Best Feature Length Documentary. What qualifies the documentary to be nominated is that it is being distributed commercially and has been screened in a theater.

Robert Flaherty's *Nanook of the North* was the first feature length documentary to run in theaters world wide. Since then there have been a steady stream of documentary films shown in theaters, however the average theatergoer can probably count on one hand how many documentaries they have seen in a movie theater.

Many documentaries make the festival and art house rounds but are not seen in regular theaters. So the financial return is limited. With the advent of DVD documentaries have the opportunity to reach a larger audience. The financial returns of the majority of feature length documentaries that get theatrical release do not gross huge amounts of money in the theaters. However there are some notable exceptions that have done exceptionally well in the theatrical circuit.

Three out of the top grossing documentaries in the US have been produced and directed by Michael Moore. The number one top-grossing documentary is *Fahrenheit 9/11,* it played in 2,011 theaters domestically, bringing in $119,195,000 at the Box Office. The production budget is reported to have been $6,000,000, prints and advertising budget, $12,000,000. In addition the film grossed another $103,300,000 internationally bringing the world wide gross to $222,414,517.

The second of the three top grossing documentaries is *Sicko,* grossing $24,540,000 in 1,117 theaters domestically. The production budget for *Sicko* is reported at $9,000,000. International gross is reported at $9,000,000 bringing worldwide theatrical gross to $33,500,000.

The third is *Bowling for Columbine* with $21,146,000 from a run in only 248 theaters nationally. Together three out six top grossing documentaries films grossed $164,881,000 released from October 2002 to June 2007

Three of the top five documentary theatrical release films have a total worldwide gross of $314,576,000.This does not include DVD Sales.

The number 2 top-grossing documentary is *March of The Penguins,* at about $77, 500,000 domestically plus $52,000,000 internationally equals $129,000,500 worldwide. *An Inconvenient Truth* is number four grossing about $24,146,161 domestically and another $25,603,190 internationally bringing the worldwide gross to $49,749,351.

While these documentary numbers may sound impressive they are small when compared to fictional feature films. For example, at this writing *The Dark Knight,* a fictional theatrical release grossed $203.8 million in its first five days in release. Of note is that *The Dark Knight* cost about $185 million to make whereas most documentaries have much lower budgets.

International release revenues often equal or surpass domestic grosses for theatrical films. Documentary films may or may not have appeal internationally since many focus on issues of interest to domestic audiences.

The next thing to consider is DVD and tape sales for theatrical release documentaries. This does not include made for television documentary films. Numbers for DVD Sales are not always available but it appears that these revenues can vary. *Fahrenheit 9/11* reportedly sold about 2 million combined DVD and VHS units—about 70% of that figure, though, was bought by rental stores. It's expected to be the best selling documentary ever --" [by the end of its first week of release].

An Inconvenient Truth US DVD Sales have reached $31,692,021. *Sicko* has gained about $13,000,000 in DVD sales in the United States.

Feature length documentary films are also made for television and may be seen on HBO, Discovery Channel, National Geographic Channel, History Channel, and on many cable and network channels. *Planet Earth* a BBC HD production was seen on HD Cable Channels and subsequently sold about 28,000,000 copies grossing $160 million in DVD sales.

What about the other documentary films made for the big screen, how do they fare in the market place? *Super Size Me* cost $65,000 to make and grossed $29,529,529 worldwide, actually making $18 million of that outside the United States. DVD sales of 100,000 copies are reported.

Spike Lee's *4 Little Girls* made $218,000 in theatrical release domestically. *Jesus Camp* grossed $902,544, Academy Award Winner; *The Fog of War* grossed over 5 million worldwide at theaters. *Hoop Dreams* released in 1994 at a production cost of $700,000 grossed $12 million in theaters Worldwide.

Grizzly Man made $3.5 Million Worldwide. Released in 2005 *MurderBall* produced by MTV for $350,000, ranks number 55 in top grossing documentaries, grossed close to $2,000,000 Worldwide. The above examples, for the main part, do not site DVD Sales that may equal or surpass the theatrical release. Going direct to DVD is a common practice for Documentaries. PBS and HBO documentary films may never play in the theaters. Popular documentaries like *The Civil War* and others by Ken Burns have sold millions of copies in VHS and DVD but actual sales numbers seem hard to find.

As you can see, from the previous examples the cost of making the documentary, the production cost, is directly related to the profit available and the type of distribution required. This is not different than the fiction theatrical film world. It's always important to determine if the production cost of a project can be recouped and a profit made from distribution. Is there an audience for this subject? If a documentary appears that it may have wide appeal a theatrical release should be followed with a DVD release.

While documentary films may at times get away with limited production value, for the best distribution possibilities, a decent level of production value or broadcast quality is necessary. Higher production value usually requires a higher budget. Shooting on film is more expensive generally than shooting on a digital format, depending on how the documentary will be released. There is also money needed for prints and advertising that is usually put up by the distribution company and recouped before any distribution of profits.

The Future for Documentary Films and Videos

Documentaries that both inform and entertain will always find some type of distribution in the theatrical realm as Michael Moore has shown. But theatrical release is only one of an ever- growing assortment of ways to bring documentary subjects to the public. Direct to DVD distribution is a viable alternative to theatrical release for nonfiction productions shot on high-end digital formats or made for television.

Audiences may be targeted and reached on the internet. In a growing number of situations documentary filmmakers are opting to offer their work for download from the internet. There are films that can be downloaded to a PC or Mac computer, iPod or to a recording device that will make a DVD.

The future, with multiple options for distribution, will facilitate independent production of nonfiction and documentary films. Independent producers should plan on ways to best market and distribute their work.

One model for producing, marketing and distributing an independently made documentary or nonfiction production is to set up a web site for that project to start building interest and an audience as shooting and post-production proceeds. By setting up a web site for the project, the subject of the documentary is made available to search engines combing the internet. One producer of political documentaries, solicits pre-release purchase of his films as the project nears completion.

Endnotes)
2
Source TheNumbers.com/box office data
Gross numbers not adjusted for inflation and not including DVD Sales   Source TheNumbers.com/box office data and BoxOfficeMojo.com
        Source TheNumbers.com/box office data
        Source TheNumbers.com/box office data
        Source BoxOfficeMojo.com --Dark Knight' Begins Smashingly Brandon Gray July 23, 2008
        Source BoxOfficeMojo.com -- Brandon Gray October 5,2004

        Source TheNumbers.com
        Sources for all gross box office receipts from TheNumbers.com and BoxOfficeMojo.com

*KeyNote® Presentation with
Audio*

CHAPTER 17

DOCUMENTARY STYLE
NONFICTION PRESENTATIONS

CHAPTER 17

Documentary Style Nonfiction Presentations

Telling the story with photographs, slides, text and voice over (VO) and multimedia techniques.

There are scenes in the Academy Award winning documentary film *An Inconvenient Truth* which demonstrate what you can do using a documentary style multimedia approach in a presentation. President Al Gore uses projection of multiple slides on a large screen to bring to life the issue of global warming.

Eric Lee/Paramount Classics

Not every presentation needs to go these lengths to be interesting and informative but there are documentary techniques that will help any presentation come alive. What ever the subject try to tell a story that makes your presentation more than a series of slides with text and charts.

Presentation slides no longer need to be silent static images. They can have sound and with Apple's Keynote application they can have video images and animation incorporated into the slide In Power Point you can also build a series of slides that has movement and sound.

Basic Power Point and Keynote presentations.

In many ways the documentary film, *An Inconvenient Truth* is a slide presentation with commentary by a speaker. This can be an informative way to present information and in the case of this documentary film, interesting. But it also could have turned out slow and boring.

A slide with a lot of text requires your audience to read the text or for you to read it to them. Most people will not read the text but listen to what is being said. The text on the screen should only highlight the main points.

Photographs, illustrations, charts and graphic examples that help explain the text, can communicate ideas better than someone basically reading slides with text on them.

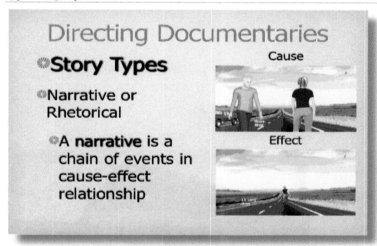

Directing Documentaries

⊕ Story - Narrative or Rhetorical

　⊕ A narrative is a chain of events in cause-effect relationship occurring in time an space. A story.

⊕ Rhetorical Exposition

　⊕ A rhetorical format consists of an introduction that explains or coveys the main idea. You then clarify the different aspects of the main idea in great detail. In the conclusion you wrap it all up and support your ideas in different words.

In actual use a color background and contrasting text might be used for the above slide. The above slide is cluttered with text.

It is easier to understand with less text (below) and some type of graphic.

Directing Documentaries

⊕ **Story Types**

⊕ Narrative or Rhetorical

　⊕ A **narrative** is a chain of events in cause-effect relationship

Cause

Effect

A transition such as a dissolve, fade-out/fade-in, wipe or other effect can be used to go from one slide to another.

Music and audio effects used purposely will improve production quality and help convey content. With Keynote presentations video clips may also be incorporated into the presentation as the whole slide or as a window in the slide. This brings a new dynamic to a presentation. Keep video clips short and at streaming compression rate since large files use more storage space.

The slide below has a small illustration and too much text bunched up and not contrasting enough with the background.

The slide below tells the story in the available space within the frame. It documents where each control is located. The illustration is larger.

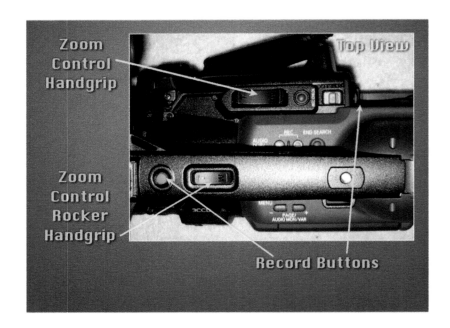

The following slides are part of a presentation that includes video, audio voice over and hyper links. It could be used as a POD Cast. The actual screen size is 1040 x 480.

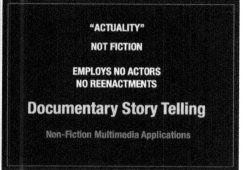

Slide 1 includes video clip   *Slide 2 includes VO*

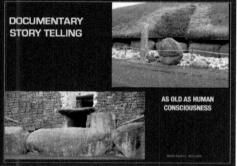

Each slide has a transition built in to move to the next slide. In this case the transitions take the form of a cube turning revealing the next slide.

Slide 3 includes VO   *Slide 4 Music and VO*

Presentation opens with 54 second clip and voice over narration.

The above slide has a lot of equipment and the text doesn't contrast with the background very well.

The slide below is better and could be used to launch into separate slides of each piece of equipment.

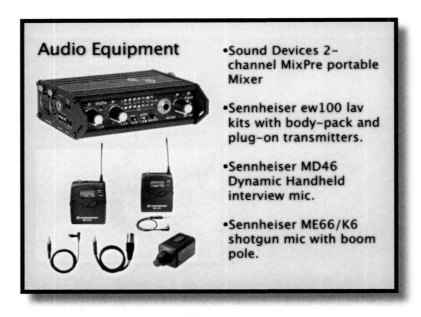

Slide 1 - Dissolve to Slide 2

Slide 2 - Dissolve to Slide 3 Note: Added labels identify inputs.

Slide 3 - Additional slides could be used to show CU's of Lavaliere microphones.

Write a script for your presentation.

A multi column script can be used for a number of different nonfiction media. For a presentation you might consider having 4 main columns. Columns, Slide number, Illustration & Audio and a forth optional column for a Story Board or rough sketch of the layout.

Slide	Text	Illustration & sound	Story Board
1	AUDIO EQUIPMENT Sound Devices - 2 channel mixer Sennheiser EW100...	Mixer, Lav's, Transmitter, hand held microphone, other parts of kit.	(Rough sketch of layout of slide.)
2	Audio Equipment Sound Devices 2 Channel mixer. (Label) 2 XLR Mic Inputs	CU Mixer with balloons naming parts.	(Rough sketch of layout of slide.)
3			

Note: A multiple column script can be easily constructed using the Table function in many word processing programs like Microsoft Word and Apple's Pages. There are also script writing programs available for AV Production. Story board programs like Story Board Quick and Frame Forge may be used to put together visualizations of frames especially if photographs are to be used.

Photographs and Video in Key Note or Power Point Presentations

Importing photographs and/or video clips for your presentation is easy to do in Key Note. The photograph or clip may occupy part of the slide frame or the entire frame. Video clips includes a bar to play and pause the clip. Video clips will also include audio if present.

If you are going to include photographs in your presentation it is usually easier and better to size, crop and prepare the photographs before bringing them in to the presentation program. Once inserted into the slide options are limited to basic re-sizing and positioning in the frame.

Video clips are best kept short (2 to 3 minutes maximum) because they will need to load and stream. The rate of streaming is related to the CPU speed, memory and size of the video file. Test the presentation out on the laptop that is being used for the presentation to see how it handles your video clips. Clips compressed for streaming on the internet should provide the best streaming speeds for a presentation. Download the presentation from external hard drives or USB devices to an internal hard drive to obtain maximum speeds.

Make sure your computer is connected to the projector and external PA or speakers systems for presentations in rooms where projectors are available. When using a Mac Book Pro you will need a video adapter to connect to a PC based monitor or projection system. Portable projectors are available and worth the price if you have a large audience.

Laptop built in speakers are small and may not convey the sound quality you would like. Small portable external speakers are an option when making a presentation in a small conference room using only a laptop screen. Also a remote allows you to change slides without being in front of the keyboard.

When traveling call ahead to find out what resources are available.

Using Other resources.

Keynote allows you to incorporate working spreadsheets and tables in the presentation. This can be a great tool for increasing participation by the audience and demonstrating variable concerns.

Using a DVD or CD for a Presentation.

A Keynote or Power Point presentation or multiple presentations could be placed on a CD and either played from CD or downloaded to another computer. Running the presentation from a CD or any external device may slow down how quickly slides change, video clips load and stream and how animation or special effects run. A Keynote presentation may be exported as a PDF file or HTML page.

Presentations can also be made in InDesign and exported as an interactive PDF with video clips, slide presentations and audio. It can also be exported in HTML format.

A slide presentation may be prepared and then incorporated into a DVD, with interactive menus, video clips, audio and other features. Using a DVD might useful in certain venues like exhibits and kiosks. DVD Studio Pro 4 is a program that is used to create full featured DVD's that can run on a computer DVD Drive and on set top devices.

Choosing Between Keynote and Power Point

Both of these programs have their limitations. Converting a fully produced presentation with voice over music and effects may be more than the program can handle when it comes to exporting it as a Quick time or other type movie. The best way to avoid problems is to be methodical in assembling the presentation. If there is voice over narration it would be a good idea to sync that up with the presentation before adding music and effects. Keep music and effects at a minimum and make sure their sound levels do not fight with the voice over.

Too much of anything is not good. To many words and crowded slides makes it difficult to read. Voice over and/or effects, used in excess can easily overwhelm the viewer.

Documentary Filmography

This is a short list of documentaries that fall into different areas of the nonfiction genre. In no way a definitive list of documentary films; this list is only a starting point with which to explore the world of nonfiction storytelling. Viewing them offers a sample of different styles and approaches to telling documentary or nonfiction stories. All films are listed in alphabetical order.

American Shopper – 2008 Cinema Libre – 87 min. Directed by Thomas Bojtar and Sybil Dessau. This is a good example of a Hybrid Documentary style story telling that creates an environment and then involves sincere participants in a staged or controlled event. Unlike Reality TV shows this style of nonfiction does not manipulate the participants or hire them to participate. American Shopper sets up a contest involving shopping in a supermarket in Columbia Missouri. It presents a humorous look a how people can get involved in what appears to be a new sport or activity.

An Inconvenient Truth – 2006 – Paramount Classics 96 min. Directed by Davis Guggenheim – "President" Al Core presents an eye opening, convincing view of the future of our planet and Global Warming. This documentary evolves around a presentation using graphics and slides that President Gore gives as he travels around the country.

Ballets Russes – 2005 –

Zeitgeist Video – 118 min. Directed by Dayna Goldfine and Dan Geller – Incorporating historic film footage, interviews and archival materials this moving documentary looks women and men who made up the Ballets Russes (Russian Ballet) companies that started in Paris and ultimately toured the world. A well made compilation documentary.

Berlin Symphony of A City – 1927 – image entertainment distributor – 62 min. Directed by Walther Ruttmann – Documentary as art, this film documents a dawn to dust day in the life Berlin, Germany set to symphony composed for the film. Ruttman was interested in light, patterns, rhythm and texture more then the subject matter itself. Today this film offers a look back in time as well as a visual and musical experience.

Bob Dylan – Don't Look Back – 1967 – Docu Rama – 96 min. Directed by D. A. Pennebaker Based on Bob Dylan's 1965 week long tour of England. Seen in this Cinema Verite or Direct

Cinema Documentary Film are Joan Baez, Alan, Price, Albert Grossman and Donavan. This film basically allows us to observe the action in a "fly on the wall" style. It is an interesting look at the tour process. There is also a famous scene where Dylan takes command of an interview with a Time Magazine reporter and proceeds to interrogate the interviewer.

Bowling For Columbine – 2002 MGM –119 min. Directed by Michael Moore – 2002 Oscar Winner Documentary Feature. A serious look at the culture of guns in the United States done with insight and humor making it a classic Michael Moore style documentary filmmaking.

Buena Vista Social Club 1999 – Road Movies/Sony/ Artisian (Spanish with English subtitles) – 90 min. Directed by Wim Wenders – Documentary reveals life stories, personalities, and music of Cuba's foremost folk musicians. This film takes the viewer from the Havana neighborhoods to Carnegie Hall in NYC and hen to Amsterdam. Great story and authentic music from Cuba.

Bush's Brain – 2004 – Tartan Video/TLA Releasing / Color – 80 min. Directed by Joseph Mealey and Michael Paradies Shoob. How Karl Rove engineered the campaign and election of G.W. Bush as President of the United States. Also explores Rove's influence on the administration and US foreign policy.

Chicago 10 – 2007 – C7 Films Inc/Participant – 90 min. – Directed by Brett Morgan – Opening night selection Sundance Film Festival - An interesting *hybrid documentary* incorporating archival footage, photographs and interviews with animated scenes. The actual court trial of the Chicago Protesters is animated but uses the actual transcripts from the trial read by actors as dialog. The animated scenes outside the courtroom seems like reenactments rather then actuality.

Children Of The Underground 2002 – Beltzberg Films/ HBO Documentary Release/ DocuRama – Academy Award Nominee – 104 min. Directed by Edet Beltzberg. - Shot on the streets of Bucharest, Romania this documentary introduces the viewer to a family of homeless children living in subway tunnels.

Comic Book Super Heroes Unmasked – 2003 – A&E TV Networks – 100 min. Looks at the history of comic book and comic book super heroes from the 60's to recent graphic novels. Good example of Cable Network historically based documentary format without recreations or dramatized action.

Crips and Bloods: Made in America - 2009 - Docuramafilms - 99 min. Directed by Stacy Peralta - Looks at a group of neighborhoods in the heart of Southern California, minutes from Beverly HIlls. This enclave surrounded by the American Dream is home to the Crips and Bloods two rival gangs that control the various sections of the area. The documentary traces the history of the neighborhoods and the rise of the gangs.

Crumb – 1995 – Sony Classic Pictures – 120 min. Rated "R" Directed by Terry Zwigoff - A profile or R. Crumb creator of Zap Comix, Mr. Natural and Fritz the Cat. This documentary looks at the life and work of this man and his often-bizarre world. It is an intimate portrait.

Dark Days – 2000 – Optmum Home Entertainment - 6 awards winner - Black & White / 94 min. Directed by Marc Singer. This documentary looks at life of homeless people who live in the dark, rat infested, unlit tunnels under Penn Station in New York City. Some of the residents have lived there for up to 25 years as the trains rumble in and out.

Dog Town and Z Boys – 2001 Sony Pictures Classic/ Vans off the wall – 91 Min. Directed by Stacy Peralta – Classic documentary about skateboarding and the "Z Boys," a group of street kids with an aggressive style of skateboarding. Their style of skateboarding has had a lasting impact on the sport and this documentary a lasting impact on dealing with the subject.

Devils Playground – 2001 – Stick Figure Productions – 77 min. – Directed by Lucy Walker This story follows Amish youth at 16 turned loose to experience the outside world until they can decide whether or not to commit to a life time within the Amish religion and culture.

Edward Hopper – 2007 - A National Gallery of Art Presentation –30 min. Directed by Carroll Moore – This film traces Hoppers varied influences and life experience. It uses archival footage and film, new footage, and actual paintings to create an insightful look into Hoppers life and work. This is an educational documentary that both entertains and informs on a number of levels. Narrated by Steve Martin.

Fahrenheit 9/11 – 2004 – Westside Productions IIC – 122 min – Best Picture Cannes film Festival – Directed by Michael Moore. "An examination of the role played by money and oil I the wake of the tragic events of 9/11. Moore at his best with satire and humor combined with revealing interviews with various people. This documentary accomplishes through satire, humor, interviews and insight the creation of objective reality that hits close to home. This documentary earned Michael Moore the wrath of the far right in the United States who has since tried to demonize him.

Farmingdale – 2004 – New Video Group/Docurama/POV – 78 min. – Special jury prize Sundance Film Festival Directed by Carlos Sandoval and Catherine Tambini. The story centers on the arrival of 1500 Mexican immigrant farm workers who settle in the Long Island, New York town of Farmingdale and the hostile reaction of the middle class community.

For All Mankind – 1989 – The Criterion Collection – 79 Min. Directed by Al Reinhart – This documentary is a compilation of NASA archival documentation of US Astronauts missions to the moon in 1969. Narrated by the Astronauts who made the historic journeys.

4 Little Girls – 1997 – HBO - Nominated for Oscar - 102 min. Directed by Spike Lee. An in depth exploration of how the death of "4 Little Girls" killed when a bomb planted in the basement of their church exploded. The documentary examines how this event had an influence on the civil rights movement. Incorporates archival photographs and film footage.

Fired-Up - Public Housing Is My Home – 1990 - J. R. Media Inc – Metropolitan Planning Council Chicago – 60 min. Emmy Award for Best Network Documentary Film. Directed by James R (Jim) Martin. This documentary examines the impact of the introduction of the concept of tenant management in Chicago Public Housing. Helping to train residents is Bertha Gilkey who successfully established the idea at Cochran Gardens in Chicago.

Food Inc – 2008 – Magnolia Pictures/Participant Media 91min. Directed by Robert Kenner – After watching this documentary it's difficult to consider eating meat or poultry again. This film is hard examination of the food processing industry and corporate farming in the USA.

Frost Nixon – 1977 – Liberation Entertainment – Directed by John Winther – First broadcast in 1977, this live broadcast interview of Richard Nixon by David Frost drew the largest world wide audience know at the time. It provides insight into interviewing techniques that might be used in a documentary film context. The interviews were used as the basis for a dramatic motion picture. This DVD Release focuses on the Watergate portion of the 28 hours of the original broadcasts.

Genghis Blues – 1999 – Wadi Rum – Docurama – 88 min. Oscar nominated – Directed by Roco Belic. Blind jazz musician Paul Pena hears singing, that he's unfamiliar with, on his radio and begins to learn the techniques of Tuvan throat-singing. The documentary takes us to the land of Tuva in Mongolia where Pena participates in the Khoomei triennial singing contest.

Gimmie Shelter- 1969 – Maysles Films Inc -
Viewing *Gimme Shelter*, A Maysles Films Inc Production, recently released on Blu-ray Disc by Criterion Collection, is a worthwhile trip back to December 1969, and the Altamonte Speedway near San Francisco, where we visit a free Rolling Stones Concert that some say ended an era. This Direct Cinema (Cinema Verite) documentary ultimately brings us to a Rolling Stones Concert, the final stop on a North American tour in 1969. There along with 300,000 mostly stoned flower children, a couple dozen mostly intoxicated Hell's Angels acting as security, *Jefferson Airplane, The Flying Burrito Brothers, Ike and Tina Turner* and of course the *Rolling Stones,* we witness chaos in the making.

Gunner Palace – 2004 – Nomados Film – Color – 87 min. Directed by Michael Tucker and Petra Epperkein. Shot by a reporter embedded with the 2/3 Field Artillery, aka. "The Gunners" for two months. This documentary gives the viewer a first person look at life for soldiers in Bagdad.

Harlan County USA – 1978 (Reissue 2004 DVD) – Criterian Collection – 104 min. Directed by Barbara Kopple – Classic Social Documentary that takes the viewer into the coal mines in Kentucky and into the lives of the men and women of Harlan County during a crucial period as they negotiate a union contract with Duke Power Company. Academy Award Winner, New York Film Festival and listed on the National Film Registry.

Hoop Dreams – 1994 – Filmline Features – Kartemquin Films and KTCA TV – Distributor Criterion Collection – 171 min. Directed by Steve James – Filmed over a five year period this film follows two young men as they navigate the complex world of
Scholastic Athletics while striving to overcome the intense pressure of family life and the reality of the Chicago Streets.

I Like Killing Flies – 2005 – New Video Group/Docurama Films/Mortal Films/Red Envelope Entertainment/ Think Film – 79 min. – Directed by Matt Mahurin. Sundance Film Festival Grand Jury Prize Winner. A cinema verite style documentary visit with Kenny

Shopsins at work in his Greenwich Village restaurant where he reins supreme. Shopsins not only cooks up food from a huge menu he philosophies on life in an often-humorous fashion.

INSIDE JOB - 2011 Oscar Winner 109 Min.- Directed by Charles Ferguson. Inside Job tells the nonfiction story of the global economic crisis of 2008 including the history that leads up to this disaster. Inside Job goes beyond documenting the event from a historical perspective; it discusses the cause of the catastrophe, and names the culprits who cashed in, benefiting at the expense of the taxpayers. The documentary does all this in a way that is insightful and not difficult to comprehend.

Into Great Silence – 2007 – Zeitgeist Films – Directed by Philip Groning --162 min. In 1984 Groning requested permission from the Carthusian order to make a documentary about them. They said they would get back to him. Sixteen years later they said they were ready. Groning went on his own and lived with the monks at the Grande Chartreuse in the French Alps. The documentary has no score, no interviews, no voice over, no artificial lighting, and no archival footage. It brings the audience in to the reality of monastic life.

Iraq for Sale – The War Profiteers – BraveNew Films – 70 min. Directed by Robert Greenwald. Greenwald is one of the leaders in attack documentaries, starting with *Wal-Mart, the high cost of low price.* In **Iraq For Sale** he makes a strong case is made about war profiteers and their gains from the Iraq War.

Jesus Camp – 2006 – A & E Cable Network – 84 min. Directed by Heidi Ewing Rachel Grady – Follows Levi, Rachel and Tory to Pastor Becky Fisher's "Kids on Fire" summer Camp in Devils Lake, North Dakota where children as young as 6 are taught to become dedicated Christian Soldiers in God's Army.

Koyaanisqatsi 1982/ Naqoyqatsi 2002/ Powaqqatsi 2002 - 87 min; 89 min; 97 min. – MGM/Buena Vista Home Entertainment/MGM - Directed by Francis Ford Coppola, Godfrey Reggio; Steven Soderbergh; Francis Ford Coppola, Godfrey Reggio. – Documentary trilogy that is both beautiful and moving in it exploration of human relationship with the planet.

Krump – 2005 – Aroustry Home Entertainment and Krump Kings Inc. 90 min. Interesting documentary about a form of Dancing called Krump.

Louisiana Story – 1948 – Home Vision Entertainment - Oscar Nominated - Black & White – 78 min. – Directed by Robert J. Flaherty. Standard Oil funded this documentary at a time when they were being scrutinized for oil drilling in Louisiana. However, they gave Flaherty complete freedom to make this documentary.

Lost Boys of Sudan – 2003 – POV/Docurama - 87 min. - Directed by Megan Mylan and Jon Shenk. Follows two teenage Sudanese boys on a journey from Africa to America.

March of the Penguins – 2005 – Warner Independent Pictures – Academy awarded - 80 min. – Directed by Luc Jacquet. This theatrically released documentary follows the migration of emperor Penguins as they walk across a frozen continent. Narrated by Morgan Freeman the film is moving and insightful.

Man with the Movie Camera – 1929 – Image Entertainment – Black & White – 68 min. – Directed by Dziga Vertov. This early documentary experimented with creating a new cinematic language that used no script and put the filmmakers in the film. Interesting special effects for its day.

Maya Lin – 1994 – DocuRama – 83 min. Directed by Freida Lee Mock – Academy Award Best Documentary 1994 – Reveals the contentious beginning of the design and construction of the Vietnam Veterans Memorial and how a young female architect's design became controversial after she won an open contest to pick the design. The documentary also looks into Maya Lin's career subsequent to the Vietnam Memorial. An excellent documentary that incorporates archival footage and interviews with Maya Lin and others involved in the process of designing and building the memorial.

Man On A Wire – 2008 – Magnolia Home Entertainment – Oscar Winner -90 min. - Directed by James Marsh.

Murderball – 2005 – Think Film/MTV Films/1 More Film - 88 min. - Directed by Henry Alex Rubin and Dana Adam Shapiro. A well made theatrical documentary that documents the US athletes involved in Wheel Chair Rugby, aka "*Murderball*" in their competition with Canada as they move toward the 2004 Olympics in Athens. This story has drama, conflict and all the ingredients you would find in a fiction film.

Nanook Of The North – 1922 – Criterion Collection - Black & White – 79 min. - Directed by Robert J. Flaherty. Considered by many as the first feature length documentary film to play in theaters this film has not lost any of its appeal. Flaherty wanted to show the Inuit way of life and preserve a way of life that was fast disappearing as European influence changed it. Flaherty had no rules about what an anthropological documentary should be and really didn't set out to make an anthropological documentary. Still he did manage to create a historical record of Inuit life at that time.

Night and Fog – 1955 – Argos Films/Criterion Collection – 32 min. Directed by Alain Resnais. This strong documentary examines man's inhumanity to man as it explores the German death camps shortly after the Second World War ended. Resnais combines archival photographs and film footage with new footage shot in the empty camps. A moving and timeless documentary statement.

No Direction Home – 2005 – Paramount Pictures - 208 min. - Directed by Martin Scorsese. Bob Dylan's life from his roots in Minnesota to Greenwich Village through to today. An in depth exploration of the man and his music.

Orwell Rolls In His Grave – 2004 – Sky Island Film - 84 min. - Directed by Robert Kane Pappas. "...explores what the media doesn't like to talk about – itself.

Parrots of Telegraph Hill – 2005 – Shadow Distribution Inc. - 83 min. – Directed by Judy Irving. Tells the story of Mark Bittner, who cares for a flock of non-indigenous parrots in San Francisco. Filmed and edited in such away that we get to know Mark and many of the parrots by name.

Planet Earth – 2006 –- BBC Natural History Series - 150 min. – Directed by BBC Natural History Unit. An amazingly beautiful documentary, that looks at the entire planet in HD. Shot 200 locations around the planet.

Primary – 1960 – Docurama/Robert Drew Collection – 60min. - Directed by Robert Drew. An American "Direct Cinema" (Cinema Verite) film, that takes the viewer on the Democratic presidential primary campaign trail in Wisconsin with John F. Kennedy and Hubert Humphrey. The "fly on the wall" style of filming shows the candidates in a candid and straight forward fashion.

Religulous – 208 – LionsGate and Thousand Words/Bill Maher – 101min. – Directed by Larry Charles – This hosted by Bill Maher Documentary takes an irreverent and comedic look at organized religion in the United States.

Riding Giants – 2004 – Setsune, llc and Studio Canal – Distributed y Sony Picture Classics – 100 min – Directed by Stacy Peralta – This film uses graphics, interviews, archival footage and documents, and other techniques to trace the history and culture of Big Wave Surfing. Excellent documentary, entertaining and informative.

Roger and Me – 1989 – Warner Bros. - 91 min. - Directed by Michael Moore. First major documentary by Michael Moore sets the mold for his particular style of in your face documentary filmmaking.

Salesman – 1968 – Maysles Films - Black & White – 85 min. - Directed by Albert Maysles and David Maysles. Visit with bible salesman as the go door-to-door selling bibles, meeting with sales managers and hanging out at local diners. Direct Cinema documentary that lets you feel what it's like to be a bible salesman.

Scratch – 2002 – Palm Pictures – 92 Min. Sundance Film Festival selection – Directed by Doug Pray. Explores the world of the Hip Hop DJ from the birth of Hip- Hop to the invention of "scratching" to its recent explosion as a musical movement called "Turntabism." This is a well directed and edited documentary.

Shine A Light – 2008 – Paramont Classics – 121 min. Directed by Martin Scorsese. Rolling Stones in concert face a few questions about how long they've survived. Great music event documentary, play it loud. Blu-ray release is excellent.

Sketches of Frank Gehry –2006 – Sony Pictures Classics Release – 84 min. Directed by Sidney Pollack – Looks inside the world and mind of Frank Gehry a world acclaimed architect who's work includes contemporary buildings such as the Walt Disney Concert Hall in Los Angeles and the Guggenheim Museum in Bilbao, Spain.

Style Wars – 1978 – Docurama/ New Video Group – Academy Award Winner - 52 min. – Directed by Arnold Shapiro. Classic documentary about the origins of the "Hip-Hop and graffiti artists movement that emerged in New York City in the late 1970's.

Sound And Fury – 2000 – PBS – 80 min. - Academy Award Nominee – Directed by Josh Aronson. Through the eyes of one family this film examines how the deaf community feels about cochlear impants a device that can help the deaf to hear.

Super Size Me – 2004 – Kathbur Pictures – 100min. – Directed by Morgan Spurlock - In this hybrid documentary the filmmaker subjects himself to a 30 day diet of eating only at McDonalds Restaurants. He explores issues involved with fast food and obesity as well as the push by Fast Food Restaurants to offer large high calorie upgrades.

The Bridge – 2006/7 – Koch Lorer films – 94 min. – Directed by Eric Steel. During a one year period this film documents daily the Golden Gate Bridge where 24 people commit suicide by jumping off the bridge. This documentary was shot from a number of camera positions and every attempt was made to call authorities about potential jumpers. Relatives of survivors are interviewed as well as one jumper who survived the fall.

The Civil War – 1990 Public Broadcasting Service (PBS) – Distributed by Warner Home Video – 11 hours – Directed by Ken Burns - "Hailed as a film masterpiece and landmark in historical story telling" this documentary employs 100% actuality materials, no re-enactments, only historic photographs, archival documentation in many forms, archival film footage, letters from Civil War Soldiers; other quotes read voice over, contemporary footage of civil war areas, paintings, graphics and interviews with scholars. Ken Burns has used this method of storytelling successfully in a large number of documentary films. According

to Erik Barnouw, author of a *History of Nonfiction Film,* the films won Burns an invitation to membership in the Society of American Historians previously only available to authors of historical books. This –"also was, recognition of documentary a medium for the writing of history." Other documentary films by Ken Burns include *Brooklyn Bridge (1981); The Shakers: Hands to Work, Hearts to God (1984) among others. More recently in 2006 he produced an 15 hour documentary on the World War II titled THE WAR.*

The Cove - 2009 - Lions Gate - 96 min. - Directed by Louie Psihoyos - Oscar Best Documentary 2010 - Tells the story of the Japanese practice of selling and slaughtering dolphins in the town Tajji in Japan. A group of documentary filmmakers goes undercover to find out what goes on in a highly guarded cove on the coast. Looking at Flipper will never be the same after seeing this documentary.

The Devil and Daniel Johnston – 2006 – Sony Pictures – 110 min. – Directed by Henry S. Rosenthal and Ted Hope. A story about underground music musician and artist Daniel Johnston, including his work and his struggle with mental illness.

The Harvest of Shame – 1960 New Video Group/CBS/ Docurama - 55 min. Directed by Fred W. Friendly – Television style documentary hosted by Edward R Murrow and Fred Friendly, presented by CBS News. Looks at the situation facing migrant farm workers living in Florida but transported north to pick crops in season.

The Fog Of War – 2003 – Sony Pictures Classic – 107 min. Directed by Erroll Morris – Academy Award 2003 – Best Documentary Feature – An interview with former Secretary of Defense Robert Strange McNamara as he reflects on his tenure during the Vietnam War. Excellent archival footage structured around eleven "rules" McNamara has learned from.

The King of Kong, A Fistful of Quarters –2007 - New Line Cinema – 90 min. Directed by Hybrid documentary look at the "cut throat " world of Donkey Kong competition. A humorous exploration of the Donkey Kong game and individuals involved the competition.

The Last Waltz – 1978 – Metro Goldwyn Mayer – Aprox. 120 minutes – Directed by Martin Scorsese – This well made documentary covers a concert that was promoted as the last performance of the Band. Shot in 35mm Scorsese lit and dressed a concert hall in San Francisco and

filmed the concert. He also did interviews with the musicians and to make this more then an event documentary. Scorsese used multiple cameras and did a shooting script on how he would shoot the film. The film has been re-released on DVD with Dolby sound in 2006.

The Plow That Broke The Plains – 1936 – U.S. Resettlement Administration/ America's National History Archives - 25 min. – Directed by Pare Lorentz. – Commissioned by the US Department of Agriculture, this film along The River, also made by Pare Lorenz, played in theaters until Congress deemed them propaganda because the US government paid to have them made. This led to laws being made about US government made films being shone in US theaters.

The Story of Anvil – 2009 – Little Dean's Yard and Amnisha Films – 80 min. Directed by Sasha Gervasi – An interesting, often humorous look at the struggles of Anvil, a heavy metal band that started out strong but never quite made it.

The US vs John Lenin – 2006 – Lionsgate – 96 min. – Directed by David Leaf and John Scheinfeld. This film explores the attempt by the US government to prevent John Lenin from living in the United States. Incorporates archival footage of Lenin and

Yoko Ono giving interviews from their bedroom.

The Weather Underground 2003 – New Video Group/ Docurama/The free History Project/Kqed Public Television/ITVS – 92 min. – Directed by Sam Green.

United States of America v. Thomas B Kin Chong – a/k/a Tommy Chong – 2006 – Blue Chief Entertainment – 78 min. – Directed by Josh Gilbert. Entertaining and informative documentary about how Tommy Chong was setup, arrested, tried and convicted of selling drug paraphernalia across state lines.

Veer – 2005 - A Series of Documentaries – A Dr. Martens Film Project – Directed by Doug Pray - A series of short documentaries previewed at Silver Doc film festival. These short documentary profiles show that it is possible to tell a documentary short story.

When The Levees Broke – 2006 – HBO – 256 min. - Subtitles: French, Spanish – Directed by Spike Lee. This is an in depth and insightful look at New Orleans and its residents during and after Hurricane Katrina.

Who Killed The Electric Car – 2006 – Sony Pictures Classics – 93 min. – Directed by Chris Paine. The history of the electric car and how GM created a

successful electric car in the 1980's, then pulled it off the market destroying all production models made.

Why We Fight – 2005 – Sony Pictures Classics – 98 min. – Directed by Eugene Jarecki -- Grand Jury Prize Sundance Film Festival. Explores issues pertaining to the US military-industrial complex.

With One Voice – 2009 – Forest Way Productions – 78 min. Directed by Eric Temple – 2009 Telly Award -- Educational and informative documentary that explores the notion of mysticism in a number of mainstream world religions. Well shot and edited.

Winged Migration – 2001 – CBC - Oscar Nominee - 89 min. - Directed by Jacques Perrin, Jacques Cluzaud and Michel Debats. Nature documentary that follows the migration of a variety of birds through 40 countries.

Wordplay – 2006 – IFC films – 85 min. Directed by Patrick Creadon – Documentary about why 50 million Americans do Cross Word Puzzles and the World of Will Shortz known to many as NPR's Puzzle Master.

General Bibliography and **Recommended** *Reading*

Alten, Stanley R. *Audio in media.* Belmont, Calif: Wadsworth Pub., 1986. Print.

Artis, Anthony Q. *The Shut Up and Shoot Documentary Guide A Down & Dirty DV Production.* New York: Focal, 2007. Print.

Barnouw, Erik. *Documentary a history of the nonfiction film.* New York: Oxford UP, 1993. Print.

Bernard, Sheila Curran. *Documentary Storytelling, Second Edition Making Stronger and More Dramatic Nonfiction Films.* New York: Focal, 2007. Print.

Carlson, Verne. *Professional lighting handbook.* Boston: Focal, 1985. Print.

Crowell, Thomas A. The Pocket Lawyer For Filmmakers. Boston: Focal Press 2007 Print

Grant, Barry K and Sloniowski, Jeannette, Documenting the Documentary Close Readings of Documentary Film and Video. Detroit: Wayne State UP, 1998. Print.

Edmonds, Robert. *Anthropology On Film.* Dayton: Pflaum, 1974.

Family of man the 30th anniversary edition of the classic book of photography. New York, N.Y: Museum, Distributed by Simon & Schuster, 1983. Print.

Frankfurt, Harry G. *On Truth.* New York: Alfred A. Knopf, 2006. Print.

Garrand, Timothy Paul. *Writing for multimedia entertainment, education, training, advertising, and the World Wide Web.* Boston: Focal, 1997. Print.

Hampe, Barry. *Making Documentary Films and Videos A Practical Guide to Planning, Filming, and Editing Documentaries.* New York: Holt Paperbacks, 2007. Print.

Hardy, Forsyth. *John Grierson.* London and Boston: Faber and Faber, 1979. Print.

Holt, Jason. *The Daily Show and Philosophy (The Blackwell Philosophy and Pop Culture Series).* Grand Rapids: Blackwell, 2007. Print.

Houghton, Buck. *What a producer does the art of moviemaking (not the business).* Los Angeles: Silman-James, Distributed by Samuel French Trade, 1991. Print.

Jacobs, Lewis. *The Documentary Tradition.* Second ed. New York: W.W. Norton and Company, 1979. Print.

Konigsberg, Ira. *The Complete Film Dictionary.* New York: Meridian, 1987. Print.

Lumet, Sidney. *Making movies.* New York: Vintage, 1996. Print.

Martin, Clifford,. *Microphones how they work & how to use them.* Blue Ridge Summit, Pa: G/L Tab, 1977. Print.

Murch, Walter. In The Blink of an Eye. Second Edition. A Perspective on Film Editing. Sillman-James Press. 2001. Print

Wiese, Michael. *Film & video budgets.* Studio City, CA: M. Wiese Productions, 1995. Print.

GLOSSARY

(Please submit additions and suggestions to jr@ jrmartinmedia.com

FILM, VIDEO, DIGITAL, MULTIMEDIA AND DOCUMENTARY FILMMAKING TERMS

1/3 - 2/3 RULE - This rule states that one-third of the depth of field is in front of the focus point and two-thirds-is behind the focus point.

16MM - The midsize film format used for many professional filmed productions. 16mm film contains two perforations on each side of a frame; it contains 40 frames per one foot of film and travels through the camera at the rate of 36 feet per minute at sync sound speed of 24 frames per second.

35MM - The standard film format for shoot most professional filmed productions. 35mm film contains four perforations on each side of a frame; it contains 16 frames per one foot of film and travels through the camera at the rate of 90 feet per minute at sync sound speed of 24 frames per second.

3/2 PULLDOWN - Since film is usually shot at 24 frames per second and video has 30 frames per second, we need to make up 6 frames per second when transferring film to video. This is done by adding an extra field to every other film frame, (there are 2 fields per video frame), resulting in a field sequence of AA, BBB, CC, DDD etc. This process is called 3/2 pull down. There is no 3/2 pull down when the film is shot at 30fps in NTSC, or 25fps in PAL because in these cases the film and video are running at the same rate, (1 film frame per 1 video frame).

4:2:2 / 4:4:4 - See analog / digital and CCIR-601

A

AATON - A French company that makes motion picture cameras. They developed Autoscore and the Key linker to facilitate easier syncing and tracking of picture and sound during postproduction. See also Arriflex.

AATONCODE - (similar in concept to Arri FIS). A code exposed along the edge of the film at the same time the image is exposed. Aaton Code contains time code; shoot date and camera I.D. information. Only certain cameras can expose this code. Aaton Code contains the same time code as that is recorded simultaneously on the audio deck. During film transfer, Aaton Code is decoded by a reader attached to the telecine, (Key linker). The audio locks to the matching Aaton Code and automatically syncs with the picture. This eliminates the need for a slate during shooting since sync can be determined at all times via the Aaton Code. (A visual/audio slate such as clapboard or smart-slate can be used as a back up.) See also Key linker.

ABOVE THE LINE - That portion of a motion picture's budget that covers major expenditures incurred or negotiated before the actual shooting begins. May also refer to the creative positions within a film crew, including the producer, director, screenwriter, and the actors.

AC-3 – Audio Compression 3 – Marketed as Dolby Digital and used in DVD, HDTV, and some movie theaters.

ACADEMY APERTURE - The standard ratio, for shooting and projecting films, set in 1932 by the Academy of Motion Picture Arts and Sciences. The ratio of width to height is 4:3, or more commonly expressed as 1.33:1. Today, films are shot and projected in wider aspect ratios of 1.66:1 or 1.85:1.

ACETATE PRINT - A slow burning film print made with an acetate base that replaced the highly flammable nitrate print in the 1940s.

ACTUALITY – A term used in documentary filmmaking to define an event which has been recorded in some way and/or observed that is happening in reality, that does not employ actors and has not been staged or scripted.

AMBIENT LIGHT - The natural light in an environment excluding the use additional supplemental lighting.

AMBIENT SOUND – The natural sounds and noises in an area where shooting is taking place. (See Audio Mix).

AMERICAN SOCIETY OF CINEMATOGRAPHERS (ASC) - An honorary organization of Cinematographers. To become a member you must be invited by the membership based on your body of work as a cinematographer.

ANALOG / DIGITAL - An example of **analog**: a plucked guitar string vibrates the air around it. These airwaves in turn vibrate a small membrane in a microphone. This membrane translates those vibrations into fluctuating electronic voltages. During recording to tape, these voltages charge magnetic particles on the tape, which when played back will duplicate the original voltages, and hence the original sound. Recording pictures works similarly, except that instead of air vibrating a membrane, fluctuating light strikes an electronic receptor that changes those fluctuations into voltages. Analog describes real world sound and images that have been translated into continually changing electronic voltages.
Composite analog - 1", 3/4", VHS
Component analog - Betacam/ SP, M2
In the **digital** world, the same varying voltages are sampled or measured at a specific rate, (e.g. 48,000 times a second or "48K"). Because of sampling, a digital signal is segmented into steps that define the overall quality of the signal. A signal sampled at 48K is better than one sampled at 44.1K. These samples are represented by bits, (0's and 1's) which can be processed and recorded. The more bits a sample has the better the picture or sound quality, (e.g. "10 bit" is better than "8 bit"). A good digital signal will have a high number of samples, (sampling rate) and a high number of bits, (quantizing). Digital processing clears the way for multiple, perfect copies or "clones", because it is the bits that are copied instead of the analog voltages.
Composite digital - D2, D3
Component digital - D1, D5, DBC, DCT, DVC

4:2:2 refers to the sampling ratio of the three parts of a component color difference signal, (one luminance channel, and two chroma channels). For every 4 samples of the luminance channel, there are 2 samples for each of the chroma channels. As the sampling rate increases, so does quality. In 4:4:4, the chroma channels are sampled equally to the luminance channel, creating better color definition. Similarly, 8:8:8 increases picture quality with an even higher sampling rate. Currently the component digital tape recording standard is 4:2:2.

ANALOG TELEVISION - NTSC – United States, Canada, Japan; **PAL** – Europe, Asia, Oceania. **PAL-M** – Brazil; **RS-343** - Military.

ANAMORPHIC - An image that is squeezed horizontally before being recorded on film or video. Later the image is un-squeezed back to the original picture for viewing. This process to is used to fit a wide picture into a smaller frame so that later it can be "unpacked" and viewed on a wide screen. The aspect ratio for anamorphic filming may be referred to as 2.35:1 or 2.40:1. If one were to view the squeezed picture before it was un-squeezed, the persons or objects in the frame would appear tall and skinny. The squeezing/un-squeezing happens by means of camera and projector lenses, or electronically in the case of video. See also aspect ratio.

ANSWER PRINT - (Trial Picture/Sound - Composite Print). A print used to identify scenes or shots that require further correction in color, density and sound quality. The final composite print has all the corrections accomplished.

See print.

ANTI HALATION BACKING - An opaque layer on the back of the film base to prevent internal light reflections in the film.

APERTURE/CAMERA - The opening in a camera that defines the area of each frame exposed and at which each frame stops during exposure or projection.

APERTURE/LENS - The opening in a lens, usually formed by an adjustable iris, which controls the amount of light passing to and exposing the film.

APERTURE/PLATE - The metal plate within the camera that limits the area of the film frame exposed to light.

APPLE BOXES - Wooden boxes used by the grip department for various functions. They come in four basic sizes - full, half, quarter and eighth (also called a pancake).

ARC LIGHT - A high intensity light used to supply very bright illumination-provided by an electric flow (or "arc") crossing between two electrodes.

ARCHIVAL FOOTAGE – Film, Video or Photographs drawn from library archives, historic sources or other sources.

ARRI FIS - Film Ident/Sync System. (Also referred to as "Arricode", similar in concept to Aaton Code). A barcode exposed along the edge of the film at the same time the image is exposed. Arri FIS contains the same time code as that is being recorded simultaneously on the audio deck. Only certain cameras can expose this code. During film transfer, Arricode is decoded by a reader attached to the telecine, (Keylinker). The audio locks to the matching Arricode and automatically syncs with the picture. This eliminates the need for a slate during shooting since sync can be determined at all times via the Arricode. (A visual/audio slate such as clapboard or smart-slate can be used as a back up.) See also Keylinker.

ARRIFLEX - A German company (Arnold & Richter = ARRI) that makes camera and film production equipment, and developed Arri FIS to facilitate easier syncing of picture and audio during post production. See also Aaton

Artifacts – Distortion that occurs when audio or video is compressed to a low bit rate, also called noise.

ASF – (Advanced Streaming Format) An audio or video file encoded for use with Windows Media Player. Also see, WMV, WMA and AVI.

ASX – (ASF Streaming Redirector File) A Windows Media container file. ASX is a metafile that provides information about ASF media files, including descriptions of multimedia content. When a browser links to an ASX file, the ASX file in turn links to an ASF file on a server that points to a Windows Media audio/video streaming file.

ASA SPEED - (See ISO, EI), or DIN). Original acronym for film sensitivity to light as rated in numbers the higher the number, the more sensitive to light. (12, 16, 20, 25, 32, 40, 50, 64, 80, 100, 125, 160, 200, 250, 320, 400, 500, 640, 800) established originally by the American Standards Association (ASA).

The International Standards Organization (ISO) has replaced ASA.

ASC - American Society of Cinematographers.

ASPECT RATIO - The width-to-height ratio of both the film frame and the projected image. In the silent era, the standard aspect ratio-devised by Thomas Edison-was 1.33:1 The 1.33:1 aspect ratio is known as the Academy aperture. Standard television aspect ratio is currently four units wide by three units high, or 4:3. Super 16mm aspect ratio is 15:9, or said another way, 1.66 units wide for every 1 unit high, otherwise listed as 1.66:1 (read 1.66 to 1), or simply "one-six-six". High definition television (HDTV) is slightly wider at 16:9 or 1.77 units for every 1 unit high ("one-seven-seven"). Even wider still are theatrical projections with common aspect ratios of 1.85:1 and anamorphic 2.35:1 and 2:40:1. An entire wide screen image displayed on a regular television will have a black band at the top and bottom. This is called letterbox.

ASSISTANT DIRECTOR (AD) - The crewmember responsible for organization and efficiency on the set.

ATTENUATOR - A filter with a continuous gradual change from a specific density to clear glass, or from heavier to lighter density. Sometimes used to designate a Graduated Filter.

AUTOCONFORM - The process of automatically conforming a show from camera original film, (transferred to video), to an edited video copy. This process is used when a client edits with work print, or a video off-line system, then returns to the lab where the original negative is cut into reels of selected takes, (arranged in order). These select reels are then transferred to videotape. The edited work print or video off-line copy is then transferred to different videotape. In on-line, the editors use an EDL disk created by the lab that allows them to find each scene on the film transfer masters (via time code), and accurately place them in the right place on the edited work print/off-line copy. (The new color corrected pictures are inserted over the off-lined pictures). This eliminates the need to eye match each scene individually, or to manually enter the time codes for each edit. Since all the information is contained in an EDL, the editor can assemble the show in "auto" mode. A half hour show might take only a few hours to assemble, (although there's a lot more that needs to happen before the show is complete, e.g. titles, credits, effects, etc.). The key to making this work is the lab. They keep track of all pertinent numbers, and deliver a package ready to roll. Careful, consistent lab work, and obsessive attention to detail are critical for a successful Auto conform.

AUDIO RECORDING -- Recording the sound for any type of project in sync or with out sound (MOS) at sufficient levels and quality that it can be used for all aspects of the project. Audio Recording includes Dialog, Effects, Live Music or Events and Ambient Sound to be used a presence or room tone if required.

AUDIO MIXER (Sound Mixer)-- An individual who mixes sound and the name of the device used to set levels and mix multiple channels of incoming audio before it is recorded. In Post-Production an editor who specializes in mixing sound and an Audio Engineer who mixes sound in a final mix. Note: The words "Audio" and "Sound" are often used synonymously.

AUDIO LEVELS – Setting audio levels begins with the notion of working toward a balanced signal to noise ratio, usually a low signal to noise ratio. If someone is speaking we want to hear his or her voice clearly and eliminate as much of the back ground noise as possible. If the background noise is important for some reason a separate recording could be made and mixed at desired levels in post-production.

Audio Gain Control (AGC) - A feature on most camcorders that automatically adjusts the recording sound levels on the camera. This feature may cause high noise problems when there is no signal and the automatic gain control searches for sound.

AUDIO CHECK or SOUND CHECK – The sound or audio technician requests to check his or her levels before actually recording them. "Quiet On The Set" except for the source of the sound is required. It is important to check both the audio going into the camera and the audio actually being recorded in a single system situation such as using a camcorder that has audio recording functions. When using a double system-recording device such as a Nagra Recorder, a switch allows the recordist to hear what is coming in and what has been recorded at any time.

AVAILABLE-LIGHT PHOTOGRAPHY and

CINEMATOGRAPHY - To shoot a film without the use of additional lamps or artificial light.

AVI – (Audio/Video Interleave) A file format containing different types of rich media data, such as audio, video, and metadata.

Avid – Widely used NLE software company.

B   **TOP**

B-ROLL – Any footage that supports the action, interviews or continuity of the story. Footage shot to complement and illustrate topics and information in the story.

B & W - Abbreviation for Black and White visual images on film or other media.

BABY LEGS - Short tripod used for low-angle shots.

BABY SPOT - Focusable studio lamp with a Fresnel lens and a 500-watt to 1000-watt bulb.

BACK LIGHT - A light source positioned above and behind the subject. It provides texture and definition to the hair and separation from the background.

BACKING - Painted or photographed background used behind set windows and doors.

Backbone – A segment of a network that is higher speed than the rest of the network that connects segments together.

Backhaul – Is a means for sending live rich media from its origination point to a point from which it can be distributed over a network. For example, backhaul is used to deliver a live SvBroadcast from Chicago, to a Smart Video data center, encoded and then be made available to viewers on their individual computers live over the public Internet anywhere in the world.

Bandwidth – In digital terms, the capacity of a connection to transmit data, expressed as data speed in bits per second (bps), thousands of bits per second (Kbps) or Millions of bits per second (Mbps). Smart Video works with Dial-Up and broadband connections 23Kbps or greater.

BARNDOOR -Two or four metal shields hinged in front of a lamp to limit and shape the pattern of light.

BARNY - A padded camera cover used to reduce camera noise.

BASE - The acetate support component to any film stock.

BEST BOY - Electrician who is second in line of command after the gaffer or key grip. Their main duties include equipment maintenance. The electrical best boy is also responsible for power distribution.

Bit – Describes the smallest unit of computer storage. A Bit may have a value of either 0 or 1. See Byte.

Bit Rate – The speed at which computer binary content is sent through a computer or over a network, usually measured in kilobits or megabits per second (Kbps or Mbps).

BLACKOUT - Covering a window or doorway with black material (visquene or duvatyne) to prevent light from entering.

BLACK WRAP - A flexible material that may be wrapped

around a light to cut or shape the light as it falls on the set.

BLOCKING - Staging the actors or subjects in relation to the camera and establishing the camera movements for a given shot.

BNC – One type of video cable connector used to connect various video equipment including monitors and cameras.

BOOM - A counterbalanced extension device, used as a support for a camera or a microphone.

BOOM SHOT - A continuous single shot incorporating any number of camera levels and angles. Achieved through the use of a boom arm, Jib or crane.

BOOSTER LIGHT - Usually a carbon arc, an HMI, or cluster quartz lamps used on exterior locations for augmenting the daylight, especially when filling the shadows.

BOSCH / BTS / PHILLIPS - (First Bosch, then BTS, currently Phillips.) Manufacturer of telecines, and other video equipment.
FDL-60 / FDL-90 - Earlier model telecines made by Bosch. Their light source comes from an inexpensive and not-so-temperamental halogen light bulb, (as opposed to the CRT's used in Ranks). These machines use CCD sensor technology.
Quadra - A newer model, high quality telecine from Phillips. The Quadra uses a Halogen light source and CCD sensor technology.
Spirit / Datacine / (Kodak "Thunder") - Top of the line telecine made by Phillips. This machine creates images for use in the high definition world. It

uses a Xenon light source, and CCD sensor technology.

BOTTOMER - A flag used to block unwanted light from the bottom of the light source. May also be called a bottom shelf or shelf.

BRACKET - Shooting at the correct exposure plus one or two stops over exposed and one or two stops underexposed.

BREAKDOWN - A detailed list of everything required for the shooting of a film, scene-by-scene and day-by-day.

BREATHING - The characteristic of some lenses which gives the illusion of zooming while changing the focus of the lens.

BRIGHTNESS - Ability of a surface to reflect or emit light in the direction of the camera. Also referred to as luminance.

BROAD - A single or double lamp designed to provide even illumination over a relatively wide area. Used as a general fill light.

Broadband – Describes a high-speed network connection (ISDN, DSL, Cable Modem, T-1) as opposed to a dial-up modem connection.

Broadcast Page – An HTML page, which is opened to facilitate the delivery to a viewer of audio, video, graphic and textural information during an SvBroadcast. When used in live broadcasts, the Broadcast Page also incorporates interactive viewer chat and live call in with subject matter experts and presenters.

BRUTE - A type of arc lamp that uses 225 am

BUCKLE SWITCH - A switch within the camera that acts as

a safety device and stops the camera in the event of a camera jam or rollout.

BUDGET – a formal document showing planned expenses for a project.

Buffering – Is similar to the concept of "pre-filling". The stream of data begins before the rich media file actually plays. Data is sent to the viewer's local computer at a rate faster than it takes to view so that incoming data always stays ahead of the actual data being viewed. Occasionally, if there is significant network congestion, or bandwidth of the viewer is reduced, a media file may stop playing momentarily so that the buffer can be refilled.

BUFFER – Memory in a camera that stores digital information before it's written to a memory card or flash drive.

BUTTERFLY - A net stretched on- a frame and supported by one stand. Used over an outdoor scene to soften the sunlight.

Byte – Describes a unit of computer storage. 8 bits make 1 byte.

C   <u>TOP</u>

C-47's – Wooden clothes pins used to clip gels to the barn doors used on lights.

Cache – The internal memory in the computer that stores data temporarily so that it can be accessed quickly. Web pages that are viewed are generally stored temporarily on the user's hard drive, for quick access on return visits. Caching can also refer to distributing Internet content (including Multimedia Files) in server storage, which is periodically refreshed.

Cable Modem – An external device that enables a computer or network to connect to a local cable TV line and receive data at high speeds. This data rate far exceeds that of the prevalent 28.8 and 56 Kbps telephone modems and the up to 512 Kbps of Integrated Services Digital Network (ISDN) and the data rate available to subscribers of Digital Subscriber Line (DSL) telephone service.

Capture – The process of inputting or transferring digital or analog audio and or video files to binary files, which can then be edited and encoded on a computer.

Capture Card – A hardware device located in a computer, facilitating the capture of analog or digital data.

CALL SHEETS - Production form which informs the cast and crew of the time they must be on set, which scenes are to be shot and anything else related to the day's filming.

CAMERA ANGLE - The camera's point of view when it is set up for shooting; the relative depth, height, or width at which an object or an action is photographed.

CAMERA BALANCE -- Balancing the camera on any type of mount so that it does not tilt forward or back, on its own, when unlocked.

CAMERA, HAND-HELD - A portable, motion picture camera that is held in the hands of the cameraman and steadied against his body without the use of a tripod.

CAMERA LEFT - The direction to the left of the camera as seen from the camera operator's point of view.

CAMERA LOCK – A camera is considered "locked" or "locked off" when the adjustments that allow it to move are tightened so as to hold in one position.

CAMERA MOUNTS - Umbrella term that includes tripods, dollies, cranes, Steadicam and any other specialized type of camera mount also referred to as camera support.

CAMERA MOUNTING PLATE – An attachment that can be fixed to the camera and then to a tripod or other mount. The mounting plate allows the camera to be quickly released from a tripod to be used handheld.

CAMERA MOVEMENT - The panning, tilting, tracking, or zooming of a motion picture camera. Camera Operators may set the pan and tilt adjustments on the camera mount so that there is a certain amount friction or "drag" to make movements smoother.

CAMERA OPERATOR - Crew member who operates the camera during filming. Composes the shot by panning and tilting the camera in order to keep the action within the frame lines.

CAMERA PACKAGE - Umbrella term for the camera, lenses, magazines, batteries, head, tripod and all other camera equipment needed for shooting.

CAMERA REPORTS - Production forms used to keep a daily record of scenes shot and amount of film used.

CAMERA RIGHT - The direction to the right of the camera as seen from the camera operator's point of view.

CAMERA ROLL - A single uninterrupted load of film. In 16mm, a roll of film can be purchased in 100, 200 or 400-foot lengths (400 feet runs about 11 minutes at 24fps). 35mm film rolls come in 400 or 1000-foot lengths (400 feet runs about 4-1/2 minutes at 24fps, 1000 feet about 11 minutes at 24fps). See also lab reel.

CAMERA TAPE - One inch wide cloth tape use for labeling and wrapping film cans along with many other uses on the set The most common colors of camera tape are white (used for re-cans or short ends) and black (ALWAYS means exposed film), but it is also available in red, blue, yellow and certain other colors.

CANDELA - A unit of light intensity. The luminance of a light source is often expressed in candelas per square meter.

CAPSTAN - A spindle that drives the tape in a sound recorder at a constant speed.

CARDIOID MICROPHONE - Unidirectional Mic with a heart shaped reception pattern.

CC Filters - Color-compensating filters. A series of filters in yellow, cyan, magenta, blue, green and red, increasing in density by small steps. Used for correcting and modifying the color of a scene either when shooting or printing.

CCD – Charge Coupled Device - One of two main types of image sensors found in digital cameras. The CCD is struck by light coming through the lens of the camera. The CCD converts the light into electrons carrying millions of pixels. More expensive cameras use 3 individual CCD chips to capture RGB colors rather just one chip to handle all three colors.

CCIR-601 – (or SDI) Specifies the image format, acquisition semantic, and part of the coding for digital standard television signals. ("Standard" television is in the resolution of PAL, NTSC and SECAM) CCIR-601 gives the specification for encoding of 4:2:2signals and a tentative specification of 4:4:4 encoding. 4:2:2 means, that the color-difference signals Cr and Cb are sampled with half of the sampling frequency of the luminance signal Y, that is 13.5MHz to 6.75MHz. It also specifies the number of samples per line for 525/60(59,94) systems and 625/50 systems. The samples per total line are different, but the samples per active line are the same for both systems: 720 samples per active line. It does not specify the number of lines for both systems; this can be found in CCIR Rep. 624-4, which gives a detailed description of all parameters of the analog television systems, as NTSC, PAL, SECAM and all of the derivates. The correspondence between the video signal levels and the quantization levels is also specified. The scale is between 0 and 255, for the luminance signal you have 220 quantization levels, for the color- difference signals

CENTER TRACK TIME CODE - A time code signal recorded along the center of a 1/4" audiotape. This signal is used as a locating tool when syncing audio to film. It is also used to make sure the tape plays back at the exact speed it was recorded in the field, (this is called resolving). Often, time code is striped onto tapes that have Neopilot before a film transfer session begins.

CENTURY STAND - A metal stand for positioning a lighting accessory such as a flag, cookie, or scrim. Also called C-stand or gobo stand.

CHARACTERISTIC CURVE - Also called sensitometric curve, H & D curve, or gamma curve. A graph representing the relationship between the film density and exposure.

CHEATING, CHEAT - Shifting elements in the composition of a shot to balance the frame or get a better angle.

CHROMA LEVEL – The amount of color saturation the picture possesses. Low Chroma levels result in more pale and muted colors. Higher Chroma Levels result in more saturated colors.

CIF – Common image Format – Internationally accepted 1920x1080 pixels.

CINCH MARKS - Scratch marks on the film, chiefly caused by pulling on the end of a loosely wound roll.

CineAlta – Family of HD/24p cameras from Sony.

CINEMASCOPE - Trade name copyrighted by 20th Century-Fox for a wide-screen process based on an anamorphic system. The system involves special lenses that compress and distort images during filming and spread them out undistorted during projection.

CINEMATOGRAPHY - The photography within a film.

CLAPPER BOARD - A hand-held board that illustrates necessary shot information for a film, photographed before each take (film title, director, take number, etc.). A wooden stick or clapstick is attached to the top of the board so that when the stick is snapped shut, there is both a sound and image that can later be used to synchronize the insulting sound and film tracks. Also referred to as a slate.

CLAW - Part of the camera pull-down mechanism, usually a metal tooth that engages t-he perforations of the film and moving them into position for exposure. Also called pull-down claw

CLONE - See analog / digital.

CLOSE SHOT (ABB. CS) - A shot closer than a medium shot but not as tight as a close-up A close shot on a person, he or she is framed from the top of the head to the waist.

CLOSE UP (ABB. CU) - A shot taken from a short distance or through a telephoto lens that brings to the screen a magnified, detailed part of a person or an object. A close-up of a person, for example, might show only his head. A close-up is used to draw attention to a significant detail, to clarify a point, designate a meaning, or heighten the dramatic impact of a film's plot.

CO-AXIAL - A type of camera film magazine, which has the feed roll on one side of the magazine and the take-up roll on the other side. It is called co-axial because the feed and take-up sides share the same axis of rotation.

CODEC – (Compressor / Decompressor) A system by which media is encoded or compressed using an algorithm or formula contained within the CODEC. The file is then decoded

or decompressed as the user views or listens to the file.

COFFIN LIGHT - An overhead light consisting of a boxlike frame with a few rows of bulbs which either point up toward a reflective surface, or down toward a diffusing screen, thus producing soft light.

COLOR CORRECTION - This term might be better thought of as "color enhancement" or "color manipulation". Why do film and video images need color correction?
A) Film has a much wider contrast and color range than video. Color correction allows the colorist to adjust these characteristics to meet the producer's needs.
B) Shooting situations are not always ideal and are often spread out over time. Color correction provides a controlled environment to match scenes from differing conditions.
C) Sometimes a special effect is needed where unusual colors or textures are desired.
The following are terms used to describe the level of color correction used for a color correction session:
Scene-by-Scene - The highest level of color correction. The colorist uses any available technique and makes as many color corrections as necessary to create the best possible image from a film or tape source. In addition, the colorist matches each scene to the rest of the project to achieve an overall look consistent with the desires of the producer. The resulting transfer will be suitable for any end use.
Best Light - The middle level of color correction. Each scene is color corrected but not matched to any other scene. The colorist will stop as often as necessary

to adjust for scene or lighting changes. The resulting transfer will be suitable for stock libraries, editing, (especially when the edit source image quality must be appealing), and final scene-by-scene tape-to-tape color correction. (Only used during film-to-tape-transfer.)

Lab Transfer - This level should be used when color quality is of minimal concern. The colorist will use an informal reference color correction setting, and may ride the level as the transfer proceeds. The intent is to transfer the film image within the contrast range of video as quickly and efficiently as possible. This transfer may not be suitable for future tape-to-tape color correction. (Only used during film-to-tape transfer.)

COLOR DIFFERENCE - See component.

COLOR TEMPERATURE - A system for evaluating the color of a light source by comparing it to a theoretically perfect temperature radiator called a black body. At lower temperatures a black body emits reddish light, and when heated to high temperatures its light changes to bluish. This is expressed in degrees Kelvin (K). A degree Kelvin is the same as degree Centigrade, but the two scales have different starting points. ($0°$ K= - $273°$ Centigrade). The bluer or "cooler" the light, the higher the number, the redder or "warmer" the light, the lower the number. A normal light bulb is around $3200°$ K, normal daylight is around $6000°$ K. Television monitors are on the cool side with a U.S. standard set at $6500°$ K, (otherwise called D65 - "D" for daylight).

COLOR TEMPERATURE METER

- A meter used to measure the specific color temperature of a light source.

COMMON IMAGE FORMAT (CIF) – Internationally accepted 1920x1080 pixels.

CMOS – Complementary Metal-Oxide Semiconductor – One of the two types of image sensors found in digital cameras. CMOS sensors are not as widely found in cameras as CCD's, the other type of sensor.

COMPLEMENTARY COLORS - Colors obtained by filtering out from the visible spectrum three primary colors, in turn. Yellow filter (minus blue) subtracts blue, but allows green and red pass through resulting in yellow light. Magenta filter (minus green) subtracts green light, transmitting blue and red seen as magenta. Cyan filter (minus red) subtracts red light, transmitting blue and green seen as cyan.

COMPACT FLASH MEDIA – Used for memory storage in all types of digital cameras. These cards can be as smaller then a postage stamp and as large as a PCMCIA or Express memory card. Memory storage capacity currently ranges as high as 64 gigabytes. The cards use solid-state memory.

COMPONENT VIDEO - Component video consists of either a separate red, green and blue signal (RGB), or a "repackaged" more robust version called color difference which also has three elements. These include the luminance channel (Y), which is a black and white version of the image, and two chroma channels called R minus Y (R-Y), and B minus Y

(B-Y) that together make up the chroma information of the image. A component signal is recorded to a video format in its separated state, but to see a complete picture, the three elements must be combined. See also composite and analog / digital. (Component formats include: D1, D5, DBC, DVC, BSP)

COMPOSITE VIDEO - A video signal where the red, green and blue elements are combined into one signal. North American televisions receive an NTSC composite signal. See also component.
(Composite formats include: D2, 1", 3/4", VHS)

COMPOSITE PRINT - A film print with a sound track printed on the film. This can be a magnetic sound track, but most often is an optical track. See also print.

COMPOSITION - The arrangement of shapes and forms within the frame.

COMPRESS – Reduce file size by using various software CODEC's to reduce the size and speed up transmission.

CONCEPT -- A short description or idea for a documentary, non-fiction project or fiction film. Usually precedes a Treatment (see Treatment).

CONTACT PRINT - See print.

CONTINUITY - The uninterrupted progression of related shots, scenes, and sequences necessary to maintain a logical development of theme or story. Since motion pictures are frequently shot out of sequence, care must be taken to avoid breaks in the flow of action and dialogue as well as discrepancies in details. The appearance of performers, props, costumes, and backgrounds 'must match exactly from one shot to the next so that the illusion of sequential filming is maintained.

CONTINUITY SHEETS - Records maintained by the script supervisor indicating scenes and slate number of each shot, the number of takes and their quality, the type of lens used and its aperture, the actual dialogue spoken, details of the action, the props, and the players' attire, etc. The sheets are used as a reference for possible retakes and inserts and for guidance for the prop and wardrobe departments and eventually the film editor.

CONTRAST-SCENE - The brightness range within a scene or the difference between light and dark areas within a scene.

CONTRAST-LIGHTING - The light intensity differences between the various light sources.

CONVERTER - A general name for electrical devices that serve certain functions in changing electrical characteristics such as conversion from AC to DC or vice versa, voltage conversion (transformer), or frequency conversion.

COOKIE - Also called Cucaloris. An irregularly perforated shadow-forming flag, opaque or translucent, made of plywood or plastic.

COOL LIGHTS - Lights designed to dissipate heat toward the rear of the lamp, through the reflector, allowing for a more comfortable temperature in front of the light.

COOP/CHICKEN COOP - An overhead, boxlike light with a

cluster of six, usually 100-watt globes, for top lighting of sets.

COPYRIGHT - Legal right of the author or other originator of a book, film, audio recording or other work to exclusively use and/or distribute said work.

CORE - Plastic spool onto which raw stock is wound.

CORE ADAPTERS - Circular device inside a magazine that allows core load film to be placed on the spindle.

CORE LOADS - Film stock wound onto a plastic core. Core loads must be loaded or unloaded in complete darkness.

COVERAGE - All the footage shot from all the angles that are foreseen as necessary for the editor to edit the project with continuity and pacing.

CRANE - A large, wheeled camera support with a rotating and high rising arm, operated manually or electrically. A platform on the end of the crane contains a mount for the camera as well as seats for the camera operator and camera assistant.

CRANE SHOT - A shot achieved by attaching a camera to a power-driven lifting device such as a construction crane or "cherry picker".

CREDITS - A list of the names of the principals involved in the production of a motion picture with their functions- e.g., the actors, the featured players, the director, producer, screenwriter, cinematographer and all other technical personnel and crew.

CRONIECONE - A device developed by Jordan Cronenweth for mounting a diffusion screen directly onto the light. It protrudes from the lamp as a widening cone so that light will not spill to the side and the diffusion screen will be a few feet wide.

CROSS HAIRS - The two intersecting lines in the center of a camera's viewing system.

CROSSING THE LINE – (See Imaginary Line)

CRYSTAL - Refers to a crystal in film cameras and 1/4" audio decks that provides a precise frequency used as a reference for speed. With film cameras the crystal frequency acts as a master clock to which the speed of the camera is matched; hence 24 fps can be timed to the 4th decimal place. The crystal frequency acts as a master clock for audio recorders as well. A Nagra pilot signal created with this frequency is used to assure that audio playback happens at exactly the same speed as it was recorded in the field. Because the crystal frequency is so dependable, audio sync with picture can be held for several hours, even though the two elements were recording independently of each other. Terms commonly used: "crystal sync", "crystal camera", "crystal audio", or just "crystal". See also Nagra.

CRYSTAL MOTOR - A camera motor operating at a precise synchronous speed, regulated by referencing an accurate crystal frequency source.

Color Temperature Gel (CTB) – Used on tungsten light (3200K) source to shift balance to daylight (5500K).
Color Temperature Orange (CTO)

– Used to shift a daylight source (5500k) to tungsten (3200k) balance.

CU - abbreviation for close-up

CUE, CUE CARDS – A signal given to talent or others to begin speaking or moving I some way. Written, drawn information, or dialog on a card held outside the camera's view.

CUT - The point of joining two shots by splicing, this creating an immediate transition, as opposed to a fade or dissolve. The command issued to cease action at the end of a take.

CUTAWAY - A shot of an action or object related to but not an immediate part of a principal scene. It is designed to draw attention from the main action temporarily. **CUTTER** - A shadow-forming device, usually rectangular in shape; a type of flag.

CUTTING COPY - See print (work print).

CYCLORAMA (CYC) - A sound stage background, usually white, with rounded corners, to create a limbo or sky effect. Made of plaster or stretched plastic.

CYC-STRIP - A lighting instrument shaped like a trough with up to 12 bulbs for even illumination of a cyclorama.

D   **TOP**

D.P. - Abbreviation for Director of Photography.

DAILIES - Originally this term referred to the "rushes" or "daily" work print created overnight - with or without synchronous sound - for a feature film director/crew to view in the morning, so they could see if they got their desired scenes before striking the sets. The daily print is later used by the editor as part of his work print in assembling the film. In the video world "dailies" simply reefers to the footage shot the previous day that is usually reviewed by the director, cinematographer, crew and others to insure nothing needs to be reshot.

DATA TRANSFER RATE– (or Data Rate) is the amount of digital data that is moved from one place to another in a given time, usually in a second's time. The data transfer rate can be viewed as the speed of travel of a given amount of data from one place to another. In general, the greater the bandwidth of a given path, the higher the data transfer rate.

DA VINCI - The color processor at the center of color correction. This box takes the signal from film or tape, manipulates the colors, and then sends it on to the recorders.

888 - Top-of-the-line all digital da Vinci color corrector. This model offers Power Windows as well as Kilovectors. Because of the high bandwidth signal the 8:8:8 processes, it can offer a very clean output. Tape-to-tape color correction from a digital source is especially easy with the 8:8:8.

Renaissance - Analog "hi-rez" da Vinci color corrector. This version takes its signal from the telecine before the digi-scan resulting in higher color resolution. The Renaissance offers Kilovectors and simple windows.

Classic - An older design of the da Vinci color correction system. This version takes its signal after the Digi-scan, (lower resolution of color compared to the Renaissance) and lacks the dedicated control panel for secondary color adjustments, (chroma, hue, luminance).

DAY-FOR-NIGHT CINEMATOGRAPHY - The process of simulating night scenes while shooting in daylight, usually with the aid of filters and through - underexposure

DAYLIGHT - A photographic light source which has a color temperature of 5600K.

DAYLIGHT SPOOL - A black metal film reel that holds 100, 200, or 400 feet of unexposed film. The sides completely shield the film from light exposure so that this spool can be loaded into a camera in subdued daylight, without ruining the roll. (The first several wraps of film might have overexposed edges.) These spools are used for older cameras, or special use cameras, (e.g. high speed) that require the easy to load spools.

Decibel (dB) - Sound is measured in decibels.

Decompress – (decompressing) expanding a compressed file to its original form and size. After Media is compressed using an algorithm or formula contained within a CODEC; media may then be decoded or decompressed so the user may view and/or listen to the file.

DEEP FOCUS - Sharp definition of all objects in front of a camera.

DENSITOMETER - An instrument used for measuring the density of a processed photographic emulsion.

DENSITY - The thickness of the silver deposit, or color dyes on the film, which affects the amount of light projected onto the screen.

DEPTH OF FIELD - The range of distance in front of and behind the principle point of focus which will also be in acceptably sharp focus. The permissible depth of field for a shot depends on the focal length of the lens, its aperture (f-stop), and the distance at which it is focused.

DEPTH OF FOCUS - The distance that the film plane can be moved toward or away from the lens before the image becomes soft and out of focus.

DESATURATION - Lowering the degree of hue in a given color.

DEVELOPMENT - The chemical process in which the latent image on the film stock is made visible. If a film has been underexposed it can be overdeveloped in order to attain the correct contrast.

DIAPHRAGM-LENS - An adjustable opening within the lens that controls the amount of light reaching the film through the lens. The size of this opening is calibrated in f-stops.

DICHROIC FILTER - A glass filter used on tungsten lamps to convert their color temperature to that of daylight. The filter reflects excessive red and transmits light that is bluer.

DIFFUSERS - For lenses: Fine nets, granulated or grooved glass, petroleum jelly or glycerin smeared on glass, positioned in front of the lens to soften the photographed image. For lamps: Diffusing materials like tight nets, spun glass, frosted plastic, and so forth, placed in front of the lamp.

DIGI-SCAN - A part of the Rank that makes the actual video picture from the high bandwidth red, green and blue signals created from the film images. The later the model the better the image quality, with a Digi-IV being the best. Better yet is the Quatroscan that offers a 4:4:4 output vs. the 4:2:2 output from a Digi-IV. (The bigger the numbers, the higher the resolution.)

DIGITAL CINEMATOGRAPHY – Digital acquisition using film style operational practices.

DIGITAL TELEVISION – Formats: **ATSC** – United States, Canada; **DVB** – Europe; **ISDB** – Japan, Brazil; **DMB** – South Korea.
DIGITAL VIDEO FORMATS --

DIGITAL WETGATE - Electronic filters in a noise reducer/enhancer (e.g. Digital Visionís DVNR-1000), that work to hide dirt and scratches on film. See wet gate for derivation of this name.
Digitize–Changing or transferring digital or analog audio and or video files to binary files, which can then be edited and encoded on the computer. (See Capture)
DIMMER - An instrument used to change the voltage of lights on the set to regulate their intensity. Not always useful for color cinematography, as the color temperature of the lights will also change.

DIRECTOR - The crewmember whose job it is to interpret the script and translate the written word to visual images.

DIRT / SCRATCH CONCEALMENT - See Digital Wet gate.

DISPLACEMENT MAGAZINE - A magazine type that contains both the feed and take-up roll within the same compartment on the same side of the magazine. As the magazine sits on the camera, the front contains the feed side, and the rear contains the take-up.

DISSOLVE – A fade out and a fade in overlapped so that one scene goes to black while the other scene emerges from black. A video transition with one scene fading down while the other is fading up.

DOCUMENTARY – A Non-Fiction story that uses actuality materials and sources in a film, video, audio, photographic, or multimedia format.

DOLBY -E – Digital audio system preferred for HDTV transmission incorporating eight channels (the six Dolby 5.1 channels plus two stereo channels}.
DOLBY 5.1 - A surround sound system using 3 speakers in front (right, center, left) and two stereo speakers in the rear along with a subwoofer.
DOLLY - A wheeled vehicle used-for mounting a camera and also containing seats for the camera operator and camera assistant.

DOLLY SHOT - Also called "traveling" "trucking," or "tracking shot." A moving shot of a moving or stationary subject exercised by mounting the camera on a dolly or camera truck. To dolly-in (or track-in) is to move the camera toward the subject; to dolly-out (or track out) is to move the camera away from the subject.

DOLLY TRACK - Special rails on which the dolly is mounted in order to achieve smooth, level dolly shots.

DOT - Shadow-forming device in the form of a small round scrim.

DOUBLE EXPOSURE - The recording of two different images on the same length of film as a result of exposing the same negative twice through the camera or a printer. Double exposure may occur accidentally, by unknowingly running previously exposed film through the camera, or by design if some special effect is desired.

DOUBLE PERF - Film which contains: perforations on both sides of the film.

DOWN CONVERSION – Reproduction of high-resolution image down to a standard definition image.

DOWNLOAD – Moving a digital media file from a server, where stored, to a local system for viewing. Also moving digital video files from camera flash media to a server, computer or external hard drive.

DOWNLOADING - The act of unloading the film from the camera and magazine.

DRAG – See Camera Movement
DRM (Digital Rights Management) - Technology that allows content owners to determine and control how users may view content such as media files on the Internet.

DPI – DOTS PER INCH – Measure of image resolution.

DREAMWEAVER – Adobe Software used to create and maintain websites.

DROP - Curtain or screen of black cloth hung vertically over the set to control the passage of light. For example, blocking the backlight from unwanted areas. Also known as a teaser.

DUBBING AND ADR (AUTOMATIC DIALOG REPLACEMENT) – Replacing dialog or mixing audio tracks. Done in editing and/or a Dubbing Theater.

DUMMY LOAD - A small roll of film that is too short for shooting. It may be used as a practice or test roll when checking camera equipment.

DUST BUSTING – Removal of film and negative dust and sparkle before telecine transfers.

DUTCH ANGLE – Diagonally tilted camera angle.

DVD (Digital Video Disk or Digital Versatile Disk) - A medium for storing large amounts of digital data, most notably movies encoded using MPEG-2 compression (a CODEC designed especially for use with DVDs). DVDs can hold several gigabytes on a single disc. Most CDs by contrast can only hold 600 megabytes each.

DVD-RAM - Writable DVD disks. Analogous to CD-R and CD-RW, but with several times the storage capacity of these older formats. Special drives are required for writing onto blank DVD-RAM disks.

DVD-ROM - Drives capable of reading DVD disks. DVD-ROM

drives are usually backward compatible, which means that they are capable of reading CD-ROMs and audio CDs.

DVD-Video - Standard that combines DVD disks, MPEG-2 video compression, and any of a number of high-quality audio formats to create a movie that is stored and played back on computers and on DVD players designed for home entertainment centers.

E   **TOP**

EASTMAN KODAK - Manufacturer of the most widely used motion picture film stock in the industry.

EDGE FOGGING - Unwanted exposure on the film edges caused by light leaks in the camera, film magazine or film cans.

EDGE NUMBERS / KEY NUMBERS - These numbers are printed by the manufacturer at 1 foot intervals, (35mm) and 1/2 foot intervals, (16mm), on the edge of raw film stock. They act not only as a footage counter and location marker on the stock, but also contain film type and manufacturing batch codes. Edge numbers / key numbers on a work print copy are used to locate scenes from the original negative. See also Keykode, a bar-coded format of key numbers.

EDGE SERVER – (Enhanced Data GSM Environment) Storage of data files on remote servers specifically designed for streaming over the Internet. EDGE is a faster version of GSM wireless service. EDGE enables data to be delivered at rates up to 384 Kbps on a broadband. The standard is based on the GSM standard and uses TDMA multiplexing technology.

EDITING - Editing is the process of selecting and assembling various motion picture shots and sound tracks into a coherent whole. The process moves from assembly, to rough-cut, then to fine cut that includes mixed audio.

EDITOR - The crew member responsible for creating a workable version of the film by assembling all of the shots in a coherent manner.

EDL - Edit Decision List. - A computer generated list that has in and out video time code points for the source material, as well as in and out points for the final video edit master. This is the "script" for an on-line editor. Reel numbers, edit types, notes, and machine settings can all be stored in an EDL as well. If a client is returning for tape-to-tape work, a copy of the EDL can be loaded into the da Vinci so that each scene is already marked for color correction.

EGG CRATE - A grid used on soft lights to control the pattern and direction of the light.

ELECTRICIAN - Crewmember whose job includes handling all electrical lamps and stands. They report to the directly to the gaffer. May also be called Spark or Juicer.

EMBED TAG - HTML tag used to place a media file (such as an audio, video, or Flash file) into a web page. The embed tag defines an area on the page in which the media file will appear if it involves graphic elements, helps the browser understand what type of file it is, and specifies other information as well, such as whether the file will play automatically when the page loads.

EMULSION - The light-sensitive substance, consisting primarily of a gelatin compound and silver halide crystals onto which the photographic image is formed.

ENCODING – The process of converting a digitized file into a streaming format.

ESTABLISHING SHOT - A shot, usually a long shot or a full shot at the beginning of a sequence - which establishes and defines the location, setting, and mood of the action. It provides the audience with an initial visual orientation, enabling it to see the interrelationship between the general setting and the detailed action in subsequent scenes.

EV (EXPOSURE VALUE) - Units used in calibrating modern reflected light meters. As with f/stops each whole number increase is equivalent to twice the brightness. For example E.V.6 means twice the light of E.V.5.

EXPENDABLES - Any supplies which are used up during a production such as tape, gels, compressed air cans, lens tissue, lens fluid, etc.

EXPOSURE - The process of subjecting the film to any light intensity for a specific amount of time, resulting in a latent image on the film emulsion. The measurement of the amount of light a film stock is subjected to.

EXPOSURE INDEX (EI) - A numerical rating of a film stock's sensitivity to light. See also ISO and ASA

EXPOSURE METER - An instrument for measuring the intensity of the light, either incident or reflected from a photographic subject. Incident light is the light falling on a subject and Incident light meters are used to take readings at the subject facing the camera. Reflective light readings measure the amount of light reflected off the subject and readings are taken at the camera facing the subject. Cameras with built in light meters are using reflected light to calculate the exposure.

EXT - Abbreviation for "exterior" found in scripts for scenes filmed outdoors.

EXTENSION SOUND - Refers to sync sound that runs on after the camera roll has run out, or before the roll starts.

EXTREME CLOSE-UP (ABB. ECU OR XCU) - A very tight close-up shot that greatly magnifies a tiny object or shows a magnified view of part of an object or a person, such as a shot of a face featuring only the eyes, nose, and mouth.

EXTREME LONG SHOT (ABB. ELS OR XLS) - A wide-angle shot providing a bird's-eye view of a vast area. Usually a static shot filmed from a high vantage point, it is most often used to establish the geography of an area or to suggest wide-open spaces.

EYE-LEVEL SHOT - Shot taken with the camera placed near the eye level of the subject being photographed.

F **TOP**

FILL LIGHT – A light used to fill-in the shadow areas caused by the main source or Key Light. Fill light is usually soft light and may be bounced or reflected from a reflector, bounce board or other sources.

FINAL CUT – Nonlinear digital editing software from Apple.

FIREWIRE -- FireWire is a standard for high-speed transfers between devices including camcorders and FireWire-enabled PCs. This standard supports data rates of 100/200/400 Mbps. The other terms referring to the same standard are iLink and IEEE (Institute of Electrical and Electronics Engineers) 1394. The latest FireWire standard (FireWire 800) is able to support data rates of 800 Mbps.

FLASHPVR -- Technology allowing Pinnacle TV Center Pro software to run from the PCTV HD Ultimate stick's on-board flash memory. Users can automatically record TV shows to the integrated flash memory or to their hard drive in a broad range of formats including iPod®, PSP®, DivX®, or even direct-to-DVD.

FRAME – One image shot as a still photograph or part of a series of images in film or television. In a digital reference it refers to unique still images in animation or video.

FPS - Frames Per Second. (Film) The number of individual images displayed every second as the film passes through the camera gate. Motion picture film of any type is shot at a standard 24 FPS This rate was established originally as a rate that would maximize the sound quality. Film is shot at 24 FPS and projected at 24 FPS. To achieve slow motion on the screen film is shot at 48 FPS or higher and then played back at 24 FPS thereby giving the illusion of slow motion. To speed up the motion we can shoot at slower then 24 FPS although the quality suffers below 16 FPS.

FPS – Frames Per Second (TV) The number of individual images recorded/displayed every second electronically for Television/Video is 30 FPS. Modern Video cameras can record at varying frame rates. Since most people perceive motion at about 16 FPS the lowest frame rate used for streaming video online is 15 fps, which reduces file sizes.

FPS AND 3/2 PULLDOWN - Since film is usually shot at 24 fps and video at 30 fps, we need to make up 6 frames per second when transferring film to video. This is done by adding an extra field to every other film frame, (there are 2 fields per video frame), resulting in a field sequence of AA, BBB, CC, DDD etc. This process is called 3/2 pull down. There is no 3/2 pull down when the film is shot at 30fps in NTSC, or 25fps in PAL because in these cases the film and video are running at the same rate, (1 film frame per 1 video frame).

FADE (FADE IN/OUT) - An optical effect that causes a scene to emerge gradually on the screen from complete blackness (fade in), or a bright image to dim gradually into blackness (fade out). The fade is a transitional device that usually signifies a distinct break in a film's continuity, indicating a change in time, location, or subject matter. A video image that diminishes in brightness to black or increases in brightness from black is a fade.

FALL OFF - Gradual diminishing of light falling on the set obtained by the use of barn doors, flags or weakening of the light intensity when the distance from the light source increases.

FAST MOTION - A technical effect that makes people or objects appear to be moving at a faster-than-normal rate during projection. It is achieved by running the camera at a slower rate than the standard 24 frames per second.

FAY - Lamp letter code designation for a 650-watt PAR bulb of a daylight color temperature.

FC - See Foot-candles.

FEED SIDE - The part of the camera or magazine that holds the fresh unexposed film.

FeRRITT - See Mag Follower / Dubber.

FIBER OPTICS - A technique that makes it possible to put light in difficult places. It uses glass or plastic fibers through which light can travel even when they are bent. A very useful device in delivering illumination to cramped spaces, such as car interiors.

FILL LIGHT - Light shining on the scene from a point near the camera and illuminating the shadows caused by the key light.

FILM CHAIN - Also called "telecine." An optical transfer process used for transferring film to videotape or more recently to digital media.

FILM GAUGE - The varying widths of film stock that are measured in millimeters the most commonly used film gauges or formats are 16mm and 35mm. Many commercials, music videos and television shows are shot using 16mm film. The majority of Hollywood films are shot using the standard 35 mm stock while some films use a wider print of 65 or 70 mm.

FILM PLANE - The place within the camera during exposure where the film is held.

FILTER - A glass or gel material placed on the camera or light source to alter the image or the quality of the light.

FINE CUT - A refined version of the editor's rough-cut that marks a substantial refinement over the rough cut and approximates the final version of the film in continuity and length. See rough-cut / fine cut / picture lock.

FINGER - Narrow rectangular shadow-casting device. See also flag.

FIREWIRE (IEEE 1394, I-Link) --

FIRESTORE –

FISH-EYE LENS - A wide-angle lens that distorts the image to great effect.

FIXED FOCUS LENS (PRIME) - A lens that has no provision for focusing and thus remains at a fixed distance from the film plane.

FLAG (OR GOBO) - Shadow-casting device made of cloth stretched on a metal frame. Specific types of flags include the cutter, finger, target, and teaser.

FLARE - Spots and streaks on the film caused by strong

directional light reflected off the lens components or filters.

FLASHING - A laboratory procedure for lowering the image contrast by exposing the film, before development, to a very weak light. This introduces a slight overall fog, which is more noticeable in the shadows than in the highlights, and makes the shadow details more marked.

FLAT LIGHTING - Shadow less, even lighting usually as a result from lighting at a low contrast ratio of not more then 2-1 (key to fill).

FLATBED EDITING **MACHINE** – An analog film-editing machine. Basically a table with multiple reels on either side of an editing station in the center. A projection screen and speakers sit on top for monitoring picture and audio. Work print and mag track sound are edited on flatbeds. This is a sprocket drive system; picture and sound are kept in sync by means of the perforations on the side of the film and mag stock. Only one or two Flatbed Editing Machines remain in circulation. They are KEM and Steenbeck and are available in various film sizes and formats. Most film editing today is done on Non Linear Editing (NLE) workstations.

FLB FILTER - Camera filter used to color correct a scene illuminated by a "cool-white" fluorescent tube, to a type B (tungsten) film stock.

FLEX FILE - A computer-generated file that keeps track of 3 different codes and other information at any given point. Most importantly, this file establishes the relationship of video time code to film Keykode, but can also include audio time

code, (or AatonCode). Flex files are used in off-line systems, or by a film lab to trace a video EDL back to original camera negative (via Keykode), so that the film can be cut into a finished print. In addition, select reels for a final film-to-tape color correction can also be made. Flex files also have the ability to log slate information such as "scene", "take", "camera roll", or "audio roll", at each camera stop. Most often only the "head punch" of each camera roll is logged to establish the video time code to Keykode relationship for each roll. (If AatonCode is on the film, all camera stops can be logged automatically). See also Keylinker.

FLOATER - A light, a flag or a net moved intentionally during the shot.

FLUID HEAD - A camera head that contains a viscous fluid. This fluid creates a slowing effect by pushing through narrow channels thereby cushioning any jerky movements and smoothing out horizontal and vertical movements.

FLYING MOON - A lighting contraption in the shape of a cube made of aluminum pipes and covered with bleached muslin. It houses four 25,000 watt HMIs and is hoisted by an industrial crane to 80 to 120 feet. Used to create artificial moonlight.

FOAM-CORE BOARD - A white cardboard with soft Styrofoam inner layer. Fomecore is the brand name for this product. Used to bounce light.

FOCAL LENGTH - The distance, measured in millimeters from the optical center of the lens to the film plane when the lens is focused to infinity. Shorter lenses are used for wide-angle shots, while long lenses are used for distance. For distance.

FOCUS - The position of an object at the exact distance to which the lens is set, so that the image of that object appears sharp through the lens.

FOCUS PULLER - A member of the camera crew, usually -the first assistant cameraman, whose job it is to adjust the lens during shooting to keep the image in focus. Prior to actual shooting, he measures and marks the distance between the lens and significant points in a 'shot, so that a smooth' follow focus can be achieved during the take.

FOCUS RING - The moveable ring on a lens that allows you to position the elements of the lens in relation to the film '-plane so that the image is kept in focus.

FOGGING - light Film density caused by unwanted exposure to light.

FOLLOW FOCUS - The continuous adjustment of the camera lens while shooting is in progress to accommodate the relative movement between camera and subject without loss of sharp focus.

FOLLOW SHOT - Shot in which the camera is panned to follow the subject action.

FOOTAGE COUNTER - Camera indicator that shows the amount of feet of film that has been shot.

FOOTCANDLE - International unit of illumination. The intensity of light falling on a sphere placed one foot away from a source of light of one candlepower, also, one candela.

FORCING - Also known as pushing. A laboratory procedure of overdeveloping the film to compensate for underexposure.

FORMAT - Referring to the size of the film stock and the size of the image. The most common film formats are 16mm and 35mm.

FRAME - One of the successive individual images that comprise a motion picture, or the space such an image occupies. Each frame is separated from the others by a horizontal border called a "frame line." The frame is the-smallest coherent unit of a film.

FRAME COUNTER - Camera indicator that shows the individual number of frames that have been shot. It is usually located near the footage counter on the camera.

FRAMES PER SECOND - The number of individual frames photographed per second. The standard-professional frame rate is 24 frames per second (fps), which gives the illusion of normal motion.

FREQUENCY - Expressed in hertz (HZ) the number of times per second that a sound source vibrates.

FRENCH FLAG - A small flag on an articulating arm that mounts on the camera, used-to cut lens flares.

FRESNEL LENS - A type of lens used on spotlights. The convex surface is reduced to concentric ridges, to avoid overheating and to reduce weight. Lamps equipped with this lens are called Fresnels in popular usage.

FROST - The term used for the plastic diffusion material that resembles a shower curtain in weight and tracing paper in appearance.

F/STOP - A number obtained by dividing the focal length of lens by its effective aperture (the opening through which light passes within the lens). F/stop represents the light transmitting capability of the lens at any given setting. The higher the f-stop number, the smaller the hole in the diaphragm, and the less light enters the camera. The standard series of f-stop numbers includes the following: 1, 1.4, 2, 2.8, 4, 5.6, 8, 11, 16, 22, 32,

FULL COAT - This is 35mm or 16mm magnetic track audio stock that has magnetic oxide coating over the entire surface. Sometimes 35mm magnetic audio comes on clear stock that has only "stripes" of oxide, which contain the audio tracks. This is called mag (magnetic) stripe. See also other definition for mag stripe.

FULLSCREEN - Viewing images in which the content (such as a CIF video file) is projected to the size of the monitor in use. This can result in noticeable distortion if the data rate of file is low.

FULL SHOT - shot whose subject completely fills the screen. When the subject is a 'person his or her full body is included in the shot.

FX - Industry slang for special effects.

G **TOP**

G (Good) - Camera report notation indicating which takes are to be used in the edited film.

GAFFER - The chief lighting technician/electrician on the film crew.

GAFFER TAPE - Two-inch wide cloth tape used for securing the lighting instruments, stands, cables, etc., on a set. The most common colors of gaffer tape are gray, black and white.

GAIN – Term used to describe the level of audio or video. Audio gain refers to the level of the sound or audio signal. Video gain refers to boosting the voltage of the video resulting in a brighter image.

GATE - The part of the camera or projector mechanism in which the film is momentarily held while a frame is being exposed or projected. It contains the aperture plate, pressure plate, pull-down claw and registration pin. Refers to an important piece of the Rank, which holds the lenses that focus and frame the film image. This brick-size piece of metal and glass is different for each film gauge. As in a projector, it is the key element that optically presents the picture to the electronic sensors.

GATOR GRIP - An alligator-type grip used to attach lightweight lamps to sets, furniture, and pipes, mainly on location.

GEAR HEAD - A type of tripod head in which the pan and tilt movements are operated by crank wheels through a gear or belt drive system. The speed of these gears can be regulated through the use of a sliding speed - control lever.

GEL - Transparent cellophane material used for changing the color of a-light either for visual effect or for correction of color temperature or exposure.

GENERATION - The levels descended from the original. The exposed negative film in the camera is the first-generation. Each successive copy has deterioration in quality from the original.

GEOFILTERING - Restricting access to media content by geographic areas.

GIF Graphics Interchange Format – File format used for images on the Web. Give's work well for images composed of fewer colors like logos or vector graphics.

GIGABYTE (GB) – One Gigabyte equals 1,000 megabytes.

GIMMICK BULB - A small bulb, like the FEV globe used in Inkies or a "peanut" bulb, used for hiding in confined spaces.

GLOW LIGHT - A very weak light source that creates a slight glow in the actor's face, usually directed onto the face from one side.

GOBO - See Flag.

GOBO HEAD - A grip head of c-stand head used as a clamping device for holding equipment.

GLASS SHOT - A shot obtained through a glass plate on which part of the scene has been painted the painting on the glass is photographed with the action seen through the clear portion of the glass, providing the illusion of a complete setting.

GRADUATED FILTER - A filter with neutral density or color covering only a certain portion of the glass. There is a gradual transition between the dense and the clear part of the filter. This bleed line may vary depending on the purpose of the given filter. See also Attenuator.

GRAIN - Fine silver halide particles embedded in the gelatin compound of the film emulsion exposed to light and developed.

GRAY SCALE - A photographic chart representing a series of distinct gray fields from white to black in defining steps. A term used to indicate that there will be shades of gray in a frame or printed document.

GREEN SCREEN – Subjects photographed or taped in front a green or blue background that can be keyed on and a substitute image Chroma Keyed in. Subjects should not be wearing Green or Blue respectively.

GRIFFOLYN - The brand name of a plastic material used for large reflecting screens.

GRIP - A member of a film crew responsible for laying camera tracks, erecting scaffolds, positioning flags and diffusion screens and moving large set pieces. A "jack-of-all-trades" on the set.

GRIP EQUIPMENT - Specialized stands, clamps and tools used to mount lighting control devices such as flags, nets, etc.

GROUND GLASS - The finely ground glass element on which the image is formed in the camera viewing system.

GUI – Graphical User Interface.

H.264 -- High-compression multimedia format/technology supported by Apple® iPod® and Sony® PSP®. H.264 encoding delivers high-quality videos with two to three times the compression efficiency of the MPEG-2 standard, which is used in DVD video.

HAIR LIGHT - A light source positioned specifically to light the actor's hair.

HARD LIGHT - Refers to a light source or lighting technique using strong bright direct and unfiltered light to simulated the quality of sunlight or direct overhead lighting.

HIGH DEFINITION (HD) -- HDTV (High Definition Television) Digital technology.

HIGH DEFINITION MULTI-INTERFACE (HDMI) – Used to connect HD components to each other.

HEAD - A camera mounting device that allows the camera operator to make smooth pan and tilt moves during 'the shot in order to maintain the composition. The two most common types of heads are fluid and gear. Heads may be mounted on a tripod, dolly or crane. A camera is attached t the head.

HEAD-ON SHOT - A shot in which the action appears to come directly toward the camera.

HIGH-ANGLE SHOT - A shot taken from an elevated position looking down on the subject or the action.

HIGH HAT - A low camera mount of a fixed height.

HIGH KEY - A lighting style in which the majority of the scene is in highlights. Usually enhanced by bright costumes and sets. A low ratio of key light to fill light lowers the contrast, helping to obtain this effect.

HIGHLIGHTS - The brightest parts of a photographed subject represented-as the heavy densities on the negative and as the most transparent on the original positive.

HIGH-SPEED CINEMATOGRAPHY - Motion picture photography of moving objects taken at a rate of speed greater than that possible with the normal intermittent-action camera

HISTORGRAM – Graphic representation showing the range of tones from dark to light in a photograph. Certain digital cameras include a histogram feature that allows a precise check on the exposure of the photo.

HMI - Hydrargyom Medium Arc-Length Iodide, a metal halide discharge lamp constituting, in effect, a mercury arc enclosed in a glass envelope. Gives off color temperature equivalent to daylight - 5,600K.

HONEYCOMB - A grid used on soft lights to control the lighting pattern and direction. It is shallower-than the egg crate grid. Hue. A scientific term for color.

HOT SET - A set that is ready for filming. Props and set pieces are established and are not to be moved because more filming is to be done.

HOT SPOT - A very bright area in the scene, caused-by excessive light or a strong reflection.

HTML – Hypertext Markup Language is the authoring language used to create documents on the World Wide Web. HTML defines the structure and layout of a Web document by using a variety of tags and attributes. The correct structure for an HTML document starts with <HTML><HEAD>(enter here what document is about)</HEAD><BODY> and ends with </BODY></HTML>. All the information you'd like to include in your Web page fits in between the <BODY> and </BODY> tags. There are hundreds of other tags used to format and layout the information in a Web page. Tags are also used to specify hypertext links. These allow Web developers to direct users to other Web pages with only a click of the mouse on either an image or word(s).

HTTP (Hypertext Transport Protocol) - The protocol by which web pages are transmitted over the Internet.

HTTP Streaming - Streaming (used by QuickTime) in which media files begin to play before they are downloaded entirely, i.e. a progressive download. These files can be sent via HTTP and don't require specialized server software.

HYPERFOCAL DISTANCE - The closest point in front of the camera, which is in focus when the lens is focused at infinity. By setting the focus to the hyper focal distance, your depth of field is from one-half the hyper focal distance to infinity. In other words, by setting your focus to the hyper focal distance, it gives you the maximum depth of field.

HYPERTLINK -- A link from a hypertext file to another location or file activated by clicking on a highlighted word, picture or icon.

I   TOP

IMAGE BROWSER – An application that facilitates viewing digital photos. Sophisticated image browsers allow you to rename files, convert photos from one file format to another, add text descriptions and do varying amounts of editing.

IMAGE EDITOR – A computer program that allows you to edit a photo to improve or change its appearance. With image editing software, you can darken or lighten a photo, rotate it, adjust its contrast, crop out extraneous detail, remove red-eye and other things.

IMAGE RESOLUTION - Number of pixels in a digital photo commonly referred to as its image resolution.

INCANDESCENT LIGHT - Electric light produced by the glowing of a metallic filament such as tungsten. Modern quartz lamps, more accurately called tungsten-halogen lamps, are incandescent.

INCHING KNOB - A device on the camera that allows you to manually move the camera pull-down mechanism. This allows for ease in loading the film as well as checking to be sure that the film travels smoothly through the camera.

INCIDENT LIGHT - Light coming directly from the source onto the object and the light meter, as opposed to light reflected from the photographed subject into the light meter.

INCIDENT LIGHT METER - A measuring device used to determine the exposure of the light falling on the subject. It is held at the position of the subject and aimed toward the camera.

INKY-DINK - The smallest focusable studio lamp with a Fresnel lens and a bulb up to 250 watts. Insert Car. A vehicle used for towing the action car (target vehicle) during certain moving car shots. Camera and lights are often mounted on the insert car.

INSERT - A shot, usually a close-up or extreme close up, intercut within a scene to help explain the action, emphasize a-point, or facilitate continuity. A typical insert may consist of a close-up shot of a newspaper' item, a hand holding a gun, or a clock on a wall.

INT - Script abbreviation for interior scenes.

INTERLACING – Television video is interlaced or progressive. Interlacing is a way to achieve good visual quality within the limitations of a narrow bandwidth. The *horizontal scan lines* of each interlaced frame are numbered consecutively and partitioned into two *fields*: the *odd field* (upper field) consisting of the odd-numbered lines and the *even field* (lower field) consisting of the even-numbered lines. NTSC, PAL and SECAM are interlaced formats. Abbreviated video resolution specifications often include an "*i*" to indicate interlacing. For example, PAL video format is often specified as *576i50*, where *576* indicates the vertical line resolution, "*i*" indicates interlacing, and *50* indicates 50 fields (half-frames) per second.

In *progressive scan* systems, each refresh period updates all of the scan lines. The result is a higher perceived resolution and a lack of various artifacts that can make parts of a stationary picture appear to be moving or flashing.

A procedure known as deinterlacing can be used for converting an interlaced stream, such as analog, DVD, or satellite, to be processed by progressive scan devices, such as TFT TV-sets, projectors, and plasma panels. Deinterlacing cannot, however, produce a video quality that is equivalent to true progressive scan source material.

INTERMITTANT MOVEMENT - The stop-and-go movement of the film transport mechanism allowing the film to advance through a motion picture camera, projector, or printer, frame by frame, so that each frame is held - momentarily motionless during exposure or projection. This action proceeds at such a speed that the film seems to be moving continuously through the camera, but in reality each frame is stopped long enough to be exposed in a manner similar to the exposure of a still photograph.

INTERNEGATIVE - A negative made from the original positive print, created for the sole purpose of producing additional positive prints for distribution

INTERPOSITIVE - A denser than-usual color print used intermediate film for making duplicate negatives. It can be recognized by its orange colored base. See print.

INVERTER - An electric device converting direct current (DC) to alternating current (AC **ISDN** – (Integrated Services Digital Network) An international communications standard sending voice, video, and data over digital telephone lines or normal telephone wires.

ISO – (International Standards Association) A rating of a film's sensitivity to light. This rating system replaces the ASA (American Standards Association) rating system. An ISO of 200 is twice as sensitive to light as film rated at 100 ISO, 400 ISO is twice as fast as 200 ISO and so on as the system follows this formula. Digital cameras have adopted the same rating system as that for film, to describe the sensitivity to light of the camera's imaging sensor. Many digital cameras include a control for adjusting the ISO speed. In film the higher the ISO number the more sensitive the film is to light. The same applies to the digital application. As in film, the higher the ISO number the more grain or noise in a digital camera image.

ISP – (Internet Service Provider) Companies that offer Internet access to subscribers.

J   **TOP**

JAM - CAMERA - Camera trouble when the film piles up inside the camera body, sometimes caught between the sprocket wheels and guide rollers of the camera.

JAM - MAGAZINE - Magazine trouble when the film piles up inside the magazine, sometimes caught between the sprocket wheels and guide rollers of the magazine.

JAPANESE (CHINESE) LANTERN - A large lightweight light made of paper, silk, or other translucent materials, housing a Photoflood bulb and producing a very soft illumination. Due to its lightweight, a Japanese lantern can be easily hung in the desired part of the set.

JAVA - An object-oriented programming language that is platform independent (i.e., works on Windows, Mac OS, Linux). Java is often used to write "java applets," which are small applications that can be embedded into web pages, giving the pages sophisticated functionality.

JAVA SCRIPT - A programming language based on Java and C++ developed by Netscape that allows web authors to give increased interactive functionality to web pages. Common functions created with JavaScript are image rollovers (an image that changes when you scroll your mouse over it), browser detection, and pop-up windows.

JPEG (Joint Photographic Experts Group) - Refers to an image file format popular for delivery over the Web because of its relatively high quality and low file size. Before uploading JPEGs to the Web, users can determine the amount of compression assigned to them- usually on a scale from 1 to 10. Recommended file type for photographic images.

JUMP CUT - A cut that creates a break in a film's continuity of time occurring within a scene, usually to condense the action in a shot.

JUNIOR - A focusable, studio lamp with Fresnel lens and 2000-watt bulb. Perhaps the most common studio lighting instrument.

K   **TOP**

Kbps – (Kilobits Per Second) a measure of data transfer speed. Modems, for example, are measured in Kbps. Note that one Kbps is 1,024 bytes.

KELVIN DEGREES - The temperature scale used for measuring the color temperature of light sources. See Color Temperature.

KEY LIGHT - The principal and dominant source of light used in illuminating a motion picture set. It determines the tone and mood of a scene and is therefore established first by the director of photography, who later builds around it the fill light and other compensating sources of illumination, such as the backlight.

KEYKODE - Eastman Kodak encodes edge numbers into a bar code format called Keykode. These bar codes are printed by the manufacturer at 1/2 foot intervals on the edge of 16mm negative, and 1 foot intervals on 35mm, along with edge numbers or ìkey numbers that are readable by eye. Keykode allows machines to electronically read key numbers as the film passes through a reader attached to the Rank. Keykode / key numbers act as a sort of time code for film, providing location information as well as film stock type and batch codes.

KEYLINKER - Computer system made by Aaton that provides a number of telecine services. This machine reads AatonCode (or Arricode), film Keykode and VTR time code. All of this information can be encoded into 3-line VITC, (vertical interval time code), and recorded onto the videotape.

This information and more can also be logged into Flex Files, Aaton Lists, or Evertz FTL files which can be used in off-line or at the film lab. The Keylinker can also make burn-in windows of just about anything either "live" or as a dub.

KICK - A reflection or very hot pinpoint spot flaring in the lens.

KICKER - A light source positioned approximately three-fourths back of the subject, usually on the side opposite the key light. Used to separate subjects from background.

Kilobyte - A unit of measure equal to 1,000 bytes.

KILOVECTORS - A feature of the da Vinci color corrector that allows precise pinpointing and modification of a specific color. The colorist can move a cursor onto any portion of the picture and capture the value of the color under the cursor. By making adjustments, the color can be separated from other similar colors, and then changed to a different value. What distinguishes Kilovectors from the rest of the color corrector lies in the surgical precision with which a color can be isolated and thoroughly manipulated.

L   **TOP**

LAB REEL - Otherwise known as "flats", refers to a load of 2 to 4 camera-rolls spliced together by the film lab. These reels usually run between 800 and 1600 feet for 16mm, or 800 to 1200 feet for 35mm.

LAMP - A term basically used for the light bulbs of various designs, but also used to describe the lighting instrument as a whole.

LATENT EDGE NUMBERS - Edge numbers that have printed through from one film stock to another, e.g. from negative to a work print copy.

LATENT IMAGE - The reaction of photographic emulsion when it is exposed to light. A latent image becomes a visible image after the development of the film

LATITUDE - An emulsion's ability to accommodate a certain range of exposures and produce satisfactory pictures. Also called Exposure Latitude.

LCD – Liquid Crystal Display - Used for video monitors, computers, and televisions.

LEGS - A slang term used to refer to the trip.

LENS - A transparent optical device, usually made of glass, which focuses light rays.

LENS SPEED - The relative capacity of a lens to transmit light. The speed of a lens is related to the size of its largest aperture or smallest f-stop number.

LENS TURRET - A moveable plate in front of a camera on which are mounted several lenses. By rotating the turret any of the lenses can be quickly brought into position for filming.

LETTERBOX – Masking a wide screen image to fit a standard television screen size. See aspect ratio.

LIGHTING - In film production, the art and craft of artificially illuminating a set to achieve a desired photographic image.

LIGHTING CONTINUITY - Creating photographic consistency between the shots. Lighting instruments the proper term in the film industry for lighting sources (luminaries) of different designs. Sometimes they are popularly called "lamps".

LIGHT LEAK - Any unwanted light striking the film, which may be caused by loose covers on the camera or magazine.

LIGHT METER - An instrument for measuring the intensity of the light, either incident or reflected from a photographic subject. Also referred to as an exposure meter.

LIGHTING RATIO - Representation of the relationship between the-key light and the fill light.

LINER - A light source to one side of the subject that produces a rim of light that will help to create a three-dimensional effect.

LOCATION - Any locale away from the studio selected for shooting. Location filming lends authenticity to a picture.

LOCATION SCOUTING - The process of finding locations suitable for shooting specific scenes or segments of a story.

LONG SHOT (ABB. LS) - A broad view of objects or action of principal interest. The shot requires a wide angle of photography and a scene in depth.

LOOK - The visual character of an individual film stock, which is determined by the grain, color separation, and how the stock responds to under- and overexposure.

LOOP - A slack length of film between sprocket wheels and camera or projector gate, designed to absorb the tension caused, by intermittent movement, thus avoiding the tearing of film as it travels through the camera.

LOT - Industry term for the space within the studio confines. All major studios have lots consisting of office space, sound stages, standing sets, and various other Hollywood necessities.

LOW-ANGLE SHOT - A shot taken from a -low -camera setup with the camera tilted upward. Often used for dramatic impact because it makes people and objects seem tall and overpowering.

LOW CONTRAST (LC) FILTERS - Screens used on the lens to reduce the image contrast.

LOW-CON PRINT - See print.

LOW KEY - The effect of keeping a scene or the tonal range of the subjects in a scene Predominantly at the dark end of the gray scale. Low-key lighting utilizes dim illumination and deep shadows to produce a "dense" atmosphere and mysterious, dramatic effects.

LUMINAIRES - The term used in the film industry for lighting instruments (lights) of different designs. Sometimes they are popularly called lamps, but strictly speaking, a lamp is just the electric bulb in the lighting instrument.

M   **TOP**

MACRO LENS - Camera lens that can focus on a subject that is extremely close to the camera.

MAG FOLLOWER / DUBBER / FeRRIT - The machine that plays mag (magnetic) track audio. This machine interlocks with the telecine for sync audio, and can handle 35mm 3 & 4 track formats as well as 16mm 1 & 2 track formats.

MAG TRACK - Audio track recorded on 35mm or 16mm oxide coated stock. Magnetic (mag) stock has the same dimensions and sprocket holes as film stock. This format is not used for original field recordings, but rather as a secondary or mix use. For those using flatbed-editing systems, original field audio is dubbed to mag stock, and then the work print (picture), and mag audio are edited in unison. 35mm mag offers 3 or 4 track formats, while 16mm offers 1 or 2 tracks.

MAG STRIPE - Refers to a thin strip of magnetic oxide on the edge of picture film that contains a single audio track. A small audio head attached to the telecine reads the audio during the transfer. See also full coat.

MAGAZINE - A detachable film chamber, which holds the film before and after it has been exposed of two areas or compartments. The feed side holds the fresh unexposed film stock and the take-up side holds the exposed film stock. Also referred to as mag.

MARCONI - Another brand of telecine. See also Bosch/BTS/ Phillips and Rank.

MARTINI SHOT - The last shot of the day or last shot of the film.

MASTER LIGHT® - A popular light using the PAR 64, 1000-watt bulb which can be boosted to higher voltage and subsequently higher color temperature, by means of an autotransformer. Manufactured by Leonetti Cine Rentals Inc. Hollywood, Calif.

MASTER SHOT - The widest angle on a scene that establishes the characters or action in relation to their environment. A shot, of any size, that contains all the action and dialog in a scene.

MATCHBACK - The process of cutting camera original film using a video EDL. Currently, more editors are choosing to work on a non-linear video off-line system like the avid instead of a flatbed editing system like the "Steenbeck". This means all film and audio must be transferred to a video format for input into the off-line system. After the off-line editing is complete, a producer may wish to return to the camera original film to either assemble a print for projection, or to assemble reels of selected takes for a scene-by-scene color correction, (before the final on-line). To accomplish this match back to the negative, a Flex File is generated during the initial transfer, to mark video time code and film Keykode relationships at the beginning of each camera roll. This provides a list so that a video EDL can be translated into a Keykode EDL which the negative conformers use to cut the film._

MATTE - A mask used on the camera or an optical printer to protect certain parts of the frame from exposure, which will later be exposed to a different scene, for-example, substituting a different background.

MATTE BOX - An attachment in front of a camera designed both, as a shield against unwanted light and as a holder of filters or mattes during filming. The matte box can be moved back and forth with the aid of guide rods and can sometimes be adjusted both vertically, horizontally and rotated.

MAXI-BRUTE - A cluster of 1000-watt PAR lamps (manufactured by Colortran).

Mbps – Megabits Per Second - Measure or data transfer speed. One megabit is equal to one million bits. Network transmissions are measured in Mbps.

MEAT AXE - A colloquial term for a small flag.

MEDIUM CLOSE-UP (MCU) - A camera setup intermediate between a close-up and a medium shot. The average MCU will cut off the figure of a man at about chest height.

MEDIUM LONG SHOT (MLS) - A shot utilizing a wider angle than a medium shot but not as wide as a long shot. The object or action of principal interest is in the middle distance rather than toward the foreground or far in the background. On a person from the knees up.

MEDIUM SHOT (MS) - A shot Intermediate between a close-up and a long shot with most camera angles, --- this shot cannot be described with mathematical precision. Generally speaking, it would cover the cut off the figure of a man at about the waist.

METASPEED - Controls the speed of the Rank from 1 to 90 frames per second. Also acts in conjunction with "Steadifilm RTS" gates to provide "Real Time Steady" transfers.

MICROPHONE (Mic) – A device that converts audio into electrical signals for amplification or recording.

MICROPHONE BOOM - A sound dolly with a long extendable arm enabling the operator to position the microphone.

MIDGET - A small but sturdy light (up to 250 watt) with a Fresnel lens, made by Mole-Richardson.

MINI DV – Camcorder format that is the most popular with cassettes coming in a few sizes holding 60 and 90 minutes of footage. Mini DV has 500 lines of resolution and can be transferred to most NLE programs via FireWire connections.

MINI-MOLE - A small Inky Dink light (up to 250 watt) with a Fresnel lens, made by Mole-Richardson, but not as sturdy as the Midget.

MIXER/MIXING – Mixing live audio sources on location or mixing audio tracks during the editing process. On location, using a device called a mixer, a sound technician adjusts the volume and balance of the audio signals before they are recorded. During the editing process the sound editor pre-mixes multiple tracks of audio in three areas; Dialog, Effects and Music. The final mix balances all three areas into a master mix.

MODEL - A scale replica, usually in miniature, used in filming to represent real objects. The design and photography of models is an essential part of special effects.

MOIRE PATTERNS -- Artifacts that occur in video under certain circumstances when an object with numerous parallel thin lines appears to crawl or move. Window blinds are a typical example.

MOLEFAY - Lighting instruments in the range from one bulb to twelve bulb clusters employing the FAY type (650 watt) bulbs. They are often used to provide a fill light in outdoor filming. The bulb has a color temperature of 5,000oK. Molepar Lighting instruments in the range from one bulb to nine bulb clusters, employing the 1,000-watt PAR lamps.

MONOCHROME - A single color. The term is usually used to describe black and white but can also apply to the gradations of a single color or hue.

MOS - Initials printed on clapboard to indicate that the scene was shot with out sound. The letters stand for "Mit Out Sound," as early foreign born, technical crew members or a director of German decent might have pronounced it. The slate or clapperboard is kept closed.

MOTION – In film and video streaming, motion is any difference between two frames. Video has difficulty streaming motion where there are an abundance of pans, zooms and other motion.

MP3 – An acronym for MPEG-1 or MPEG-2 audio layer 3. MP3 is the file extension for MPEG audio layer 3. Layer 3 is one of three coding schemes (layer 1, layer 2 and layer 3) for the compression of audio signals. Layer 3 uses perceptual audio coding and psychoacoustic compression to remove all superfluous information (more specifically, the redundant and irrelevant parts of a sound signal. The frequencies the human ear doesn't hear anyway). It also adds a MDCT (Modified Discrete Cosine Transform) that implements a filter bank, increasing the frequency resolution 18 times higher than that of layer 2.

MPAA – MOTION PICTURE ASSOCIATION OF AMERICA -- An Association of major film producers that amongst other things is a self-regulatory entity that give films ratings.

MPEG – Moving Picture Experts Group -- Standards developed for digital video and digital audio compression. MPEG standards are an evolving series of Codec's, each designed for a different purpose. To use MPEG video files, you need a personal computer with sufficient processor speed, internal memory, and hard disk space to handle and play the MPEG file (which has a file name suffix of .mpg). MPEG viewer software is required that will play MPEG files.

MULTI-CAMERA - The use of two or more cameras simultaneously to shoot a scene from more than one angle. - Scenes must be carefully planned and cameras placed so that one camera does not appear in the viewing field of another during filming.

N TOP

NAGRA –AUDIO RECORDERS

– Originally a 1/4" audio machine made by "Nagra-Kudelski" of Switzerland. Those who record 1/4" audio in the field use a Nagra almost

exclusively. The pilot system allows for the playback of audio at the precise speed it was recorded on location. Audio quality is excellent as well as reliability of the recorders.

Nagra VI Portable, battery powered six-channel hard disk/ compact flash digital audio recorder. Principal applications: On-Location Film / TV Production Portable

Music Mastering / Wildlife recordings Special Features: 6-Channels, SMPTE Time code, 24/96, iXML compatibility, BWF files battery powered.

Nagra V
Portable battery powered two-channel digital audio recorder using removable Hard Disk drive.
Principal applications:
On-Location Film / Documentary / TV Production
Portable Music Mastering / Wildlife recordings Special Features: SMPTE

Time code, 24/96, BWF file

format, M/S decoder, Pre-recording buffer, Battery powered, Lightweight

Ares-BB+
The NAGRA ARES-BB+ is designed as a compact, high quality, easy-to-use portable digital recorder.
Principal applications:
Any ultra-portable recording application
Special Features:
Instant start-up, one button recording, take directory and titling, USB port, Phantom powering, Linear Mono / Stereo and optional compressed recording and built-in editor. Built-in charger, optional lithium-ion battery packs.

Nagra 4.2
Portable mono full track 6.35 mm (1/4 inch) analog audio tape recorder with or without NEOPILOT.
Principal applications:
On-Location radio journalist recording (Non Pilot version)
On-Location film and TV production (Pilot version)
Special Features:
Three tape speeds, two microphone inputs, NAB/CCIR Equalization, filters, battery operated, rugged construction

NEGATIVE COST - The final cost of a completed film before the additional charges of print reproduction, advertising, distribution and exhibition.

NEGATIVE CUTTING - The process of matching negatives frame by frame with a work print, using edge numbers as a guide, so that the negative may be correctly spliced for subsequent printing. AKA Film Conformi**NEGATIVE FILM** - Film stock which renders all lights, darks and colors as their opposite on the developed original. A positive print must be made from the original in order to view the image with all colors rendered correctly.

NEGATIVE / POSITIVE - Film has two polarities: negative and positive. A positive image held up to a light source, would look normal as though one were looking at an actual scene, (e.g. film slides). Negative images are the reverse of a positive image. Brights are dark, darks are bright, blue skies appear yellow and green grass is magenta when the film is viewed through a light source. Camera original film can be either positive, ("Ektachrome" or "reversal") or negative, (like the film shot in a 35mm still camera). Most film transfers are from camera original negative that the telecine electronically reverses so that we see a positive image. Negative is a superior medium since it can capture wide latitude of exposure; whereas reversal, or Ektachrome stock is more limited in the range it can reproduce. Both film stocks can be copied to another stock of the opposite polarity at a film lab. (Projection prints are made using this process. Transferring to tape from a projection print is less desirable than transferring from negative since prints can be 3 or 4 film generations down from the original negative.)

NEOPILOT - See Nagra.

NEUTRAL DENSITY (ND) FILTERS - Colorless filters of graduated densities, used to cut down the amount of light entering the lens. They can be employed on either the camera or on windows. They are used when light is too intense for a given film or required f/stop.

NG (NO GOOD) - Camera report notation indicating which takes will not be used in the final edited film.

NITRATE - The shortened name for "cellulose nitrate base," the material used in the manufacture of most 35 mm film until 1950. Highly flammable and quick to deteriorate, it requires precautionary measures in storage and handling.

NOISE REDUCER / ENHANCER - The magic box in telecine that reduces electronic "noise" and film grain, while simultaneously enhancing or sharpening the picture. Both attributes can be dialed in to varying degrees. The telecine signal always passes through this box, with "normal" settings for noise reduction and enhancement in place.

NON-LINEAR-EDITING (NLE) – Editing using software programs installed on computers to edit digitized film and video. Popular NLE editing being used are Avid and Apple's Final Cut Studio.

NOOKLITE - An open-ended lamp with narrow housing designed primarily to fit into wall and ceiling corners but often used in studio-built overhead coffin lights.

NORMAL LENS - A lens that essentially gives a normal representation of the space being photographed. It approximates the normal field of view as seen through the human eye.

NTSC - North American broadcast standard; 4:3 aspect ratio, 525 lines in each complete video frame, 30 frames in each second (or 60 fields each second).

Time code and scan rate is 29.97 frames per second. NTSC is based on a 60Hz power source.

O   **TOP**

OFF-CAMERA - Not within the field of view of a shot, such as an actor who does not appear in a shot but whose presence is felt either by implication or by the fact that you hear his voice in the shot.

OFF-LINE - The part of the editing process where creative decisions about the assembly of the program are first made. Off-line rooms provide a place to work out the time consuming tasks of editing before entering the more expensive, fully equipped postproduction on-line suite.

ON-LINE - The part of the editing process where the final assembly of the program takes place. Titling, special effects, and possibly a final audio mix may also be added during on-line. If the show was off-lined, a video EDL will be used to direct the editor to the selected scenes on the film transfer masters, or video source master tapes.

OPTICAL PRINTING - A machine that makes duplicate copies of the original print. Various technical tasks are performed on this machine including opticals, contrast correction, and the balancing of color values. See print.

OPTICAL TRACK - An audio track in the form of a stripe down the side of a film prints. A light source on the projector or telecine shines through this stripe. Because of changes in the pattern of the optical track, the light is modulated as it strikes an electronic receptor, which translates the information into an audio signal. A film print with an optical track is also referred to as a composite print, or called a print SOF that stands for "sound on film". Most release prints have optical sound tracks, e.g. movies at theaters.

OPTICALS - Optical effects a general term for such special effects and transitional effects as the fade, the dissolve, and the wipe, usually made in an optical printer.

ORIGINAL - Negative or Reversal film stock that was exposed in the camera and processed to produce either a negative or a reversal picture.

ORTHOCHROMATIC - A black and white film stock that is sensitive to blue end green but not to red.

OUT-OF-SYNC - A term used to describe a section of film in which the sound track is not exactly synchronized with the action. The error is particularly noticeable with lip movements.

OUT-TAKES - Unused shots or takes that are rejected and not used in the final version of a film.

OVERCRANK - To speed up the camera (by shooting faster than 24 frames per second), causing a shot to appear in slow motion when projected.

OVER-EXPOSURE - A film image which has been exposed to too much light, either intentionally or accidentally, resulting in overly bright images.

OVERHEAD - A large frame, supported by two stands or ropes, with white silk or black cloth, to diffuse or block out the direct sunlight on an exterior scene.

OVER-THE-SHOULDER SHOT (ABB. OTS) - A common shot in dialogue scenes in which the subject is viewed from an angle just over the shoulder of another performer.

P   **TOP**

P2 CARD -**Panasoncic** PCMCIA memory card used for their camcorders. Cards available with eight, sixteen, and 32 gigabyte data storage.

PAL - Phase Alternating Line. A European TV standard; 4:3 aspect ratio, 625 lines in each complete video frame, 25 frames in each second (or 50 fields each second). Time code and scan rate is 25.0 frames per second. PAL is based on a 50Hz power system.

PAN - A camera movement on a horizontal plane from one part of a scene to another. A contraction of "panorama" or "panoramic," the term is sometimes used to describe any pivotal movement of the camera.

PAN AND SCAN - A process that reframes a wide-screen or anamorphic film to conform to the limits of the television screen. A considerable fraction of the image may be sacrificed when shrunk to television's aspect ratio of 1.33:1.

PANCHROMATIC - A black and white film stock that responds equally to all colors of the visible spectrum. See orthochromatic.

PAR (PARABOLIC ALUMINIZED

REFLECTOR)-A lamp designation for a bulb with a self-contained reflector and lens, similar to the automobile headlight.

PARALLAX - The apparent displacement between an area observed through a camera viewfinder and the area actually being photographed.

PEANUT BULB - A small bulb used for hiding in confined areas. GE 6S6 is one example of such a bulb.

PERFORATIONS - Equally spaced holes along one or both edges of the film stock, used to position and move the film through the camera. Also called perfs.

PERSISTANCE OF VISION - The phenomenon of the eye retaining an image for a short time after it has been seen.

PHANTOM POWER – Certain microphones require external power from a camera or other source. This is known as Phantom Power. Certain XLR ports can furnish "phantom power," however, if the microphone has its own power source, the phantom power should be switched off.

PHOTO HOOD - A type of light bulb in which the light output and color temperature are higher than that of a comparable household bulb but with a shorter life.

PHOTOSHOP – Adobe photographic editing software for editing photographs. An important tool for documentary postproduction when using archival and recent photographic and document resources.

PICKUPS - Shots filmed after the completion of the regular shooting schedule, usually in an effort to fill in any gaps in continuity that are discovered in the cutting room.

PICTURE LOCK - See rough-cut / fine cut / picture lock.

PILOT - A signal recorded on a Nagra, on 1/4" tape to ensure that audio will play back later at precisely the same speed it was recorded in the field. When a playback Nagra locks onto this signal, the pilot is being resolved, or played back at the proper speed so that the sound will stay in sync with the picture. There are two types of pilot in use. The more common version is neopilot that is used on mono audio recordings only. F.M. pilot is used with 2-track or stereo recordings. To be able to sync audio in telecine, time code is needed on the tapes instead of pilot. Neopilot tapes are striped with center track time code, whereas F.M. pilot tapes need to be dubbed to another audiotape because of technical reasons. All striping and dubbing should happen before the transfer session.

PLATE - Film shot for front or back projection.

POINT-OF-VIEW SHOT (POV) - A shot filmed at such a camera angle that an object or an action appears to be seen from a particular actor's viewpoint. This is usually accomplished by placing the camera alongside the player (or at a spot he would have occupied if he were present on the set) from whose viewpoint the scene is shot. Other players look at the point designated as the player's position (or at the player, if he is present) but not into the lens.

POLARITY - Connecting the batteries or other power sources correctly, meaning that the plus terminal on the power source is connected to the plus terminal, on the equipment and the minus terminals are connected accordingly. Also refers to the image rendition orientation of the film stock.

POSITIVE - A projection print in which the lights and darks conform to the scene as originally photographed. See Negative/Positive.

POST-PRODUCTION - The period after principal photography when the film undergoes editing, sound dubbing, and optical effects. The post-production time period is often equal to that of the initial shoot. See pre-production.

POWER WINDOWS - A feature of the da Vinci color corrector, also called "area isolation". This allows the colorist to position a variably shaped window around a section of the picture and adjust all attributes inside the window separate from the rest of the image. The window can be programmed to move or "track" an object while the scene is running. The edges of the window can also be softened to smooth color transitions within the scene.

PRACTICAL - A lamp on the set that is rigged to be operational as a luminaries' during the scene action.

PRACTICAL SET - The realistic construction of a film setting where, objects such as doors, lamps, stoves, and sinks actually work.

PREPRODUCTION - The period before photography beams when final script changes are made, the cast and crew are hired, locations are scouted, and other preliminary work is finished.

PRESSURE PLATE - The part of the film gate in the camera that puts pressure against the film, holding it against the aperture plate during exposure.

PRIMARY COLORS - The three primary colors of light are Red, Green and Blue. By combining these three colors in varying amounts all other colors can be obtained. See also Complementary Colors.

PRIME LENS - A lens of a single, fixed focal length.

PRINCIPAL PHOTOGRAPHY - The primary shooting schedule, which does not include second unit photography or pickups.

PRINT - A film with a positive image that has been printed from another piece of film, (usually negative). Prints are generally easier to transfer than negative because they could have already been color timed at the lab, where red, green and blue light adjustments were made for each scene as it was printed. (This is a simpler version of telecine color corrections.) There are different kinds of prints that can be one generation or many generations away from the original film:

An **interpositive** is a high quality copy of the original negative, used mostly in film labs for printing. Interpositive images retain most of the wide exposure range of the original negative, but with the advantages of a positive image, (better reproduction of highlights, and film dirt is black instead of white which is more visible). Interpositives are expensive to make, and hard to make well, but they are often the colorists' choice if the original negative is not available for transfer.

Work prints are made from the original negative for editors to cut or mark to create a finished program. This print, made right after the developing process, can be color-corrected ("timed") or un-color-corrected (normal). The edge numbers and Keykode from the negative print through to the work print. When editing is complete, the work print is sent to the lab where conformers use the Keykode / edge numbers to cut the original negative for final printing, or to create a select reel for final film-to-tape transfer. A Work print is also called a cutting copy or workpix, after editing has begun.

Before a print is released for projection in theaters, aspects of the printing process need to be O.K.'d by the filmmakers. Items like color timing, dissolves, titles, and optical-track audio are checked before multiple prints are made. The first print, called an answer print is viewed by the client for an "answer". If changes need to be made, a second answer print might be screened, and so on until the client is satisfied. After the client has signed off on the final answer print, the lab makes release prints for distribution. Because they are made to project over a large area, heavier contrast is built into release prints so that by the time they reach the screen, they don't appear washed out or faint. Because of this extra contrast, colorists prefer, (but don't require) a low-con print, (low contrast), for film-to-tape

transfer, (if an interpositive is not available). Most finished answer and release prints have sound that is printed onto the film, (SOF or sound on film). This can be a magnetic track, but most often is an optical.

There are two processes used to make prints. In contact printing, two film stocks are pressed together to copy the image from one to the other. In optical printing, the original film is projected into a camera that exposes the image onto print stock. By using this process, various effects can be achieved such as re-framed scenes, or blow-ups (e.g. from Super-16mm to 35mm). Because the two films are not in direct contact with each other, this process allows for printing of segments instead of the entire roll of film. Optical printing offers flexibility, but is slower, and more expensive.

PRINTER - A machine that reproduces images from one film onto another.

PRINTER LIGHT SCALE (PRINTING LIGHTS) - A graduated scale of printing light intensity, allowing one to print the original images brighter or darker to obtain an evenly exposed print from an original with uneven exposures. The light scale is also used when executing optical effects such as fades and dissolves.

PRINTING - The laboratory process of exposing raw stock by using the image of another film as the light modulator. Through printing, one may produce a positive print from negative film; negative film-from positive film; and when using a reversal process, positives from positives or negatives from negatives.

PROCESS SHOT - A technique of filming live action staged in front of the screen on which the background view is projected. This background plate can be projected either from behind the translucent screen (back projection), or from the front on a highly reflective screen (front projection).

PROCESSING - All the chemical and physical operations necessary to convert a latent image into a satisfactory visible image on film.

PRODUCT PLACEMENT - The selling of rights for products (soft - drinks, cologne, clothing) to appear in a film.

PROPS - An abbreviated term for properties: furnishings, fixtures, decorations or any other movable items that are seen or used on a motion picture (or stage) set but that are not "structurally parts of the set. Anything that an actor picks up in a scene may be considered a prop ' an abbreviated term for "prop man."

PTRs (Particle Transfer Rollers) - The tacky surface of these "gummy" rollers lift loose dirt and dust from the film while it's running on the telecine. There are usually four PTRs on a telecine, with 2 before the film gate, and 2 after the gate.

PULLBACK SHOT - A tracking or zoom shot that moves away from the subject to allow the full context of the scene to come into view.

PULL-DOWN - The action of moving the film one frame at a time for exposure or projection by the intermittent movement of the camera or projector.

PULL-DOWN CLAW - The metal claw or hook that is part of the intermittent movement mechanism that pulls the film into position in the gate so that I frame may be exposed.

PUSHING - See Forcing.

Q   **TOP**

QUADRA - See Bosch / BTS / Phillips.

QUANTIZING - See analog / digital.

QUARTZ LIGHTS - A popular name for tungsten halogen lamps.

QUATROSCAN - See Digiscan.

QUICK RELEASE PLATE - A detachable plate that is used to secure the camera to the tripod head. It allows for quick and easy removal and attachment of the camera.

QUICKTIME – Movie file format (mov) used widely for both Macintosh and Windows systems. Can be imported into Final Cut Pro.

R   **TOP**

RACK FOCUS - Physically shifting the focus ring of the lens during shooting usually to change the critical focus from a far object to a close one or from a near object to a distant object.

RAKING SHOT/ TWO SHOT - A shot of usually two people taken from one side, with the foreground head in profile. Example: A shot through the side window of a car with one or both persons in profile.

RANK CINTEL (now called CINTEL) - The English company that makes telecines (the machine that transfers film pictures into video pictures), and other related equipment:

Mark III-C - Considered the workhorse of the industry, these machines are found in a lot of post-houses. Used as platforms for newer or third party improvements, Mark III-Cs are often modified, making no two exactly alike.

RAW STOCK - Film stock, which has not yet been exposed or processed.

REACTION SHOT - A close shot ' of the person (or persons) reacting to something that is said or done off scene or in a previous shot.

REFLECTED LIGHT - Light that bounces off or is reflected from a subject.

REFLECTED LIGHT METER - A measuring device used to determine the exposure of the light bouncing off or reflected from the subject. It is held at the position of the camera and aimed toward the subject.

REFLEX VIEWING - The industry standard viewing system, which allows the camera operator to see the image through the lens exactly as it is recorded on the film.

REFLECTOR - A board with a light-reflecting surface most often used for re-directing sunlight. A reflector board may have a "hard" and a "soft" side.

REGISTRATION - The exact positioning of a frame of film in the picture gate of a camera projector, or printer.

REGISTRATION PIN - The part of the intermittent movement mechanism that secures the film by engaging in a perforation during the period of exposure.

RELEASE - In film industry terms, the official launching of a motion picture into general distribution

RELEASE PRINT - A positive print that is ready for distribution and exhibition. See print.

RESOLUTION - A definition of lens quality, measured by the number of lines per millimeter which can be separately identified. A higher resolution results in better picture quality.

RE-TAKE - The re-shooting of a scene previously filmed but not satisfactorily

REVERSAL - A type of camera-original film stock that is developed into a positive image. Most older family films, and "news films" are recorded on reversal. Even though not as high quality as negative film, reversal film is still useful for scientific applications, or special effects or looks in music videos, reenactments etc. See also negative / positive.

REVERSAL FILM - A type of film stock that after exposure and processing becomes a direct positive print without first going through a negative stage.

REVERSE ANGLE SHOT - A shot taken from an angle-opposite the one from which the preceding shot has been taken. The reverse angle technique is frequently employed in dialogue scenes to provide the editor with alternate facial shots of the actors speaking.

RE-WASH - Film can be re-cleaned by running it through part of the film-processing machine again. This softens the emulsion of the film to remove embedded dirt. Re-washing is more thorough than an ultrasonic film cleaning, but is only performed by a film lab on an as needed basis.

REWINDS - Mechanism on a viewer or an editing bench for hand winding the film.

RIGGING - Positioning lamps in the studio according to the preliminary lighting designed by the D.P. and gaffer.

RISER - The extending part of a lamp stand or century stand.

ROOM TONE - The acoustic modulations characteristic of the enclosed environment in which sound film is shot.

ROUGH CUT / FINE CUT / PICTURE LOCK - Stages of the off-line edit. First is the rough cut in which basic layout decisions are made, then the fine cut in which the timing and flow of the show are polished. The final stage is picture lock where no more changes may be made to the sound or picture. From here the off-line copy moves onto final finishing, (e.g. on-line, graphics, color correction etc.).

RTS SYSTEM - Real Time Steady film transfer system that uses a specially designed film gate in conjunction with Metaspeed to produce a steadier than normal image.

RULE OF THIRDS - A rule of composition which says you should divide the frame into thirds horizontally and vertically, to use as a guide for creating' balance in your composition.

RUN-AND-GUN – Shooting documentary footage on the move similar to ENG style gathering of news.

RUNNING SHOT - A traveling shot in which the moving camera keeps up with the pace of a moving person or object.

RUN THROUGH - Rehearsing a scene at normal speed, generally used to watch for any technical problems.

RUSHES - Immediate prints of a single day's shooting that may be viewed before the next days shooting. See dailies.

S   <u>TOP</u>

SAFETY FILM - Film whose base (usually cellulose or acetate) is noncombustible.

SAMPLES / SAMPLING RATE - See analog / digital.

SANDBAG - A grip device used to secure light stands and C-stands against tipping over.

SCOOP - A studio lamp with a soft, wide round throw of 500 to 2000 watts.

SCOPE - Abbreviation for Cinemascope and all other anamorphic processes.

SCENE - The basic unit of a script, with action occurring in a single setting and in real time.

SCOUT - The process of going to different locations and evaluating them for film production requirements.

SCREENPLAY - The written text upon which a film production is based.

SCRIM - A lighting accessory of wire mesh or net, positioned in front of a light source when attenuation of light is required.

SCRIPT - A written screenplay that undergoes several phases from outline and treatment to the final shooting script.

SCRIPT SUPERVISOR - The crew member responsible for maintaining continuity and keeping records of all information relating to each scene including scenes and slate number of each shot, the number of takes and their quality, the type of lens used and its aperture, the actual dialogue spoken, details of the action, the props, the players' attire, etc.

SELECTS - Scenes chosen from the original material for use in the final master. If on film, these scenes are assembled by the lab into a select reel for easier transfer and color correction. In other instances, a colorist would cue to, and transfer select scenes from uncut negative using locating tools like time code, Keykode, or a film counter.

SENIOR - A focusable studio lamp with a Fresnel lens and 5000-watt bulb.

SEQUENCE - A number of scenes linked together by time, location, or narrative continuity to form a unified episode in a motion picture.
SET - A construction representing an interior or exterior locale in which the action of a motion picture takes place.

SET-UP - The basic component of a film's production, referring to each individual camera position,

placement or angle.

SIGNAL-TO-NOISE (S/N) RATIO – The ratio of amplitude in decibels between a transmitted signal and the noise around it without the signal. If the signal is a voice then everything else is noise. There might also be noise inherent in the recording apparatus. In Documentary work there is often a lot of noise in the environment so that special effort needs to be made to make sure the ratio between the signal (a voice) and everything else is large.

SHOOTING SCHEDULE - An advance schedule for work assignments and equipment needed for a filming session.

SHOOTING SCRIPT - The approved final scrip, broken down with full dialogue and detailed camera setups and other instructions, which is used by the director in the-production of a film.

SHORT ENDS - Short lengths of un-exposed film that are remaining from a full roll of film or at the end of the day's filming. These may be saved for later use in shooting pickup or insert shots.

SHOT - A single continuous take filmed in a single session from one camera setup.

SHOTGUN MICROPHONE – A name for a hypercardioid mic that has a very narrow pick-up pattern. Used in documentary filmmaking in many run-and-gun situations.

SHUTTER - A mechanism that controls both the opening and closing of the aperture on a camera, thereby controls the light striking the film for the exposure.

SHUTTER SPEED - The amount of time each frame of film is exposed to light. The standard shutter speed for motion pictures is 1/50 of a second at sync speed of 24 frames per second.

SIDER - A flag placed on the side of a light source to shape or block the light.

SILVER HALIDE - Light sensitive silver compound such as silver bromide, silver chloride, silver fluoride, or silver iodide, used in photographic emulsions.

SKYPAN (SKYLITE) - A non-focusable studio lamp with a 5000-watt to 10,000-watt bulb providing illumination over a broad area, such as set backings.

SLATES - A visual marker used during filming to provide production and scene information. Also a visual and audible marker for syncing picture and audio later in postproduction. There are several different methods of slating: A smart slate provides a readable time code display on a clapperboard. This time code is the same that is being recorded simultaneously on the audiotape. By stopping on any frame and reading the displayed time code, one can find that exact point on the audiotape, and then lock the audio to the film for sync sound. A bloop slate is basically a box with a light bulb or a 2 digit number display. When a button is pressed the light(s) illuminate and a tone is recorded onto the audiotape. By lining up the light with the sound beep, sync is achieved. Clap sticks are the most traditional, with the clap of the wood as the sync reference. Of these methods, smart slates are the fastest and most accurate.

Head slates, those that appear at the beginning of a sound take, are far preferred over tail slates in which the marker is provided at the end of the take (usually with the slate upside down to denote a tail mark).

The AatonCode or Arri FIS sync systems in which slating is not necessary, surpasses all of these methods for speed in transfer, especially when used with a digital disc recorder for instant audio sync during lay to tape.

SLOW MOTION - An effect resulting from running film through a camera at faster-than-normal speed.

SNOOT - A funnel-shaped light-controlling device used on lamps in place of barn doors for a more exact light-beam pattern.

SOF - Acronym for "Sound On Film". See also optical track and mag stripe.

SOFT FOCUS - An effect obtained by shooting slightly out of focus by using a special filter, or by placing gauze or other diffusing material in front of the lens. The technique causes an image to appear diffused and lacking in sharp definition.

SOUND SPEED - The rate at-which film passes through a motion picture camera to make it compatible with minimal quality sound. It has been standardized since the advent of sound at 24 frames per second. Also called sync speed.

SOUND STAGE - A soundproof building for constructing sets and for shooting motion picture productions.

SPEED-CAMERA - The rate at which the film moves through the camera expressed in frames per second.

SPEED-FILM - The film emulsion's sensitivity to light expressed as an ASA value or EI value.

SPEED-LENS - The full amount of light that a lens is capable of transmitting

SPILL - The light "leaking" from the back, sides or front of a lamp onto an object.

SPLICE - The joint between two pieces of film.

SPREADER - A three-armed device placed on the floor and used to hold the legs of a tripod in place for filming. May also be referred to as a triangle.

SPROCKETS - The uniformly shaped and spaced holes on the edges of film stock that enable the film to advance. Also called perforations or sprocket holes.

SPUN GLASS - A diffusion material made from glass fibers. Extremely heat resistant but like fiberglass it irritates the skin and eyes. It is generally replaced now by Tough Spun which is nonirritating.

STANDARD LEGS - A tripod that extends from approximately four feet to six feet and used for shots at a standard or normal height.

STEENBECK - See flatbed-editing machine.

STOCK FOOTAGE - Existing film footage, previously shot that is taken from a company's archives, or a library and incorporated into a new production.

STORYBOARD - A series of drawings used as visual representation of the shooting script. The sketches represent the key situations (shots) in the scripted scenes. They indicate the framing, camera angle, blocking, gross character movement in the frame and basic props and sets. Dialogue, effects, and so on, appear below the pictures.

SWISH PAN - A quick movement of the camera, causing the image to blur and not be easily identified. A psychological approximation of the movement of the human eye as it moves from subject to subject.

SYNC TAKES - Segments of film with simultaneously recorded audio that are marked with a slate so that they can be easily synced or "locked" together in post production.

SYNCHRONIZATION - In motion pictures the process of aligning a picture and sound track in correct relationship so that an action and its corresponding sound coincide. Also referred to as sync.

SYNCHRONOUS SOUND - Sound that is matched with its visible source on screen.

SYNC MOTOR - A camera motor that can be electrically or mechanically synchronized to run at the same speed with the sound recorder.

SYNC SPEED - Camera speed of exactly 24 fps, which is synchronized with the sound recording.

T   <u>TOP</u>

T-STOP - The calibration of the actual amount of light transmitted through the lens at a particular diaphragm opening. The standard series of t-stop numbers include the following: 1, 1.4, 2, 2.8, 4, 5.6, 8, 11, 16, 22, and 32.

TACHOMETER - The meter-on the camera that indicates the camera speed in frames per second.

TAIL SLATE - A slate that is photographed at the end of a shot as opposed to at the beginning of a shot.

TAKE - A single continuous shot taken by a motion picture camera without any interruption or break.

TAKEDOWN - To reduce the light on an object by the use of nets, scrims or by wasting the light.

TAKE-UP SIDE - The part of the camera or magazine, which holds the exposed film.
TAPE FORMATS (SEE VIDEO TAPE FORMATS)

TARGET - A solid or net disc, up to 10 inches in diameter, used to control the lamp beam and create desirable shadows. A type of flag or scrim.

TEASER - A large black cloth screen for controlling soft light - often put on stands or hung over a set.

TECHING DOWN - The method of treating costumes and draperies to better accommodate them to reproduction on color film. For example, rinsing white fabric in weak tea lowers the highlighting tendency of pure white. The term comes from the process originated by Technicolor.

TELECINE - 1 the machine used to transfer film to videotape. The telecine acts as an electronic film projector, shining light through the film, and then turning it into an electronic signal. After color correction, the signal is formed into a video picture that can be recorded onto videotape.

TELECINE – 2-- The room or environment where film-to-tape transfers and tape-to-tape color correction sessions occur.

TELEPHOTO LENS - A lens that acts like a telescope in its magnification of distant objects. This provides a narrow angle of view and minimizes depth perception.

TENER - A focusable lamp with Fresnel lens and 10,000-watt bulb.

THREADING - Placing film in a proper way for correct passage through all of the film transport mechanisms of the camera, projector or other film handling machines.
THREE-POINT LIGHTING - The use of a key light, filler and back light to illuminate a subject within a scene.

THREE-QUARTER VIEW - A camera shot in which the actor or subject in the frame faces the camera at about a 45-degree angle, offering three-quarter-view of the face or subject. Compare full face shot, side view.
TIGHT SHOT - A shot in which the subject matter fills almost the entire frame.

TILT - The pivotal movement of a camera in a vertical plane. In a tilt shot, the camera is moved up (tilt up) or down (tilt down), in contrast with a pan shot, in which the camera is moved horizontally.

TIME CODE - An electronic code recorded on audio and videotape that acts as a location marker or time reference for the recorded material. Professional video systems rely on time code for cueing and editing. A video EDL consists mainly of time code ins and outs to direct an editor to the beginning or end of scenes.

TIMING (GRADING) - A lab operation before printing to select printer lights and color filters to improve the densities and color rendition of the original footage and thus obtain a more visually satisfactory print. The technician in charge is called a timer (in Britain, grader).

TLC - Time Logic Controller, the editing system for telecine. This machine controls the Rank and up to four VTR's simultaneously with field-accurate editing and full 3/2 pull down management.

TOUGH SPUN - A diffusing material made of synthetic fibers. Highly heat resistant.

TRACKING SHOT - A shot in which a camera-mounted on tracks, on a vehicle, or on a dolly-moves forward, backward, or sideways, to follow the action and the movements of performers. The camera is said to "track in" when moving closer to the subject, to "track out" when moving away and to "track with" when moving with the subject.

TRAILER - A short publicity film, shown as part of a regular program at a theater, advertising a forthcoming motion picture.

TRANSLITE BACKING - Backing for windows and doors prepared from large photographic enlargements and lit from the back for a desired effect.

TREATMENT - A written presentation outlining the look and feel of the project, film, video, multimedia, documentary or fiction. The treatment covers what the story is about, beginning middle and end and what the approach will be in shooting it. Usually follows a short Concept statement.

TRIMS - Sections of film cut from a scene by the editor and left over after he has made his selection of the footage he wants used in the work print. Trims, also called "out-takes" must be carefully classified and preserved in the event that they will be needed for incorporation into the final film.

TRIPOD - A three-legged camera support that can be adjusted in height for filming various shots.

TRUCKING SHOT - Essentially the same as tracking shot, but more specifically used to describe a shot taken from a moving truck, van, or some other motorized vehicle rather than a dolly.

T/STOP - Calibration of the lens light-transmitting power arrived at by an actual measurement of the transmitted light for each lens and each stop individually. T/stops are considered more accurate than f/stops.

TUNGSTEN - Standard studio light sources that have a color temperature of 3200K.

TUNING - The lab operation before printing to select the printer lights and color filers to improve the densities and color rendition of the original footage.

TWEAKING - Fine-tuning what each instrument is accomplishing in a lighting setup.

TWO-SHOT - A close camera shot just wide enough to keep two persons within the limits of the frame.

U   TOP

ULTRASONIC FILM CLEANER - A device that runs film through a heated bath of fluid, which is vibrated at ultrasonic frequencies. Jets of fluid and swirling buffers add to the cleaning power. Finally, the film is run through a heated air-dry system before winding onto a take-up reel.

UNDERCRANK - To operate a camera at a slower than normal speed so that the action appears accelerated on the screen. The term has remained in use since the -early silent days, when cameras were cranked by hand.
UNDER-EXPOSURE - A film image that has been exposed to too little light, either intentionally or accidentally, resulting in overly dark images.

USER BITS - A section of the time code signal that provides 8 digits, which can be programmed by the user for organizational purposes, (e.g. show codes or tape reel numbers). User bits are limited to the numbers 0-9 and letters A-F, and usually remain static, (as opposed to "running" like time of day).

V   TOP

VARI-SPEED - Refers to film or tape running at any non-standard speed. The Rank has a standard vari-speed feature that allows speeds between 16 and 30 fps, (frames per second). Metaspeed extends the vari-speed range from +1fps to +90fps. On video or audiotape, vari-speed range changes according to format. Most often, this feature is used to slow down a scene for effect, or to perform a "fit-fill".

VARIABLE SHUTTER - A shutter that enables you to change the size of the opening thereby regulating how long each frame of film is exposed.

VARIAC - Trade name of a popular variable transformer for manual AC voltage regulation.

VIEWFINDER - The eyepiece of the camera that enables the camera operator to view the image befog photographed.

VIGNETTE - Blurring of the photographic image on the sides of the frame, caused by close range objects obscuring the view. It may often be caused by the camera matte box being positioned incorrectly.

VIDEO TAPE FORMATS –
ANALOG TAPE FORMATS –

No longer used in most production sitations.

1" Type B videotape (Bosch)
1" Type C videotape (Ampex & Sony)
2" Quadruplex videotape (Ampex)
Ampex
Betacam
Betacam SP
Betamax (Sony)
S-VHS (JVC)
U-matic (3/4") (Sony)
VCR, VCR-LP, SVR
VHS (JVC)
VHS-C (JVC)

Video 2000 (Philips)

DIGITAL TAPE FORMATS
BETACAM IMX (Sony)
D-VHS (JVC)
D-Theater
D1 (Sony)
D2 (Sony
D3
D5 HD
Digital Betacam (Sony)
Digital 8 (Sony)
D
DVC-Pro (Panasonic)
HDV
ProHD (JVC)
MicroMV
Mini DV

VITC - (Pronounced "vitzee".) Vertical Interval Time Code. Standard VITC contains video time code and user-bits in 1 line of code that appears in the vertical interval, (a part of the video signal just above the visible picture). This code is the width of the screen, and one video line thick. It is used by videotape controllers to help read accurate time code even when the tape is in "jog" mode. With 3-line VITC, video time code/user-bits, Keykode and audio time code can be encoded into the vertical interval using 3 lines of code. 3-line VITC packs information into a film transfer that can be decoded la

W   TOP

WALKTHROUGH - First rehearsal on the set, for camera positions, lighting, sound, etc., where the director describes the scene in detail to the crew and the actors.

WASTE - Shining all the light on an object and then slowly turning the lamp head so that some of the light is lost, misses or falls off the object.

WETGATE - A device that allows film to be projected through a chamber of liquid in order to produce a scratch and dirt free transfer or print. A scratch or mark in the film is visible because light refracts on the edges of the scratch itself. As light passes through the image using the Wet gate system, fluid fills the scratch and stops the refraction so that the imperfection is invisible, (some scratches on the emulsion side may not be removed). A Westgate is a good problem solver, but has a few disadvantages. Because the film passes through a fluid, and needs to dry before winding on a take up reel, high-speed winding is not feasible. Also, the fluid used in these gates is an ozone depleter, and very expensive since its production has been restricted by the government. See also Digital Westgate.

WHITE & BLACK BALANCE – Adjusting the colors to the prevailing color temperature of the location. Most modern professional camcorders have switches that will allow the user to let the camera automatically adjust the white balance by pointing the camera at a white card or other white object in the scene.

WIDE-ANGLE LENS - A lens of shorter-than-normal focal length and magnification power that covers a large field of view and tends to exaggerate perspective, making an area appear larger than it actually is.

WILD MOTOR - Camera motor that does not run at an exact synchronous speed. Usually adjustable for different speeds.

WILD WALL/CEILINGS - Walls and ceilings made to be moved at will, even during the shot. This allows camera positions and angles that would be otherwise unattainable on a practical set.

WILD SOUND - Sound that isn't meant to sync with picture, e.g. room tone, birds chirping, flags waving in the wind etc. This sound is used as background or as ambience. Wild sound might also include voice-over audio that was recorded without picture, e.g. off camera interviews or spot disclaimers.

WIND - (As in wind a clock.) A-wind, B-wind refers to the way an image is seen on the film. On A-wind film, the image is correct when looking directly at the emulsion. B-wind is correct when viewed through the base side of the film. Most original film is B-wind. Most print film is A-wind since it is a copy of the B-wind original. Intermediates, (lab film elements) could make prints A or B wind. The standard for 35mm theatrical release is A-wind with emulsion out. This is not true for 16mm.

WINDJAMMER - Used to cover a zeppelin or blimp housing to help block wind noise.

WING - To turn the top half of a egged C-stand away from a light in a semi-circular motion in order to check the lamp setting and not change the position of a flag or cutter.

WORKPRINT - The print of a film with which the editor works in the process of editing a motion picture. It is composed of selected takes from the dailies and is gradually "rimmed" from

a rough cut to a fine cut stage. See print.

WRAP - The ending of principal photography on a feature. Putting away all of the equipment for the day.

X   **TOP**

X-Y-ZOOM - A feature of the Rank telecine that allows the image to be moved left or right (X), up and down (Y), or in and out (Zoom). Although the picture can be degraded if zoomed in too far, it is better for an image to be re-framed in telecine rather than with a DVE in edit.

XENON LAMP - A lamp filled with xenon, an inert gas that produces a bright light of controlled color temperature. The xenon lamp has replaced the arc lamp in the majority of lighting situations.

Y   **TOP**

Z   **TOP**

ZEPPELIN – Also known as a blimp. Used to house and shield boom microphones from wind noise.

ZINGER - Any directional light source used to highlight a scene predominantly lit with soft light.

"ZIP" SOFTLIGHT - A narrow, 8" x 17 1/2 soft light with 2000-watt bulb, made by Mole-Richardson. Useful in a low ceiling situation.

ZOOM – The act of using a multi-focal length lens to push in or out on a subject. To go from a wide angle shot to a telephoto shot in one smooth movement. This is not the same as a push in or out with a dolly or tracks. It is an optical move and changes the relationship between the subject and the background by compressing or expanding the shot.

ZOOM LENS - A variable multi-focal length lens that is designed to provide various focal lengths within a range of lens sizes. For Example: 12mm to 120mm. Also able to be used for continuous shot with no loss of focus from the telephoto end to the wide Angle end of the lens.

INDEX

A

A/B roll editing machines 223
AC, second 55
Academy Award Wining Film 30
action coverage 102
action footage 84, 134
  unused 134
action scenes 135
actors 4-5, 11, 30, 44, 136-7, 156
actuality 3-5, 7-8, 12, 14, 16, 31, 33,
  44, 53-4, 261
actuality documentation 15
actuality footage 116, 135
actuality material 5, 31-3, 44
AD *see* Assistant Director
Additional Crew 189
administration 18, 210, 212
**ADR (Automatic Dialog
  Replacement)** 105
adult interviewer 118
advocacy 15, 17-18, 29, 32, 200
Africanized bees 40-2
agencies 218-19, 238
agenda, social 112
agreement 51, 59, 79, 122, 196, 206-
  7, 221-2, 256
  letter of 195, 220-1
air 12, 78-80, 82-3, 99-100, 104, 195,
  223
air fares 65
airport 224, 227-8
Alexandroff 181
ambient light sources 128
ambient sound 45, 104, 109, 116,
  134
American crew 247
American Film Festival 113
amp 156, 246
anger 122
angles 22, 103, 163, 169, 225-6
  reverse 102-3
answers 38, 45, 55-6, 67, 81-2, 109,
  116-18, 120, 135-6, 142, 155, 213,
  219
Anthropological documentary

film 24
Archival Documentary 240
**Archival Documentation of
  events** 239
archival film footage 26
archival footage 40, 44, 135, 137,
  239
  black and white 15
areas
  highlighted 134, 210
  shadow 141, 144, 168
arena 225, 227
Argumentative interviewers 117
arms 121-2, 125, 159
Art Director 56
artificial situations 25
ASCAP 113
Aspect Ratio 165
Aspect Ratio of Frames 165
assignment 173-4
assistant 51, 56, 64, 124-5, 168, 189,
  209, 211
  producer's 52
assistant camera 64, 225
  first 98, 205
assistant camera person 101
  first 55, 64, 176
assistant director 64, 247
  first 50, 52, 54, 57, 190, 223, 226
  second 64
Assistant Director (AD) 50, 52, 54,
  57, 64, 98, 101, 189-90, 223, 226,
  247
**Assistant Director/Script/
  Coordinator** 189
**assistant Director/Script
  Supervisor** 101
**assistant director/script
  supervisor/continuity/PA** 98
Assistant editors 57, 66, 68, 194,
  213
assistant producer 50
Associate Project Director 184
Attackumentary films 32
attendees 112, 174, 244-5
audience 14, 35-7, 42, 70, 78-9, 82,
  98, 112-13, 172, 176-7, 182, 193,
  219, 254-5, 257, 264
  large 275

INDEX

INDEX

INDEX

INDEX

Rationale 77-8, 182, 201, 203, 221, 234, 244, 254

re-editing 195-6

reactions 18, 36, 79, 110-12, 157, 177, 213

reality 2-8, 10-11, 13-16, 18, 20, 25-6, 29, 31-2, 36, 38-9, 41, 43, 148, 172-3, 218, 261

convey 25

distort 8, 25

fictional 8

historical 21

human 13

manipulated 261

new 38

nonfiction 2, 4-5, 23

objective 6-7, 16, 116

recording 21

recreate 5

skewing 7-8

subjective 116

visual 30

reality based 53, 63

Reality Check 78

reality programming 10-11, 16

reception 105, 244-5, 249

recipient 224-5, 227-8, 231

record 4, 14, 20, 55-7, 104, 147, 149, 226, 248

audio recorders 195

record deck 223

record video 31, 56, 66, 100, 104-5, 116, 148, 156, 242, 247

recording medium 150, 154, 188

recording studio sound booth 149

recreational boating 254-5, 257

reel-to-reel audiotape 188

reenactments, based on a true story 12, 30-1

reflectors 127, 168-9

refrigerators 210, 212

relationship 28, 79, 84, 119, 163, 165, 193, 206-7, 220-2, 257

relaxes 116, 119, 157

release 51, 67, 142, 150, 174, 194, 245, 262-3

religion 8, 18, 29, 185, 193

renewal, urban 234-5

rentals, editing equipment 66

renting equipment 51, 65, 68, 75, 208, 211, 246-7

research 13-14, 26, 36-40, 42, 48, 51, 54, 59, 77, 79-81, 85, 118, 173, 184, 234, 255

basic 225

field 38

initial 39

scholarly 30

scientific 14

research team 52

Resettlement Agency (RA) 15

residents 180, 185-7, 201, 203, 205, 207-9, 214-15, 235, 238

resolution 144-5, 151, 250

resources 4, 25-6, 36, 50-1, 68, 104, 223-4, 272, 275

using digital production 150

response 118-19

responsibilities 49, 53, 55, 62, 157, 171, 183, 189, 207

camera department 64

director's 46, 52, 84

producer's 53

second assistant camera person's 57

review 39, 62, 70, 108, 142, 193, 196, 231, 256

rewinds 142-3, 194, 204

rhythm 26, 57, 111

rig lighting 56

rights 220

Right-to-work 69

rods and cones 6

role 29, 80, 85, 181, 186

photography's 19

producer's 53, 63

roll 45-6, 84, 105, 108-9, 130, 134-6, 142, 173, 176, 195, 221, 225-6

Roll and Action coverage 102

roll footage 54, 108, 134, 175, 225

room, crowded 6, 78, 111, 126-7, 142, 156, 160, 168, 170, 175, 248, 275

room tone 105, 111, 148

Royal Marine Marching Band 244, 246

royalties 112-13, 214

Russian Film-Truth philosophy, early 16